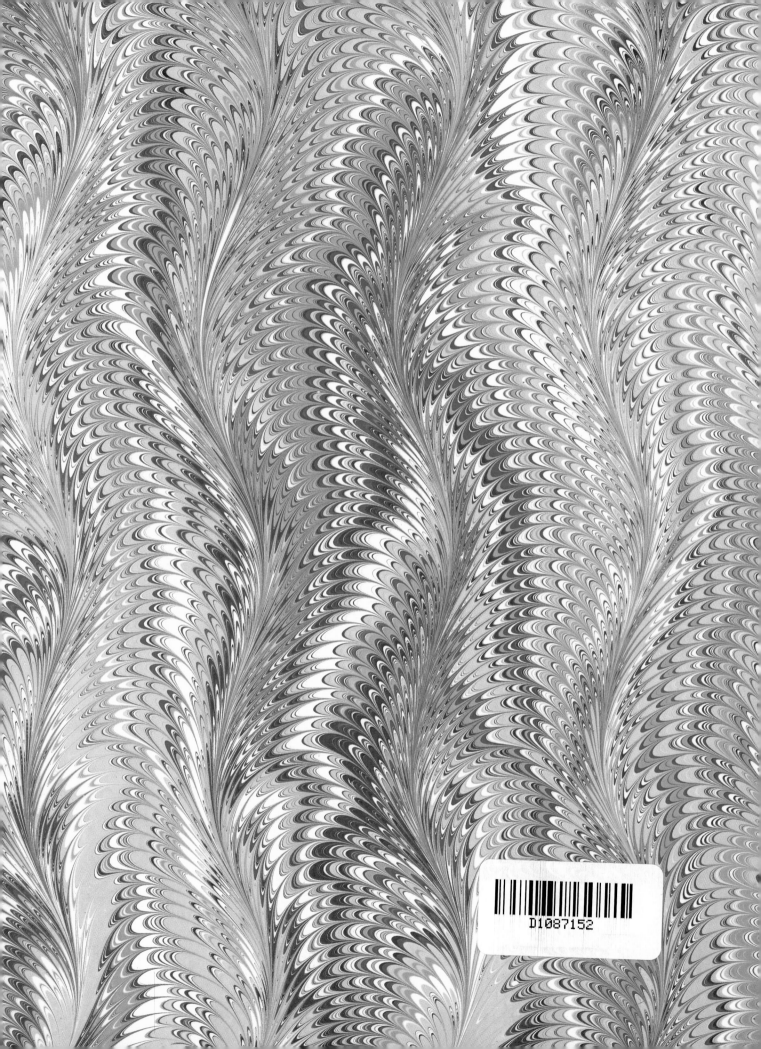

NORITAKE

Dinnerware

IDENTIFICATION MADE EASY

Robin Brewer

Schiffer Publishing Ltd

4880 Lower Valley Road, Atglen, PA 19310 USA

Copyright © 1999 by Robin Brewer
Library of Congress Catalog Card Number: 99-63737

Permission to reproduce Noritake patterns given by Noritake Co., Limited, Japan.

Designed by Bonnie M. Hensley
Type set in Korinna BT/Dutch 801 RmHdBT

ISBN: 0-7643-0925-0
Printed in China
1 2 3 4

Published by Schiffer Publishing Ltd.
4880 Lower Valley Road
Atglen, PA 19310
Phone: (610) 593-1777; Fax: (610) 593-2002
E-mail: Schifferbk@aol.com
Please visit our web site catalog at **www.schifferbooks.com**

In Europe, Schiffer books are distributed by Bushwood Books
6 Marksbury Avenue Kew Gardens
Surrey TW9 4JF England
Phone: 44 (0)181 392-8585; Fax: 44 (0)181 392-9876
E-mail: Bushwd@aol.com

This book may be purchased from the publisher.
Include $3.95 for shipping. Please try your bookstore first.
We are interested in hearing from authors with book ideas on related subjects.
You may write for a free printed catalog.

CONTENTS

ACKNOWLEDGMENTS

I would like to thank my mother, Nan Hall, and, my friend, Javena Conlee, who trudged through every garage sale, flea market, and little shop with me, turning over every piece of china we could find. My gratitude, also, to my friends, relatives, and co-workers who lent me their Noritake to photograph, and to everyone who suffered through my obsession with finding documentation on the Noritake Company. Last but not least, I would especially like to thank my friend Christel McCanless, who critiqued the manuscript and encouraged me.

This book would not exist without the wonderful dinnerware produced by the Noritake Company. I would like to thank Keishi Cuzuki, "KC," for helping me write the company history and helping me to get in touch with the right people there. I would also like to say a special thank you to Tadashi "Tony" Kawamura of Noritake for giving permission to use some of the copyrighted material in this book.

NTRODUCTION

I would like to explain how I came to write this book. My philosophy has long been "If you're not part of the solution you're part of the problem." The problem was *locating more information about the beautiful new piece of Noritake china I just bought.*

I bought Aimee Neff Alden's *Early Noritake Identification & Values*, and I purchased Joan Van Patten's *Collector's Encyclopedia of Noritake*, and all three of Carole Bess White's *Made in Japan Ceramics Identification and Values* books. My study of them revealed that there was no easy way to look up and identify a single piece of Noritake dinnerware.

To understand where I am coming from, let me give you some background. I grew up as a middle-class child of the fifties with working parents. I grew up without tea parties or large formal dining experiences. My mother's china was white Russel Wright Iroquois Casual, part of the modernist movement. On special occasions, we enjoyed a tablecloth, sterling silverware, and the same white dishes. In the 1970s, I jumped right into raising a family while pursuing an education and a career. A hectic life pace goes with that lifestyle. As a wedding gift, I received a twelve-place setting of Noritake Oriental 6341, which I used as everyday china. It survived small children and a dishwasher, because of its durability not because of my care.

With the introduction of microwaves, my beautiful, gold-edged Noritake china was relegated to the china cabinet to be used only on special occasions. I was always in a hurry in those days, so I hurried out and bought a cheap pattern of stoneware for everyday use, and we ate off stoneware for the next twenty years. I did not know what I was missing, but then ignorance is bliss.

After my children grew up and left home, I was lucky enough to be sent to a business convention in San Francisco. My traveling companion, another woman, and I enjoyed the sights in our free time – Saks Fifth Avenue, the Coach Store, FAO Schwartz, etc. When the convention was over, we decided to treat ourselves to High Tea at the Weston St. Francis Hotel on Union Square. Were we in for a treat! Sitting and enjoying the ambiance, feeling pretty hoity-toity, I realized how wonderful tea tasted in a delicate china cup. The silver strainer and strawberries with cream helped, too!

After that experience, I began to look for and collect teapots and cups and saucers with the idea that I could serve High Tea at home. I purchased a couple of English teapots and some bone china cups and saucers. I had inherited from my father's

mother a brown betty teapot marked "Japan." My mother offered me the remains of a tea set that her brother had brought back from Japan in the 1930s as a gift for their mother, my other grandmother. There was a teapot, creamer, sugar and two of the finest, thinnest, porcelain teacups and saucers I had ever seen. By the end of my first tea party, the English teapots had dribbled and the two Japanese teapots had not. I am sure some English or American teapots pour perfectly, but I was impressed with my Japanese teapots.

As I shopped further for accessories for my tea parties, a hobby was born. I touched, examined, and admired every teacup in every store in my hometown. I was attracted again to Noritake for its fine detail and satin smoothness. Long before I had to add bookshelves to our empty bedrooms to display my growing china collection, I was hooked. As I collected more and more of the older dinnerware, I gradually developed a method of organizing my collection so I could more easily identify each different pattern. How easy it would be if all the pieces had a name and number on it! But, since that is not the case, another method of identifying patterns was needed.

I have enjoyed my method of identifying Noritake dinnerware, and I want to share it with others who enjoy and collect this beautiful china. My simple method should help you do the following:

Date the piece.
Find replacement pieces.
Learn what pieces were available in the pattern.
Locate compatible patterns.

I hope you will enjoy using my "solution" to the problem of locating more information about your own beautiful piece of Noritake china.

I am always on the look out for more information about Noritake China. Should you have a catalog, old paperwork about a pattern, an advertisement, anything about Noritake I would love to hear from you. You may contact me by: E-mail at BrewerR@Hiwaay.net; Phone at (256) 337-4665; or Robin Brewer, 12012 Queens Place Huntsville, AL 35803-1822. I cannot be responsible for returning original items to you. So please send me only a copy of your information, and keep the originals for your own files. Thank you for any information you can share. We will all benefit from knowing more about Noritake.

CHAPTER 1.

CHINA MAKING AND THE HISTORY OF THE NORITAKE CO.

The year 1717 is the date given as the earliest true porcelain production in Germany. A German named Bottger in Dresden, working for the King of Poland, came upon a substance that made it possible to work with white clay and keep it white after firing. Soft paste porcelain is made of kaolin, and is mixed with bone ash to make bone china, or other ingredients to harden it. This type of china is not as translucent or hard as porcelain. The French were making a soft paste porcelain by the mid-1700s, as were the English and the Italians. Everyone vied to compete with the Chinese for their fine potting and glazes. Soon clay and later plaster-of-paris molds were created so that an endless variety of shapes and sizes of china could be made. This led to the setting of tables with services of china in every shape and size. An unbelievable number of pieces were developed for separate specialized uses, such as celery dishes and oyster plates. East India Company was formed in Holland and England to trade in Chinese porcelain. The Chinese originally made the porcelain and decorated it in the Chinese manner, but soon began taking orders for European patterns; many of these sets ran into hundreds of pieces. The stylized patterns known as the Willow Patterns were produced by the Chinese and were imported as Canton and Nanking wares into America, literally, by the boatload. By the late 1770s, American sailing ships were being designed with sleek lines that enabled them to sail with larger holds. The American ships were the fastest ships on the seas. They could outrun almost everything else afloat, so importing china was becoming more affordable, as the trips becames less expensive. America developed a prosperous middle-class with a taste for the finer things, including Chinese porcelain. English and Chinese china were still better and less expensive than anything the Americans were able to produce.

American china factories started up. But they produced less attractive wares, at higher prices, so they did not suceed. In the 1840s David Haviland opened an import shop in New York City. Later, because he was so impressed with the porcelain made in France, he opened a factory in Limoges, France. His company, Haviland & Co., produced porcelain that was designed for American export and American tastes. Limoges was the center of the French kaolin-based porcelain industry. For the first time there was fine porcelain made in quantity by an American, but it was not American-made. It was not until 1906 when Walter Scott Lenox organized the Lenox Co. in Trenton, New Jersey, to make fine, hard-paste translucent, ivory-colored, true china that there was any appreciable competition from American producers.

The Chinese export trade was still strong, but then another country was heard from. Japan had a closed-door policy with the West for more than 214 years, until the signing of the trade treaty with America in 1858. The next year a Japanese delega-

tion of 77 members was sent to the U.S. Although Ichizaemon Morimura was not a member of this delegation, he had provided the gifts and souvenirs from the Japanese government for U.S. officials. The Nagoya Area in central Japan has been Japan's leading ceramics producing region since the eleventh century, and is the site of one of the oldest kilns known in Japan. In 1876 Morimura and his younger brother, Toyo, founded an export trading firm called Morimura Gumi in Ginza, Tokyo, and in the same year they also opened a Japanese retail shop in New York City, which later became Morimura Brothers. The shop handled traditional Japanese antiques, such as lacquerware, ornaments, vases, medicine cases, porcelains, picture frames, hanging scrolls, etc.

Morimura Gumi had owned several painting factories in Tokyo, Kyoto, and Nagoya since 1884. In order to increase efficiency and reduce expenses, in 1896 Morimura Gumi consolidated these operations into the Shumokucho and Chikaramachi areas, Nagoya, near the Morimura Gumi office facilities.

Soon Morimura Brothers started exporting fancy ware such as tea sets, chocolate sets, dresser sets, perfume bottles, and vases. When they began to export fine kaolin-based porcelain to the United States, they did not specialize in dinnerware. But soon the Morimura brothers recognized the flourishing demand for china in the United States, and they were determined to produce a line of fine white porcelain dinnerware to replace their porcelain, which was grayish.

To accomplish this, Morimura Gumi constructed a test kiln in an area of their consolidated painting factory in 1904. Despite their efforts, which included sending some engineers to Germany to study porcelain-making, the production of white body china made no visible progress for over five years. After intensive research, eventually, with the help of Rosenfelt's factory in Carlsbad, Austria, and from other porcelain-makers in other locations in Germany, Morimura Gumi developed new methods of producing white body porcelain. More than ten years had passed since their decision to create white porcelain. As a result of this research, around the turn of the century, a perfect blend was discovered.

In the year 1912, in Nagoya, Ichizaemon Morimura and five others, with the intention of producing porcelain tableware for export founded the Nippon Toki Kaisha, Ltd. This later became Noritake Company, Ltd. The research for production of white porcelain continued with the help of the Rosenfelt factory in Carlsbad, Austria. Although a white blend had been found, Noritake soon discovered that they could not produce 9-1/2 inch dinner plates with the new white body composition. Because of the larger bottom area, the form sagged and was unacceptable. This was a huge problem—how to complete a dinner set without dinner plates! But research continued, and in June of 1914 a long-awaited complete 93-piece dinner set was produced and shipped to the United States. (As a comparison, please note that Lenox first offered a complete set of dinnerware in 1917.)]

Noritake had beautiful porcelain tea sets, cups and saucers, and dresser sets in production during this time, but the western style china was made exclusively for export. In accordance with U.S. import laws, until 1921, the pieces were marked Nippon (meaning Japan) as the country of origin. An amendment to the import laws in 1921 required the country of origin to be written in English. After 1921 imported Noritake china was imprinted Made in Japan. The Noritake Company also exported many undecorated pieces, which were painted later by hobbyists in Europe and in the United States as well as by manufacturers such as Pichard China.

Magobei Okura and his son Kazuchika, who were among the six founders of the Noritake Company, first established Okura Art China in 1919 near Tokyo. The company was founded for the purpose of creating and manufacturing genuine art china to compare with the leading European art china makers of the day. In 1960 the Okura factory moved to Totsuka in Yokohama. Okura Art China is made by hand from choice materials with limited production. Some of it is marked O.A.C. Noritake or with their own five-lobed trademark, a plum blossom which is the Okura family crest. Okura is not a mass-production factory like Noritake, but a smaller type called a craftsmen shop. In 1917 Okura wares were exhibited at the Philadelphia International Fair and won the Best Prize. Okura China Inc. is still in production today, supplying their products to the Japanese royal family among others. The Noritake logo was added to Okura products for the U.S. markets to help introduce their products. An early competitor in the dinnerware field was the Meito Company, which went out of business in the 1940s.

From about 1921 into the 1930s Noritake made a luster ware using a metallic film over the glaze. Some pieces had painted floral, animal, geometric, portrait, and scenery decorations, which reflected the Art Deco styles popular at this time. In 1924 the Larkin Company, an American manufacturer, sold cleaning products directly to consumers though catalogs. To stimulate sales, customers were given coupon dollars that equaled the amount of their purchase. Housewives saved Larkin coupons so they could acquire the items of their choice from the Larkin premium catalog. Larkin offered Noritake's Azalea pattern china for the first time in its 1924 catalog. By 1931, Larkin identified the Azalea pattern as "Our Most Popular Pattern." Later Green Stamps also offered Noritake vases and other products as premiums.

It was not until 1928 that Noritake started to produce for the Japanese market. Noritake's hard porcelain was of a quality to compare with Germany, France, Austria, Italy, and Czechoslovakia. In 1935 the first bone china dinner sets were produced and marketed under the trademark of Royal Bone China. The New York office of the Morimura Brothers closed in 1940, shortly before the United States entered World War II. During the war years the Noritake factory in Japan produced abrasive grinding wheels (for cutting, grinding, and polishing) for heavy industries. They produced very little chinaware, and only for the Japanese market. When the war ended, the porcelain business in the Nagoya area was not able to begin production immediately. Damaged factories had to be rebuilt, necessary materials procured, and personnel readied before production could resume. The Noritake factory had sustained almost no damage during the war. Therefore, Noritake could start production sooner than other manufacturers.

In 1946 and 1947, Noritake products carried the name "Rose China," since quality was not up to factory standards because of material and equipment shortages. In November of 1947, Noritake, Inc., of the United States was reopened in New York and began to do business with major department stores and specialty shops.

Noritake had improved its porcelain formula and had new production techniques for fine china. They manufactured and supplied this new porcelain to the American pottery company Gladding McBean in 1958; this sold under the trade name of Franciscan Cosmopolitan China by NTK, Japan. Beginning in 1959 a new ivory china was produced and continued to be supplied to Gladding McBean until 1964. Noritake began marketing its own ivory china around 1962. In 1967 Imari Porcelainware Mfg. Co. was established (presently Noritake Imari) and took charge of the production of the ivory china. To keep up with the times, Noritake succeeded in the development, in 1964, of Progression China, a heat and serve product. This china was capable of going from the refrigerator to the oven and back to the freezer. It was designed to compete with Corning ware.

American Noritake offices opened in Los Angeles, Chicago, Dallas, Atlanta, Seattle, and Cincinnati between 1960 and 1970. The Noritake Company expanded its exports to include crystal glassware, stainless steel flatware, and Melamine products. Melamine is a plastic dinnerware designed for the on-the-go lifestyles of the TV generation. The Noritake Company has continued to develop new and beautiful products, which reflect the fashions and tastes of the times.

Noritake Oriental Number 6341. My original set of Noritake china. Service for 12 with serving pieces. Cost? It was a wedding gift; to replace today $1,500.00.

Noritake Nippon tea strainer, circa 1910. $75-100.

CHAPTER 2.

SETTING AN ELEGANT TABLE

During Queen Victoria's reign, industrialization brought affluence, and people in Europe and America sought ways of displaying their wealth. Formal Victorian dining required a staggering number of service pieces, depending on the menu. China was changed for every course. In the mid-nineteenth century, servants served from a sideboard, leaving ample room to set the table with many objects. There was a plate, cup or service dish for every item on the menu.

Starting with breakfast, the china included toast racks, egg cups and egg warmers. A full table setting included china, sterling silverware, and crystal. (Even orange juice tastes better in a cut glass goblet!) Jam was served in a pot with its own porcelain spoon. The table might be set with a sugar dish, milk pot, teapot, slop bowl (for the tea dregs), a coffeepot and any number of other specialized china items. Noritake even made pancake sets, which included a plate with a vented cover for keeping the pancakes warm on the way to the table, a tall shaker for powdered sugar, and a stylized pitcher for syrup. Some syrup pitchers were small and squat like the creamers, but unlike creamers they had lids and usually an underplate to catch any stray drips.

China pieces were produced for every conceivable use on the table. Condiments were served on individual trays with an open master salt, a pepper shaker, and a mustard pot with it's own ladle. In the early 1900s, butter was stored in round china tubs that kept it cool and protected. As butter was expensive, it was served in a dish with a cover, and each guest was served one delicate curl of butter on a porcelain butter plate, ensuring that no one would overindulge.

Luncheon sets were often smaller plates than dinner sets, with smaller pieces of silverware alongside. A luncheon napkin is described as fifteen inches square and a dinner napkin as twenty-four inches. Special dishes were crafted for every imaginable type of food, for example, asparagus and pickles. Lemonade sets were designed with cups reminiscent of chocolate cups but were slightly taller. Coffee was served in cups the size we use for tea today. Breakfast coffee was in larger cups, and after dinner coffee was in smaller or demitasse cups.

Afternoons were time for tea, where the porcelain tea service was the centerpiece. Tiered trays with small sandwiches, pastries, and cookies accompanied small snack plates for a light meal. If the afternoon snack included celery it was often served in its own bowl with small salt dishes available at every place. The meal might take on the elegance of a mini-dinner party, with double-handled bouillon cups, progressing though an array of small side dishes and finishing the meal with decorated cakes and molded ices.

On some winter afternoons early in the 1900s, Americans enjoyed cups of hot, thick, sweet chocolate, a beverage that has been somewhat neglected in recent years. It was made from a thick paste of cocoa or chocolate to which warm milk was added. Frothy chocolate was made with whipped egg whites, while milled chocolate required whisking the mixture in the pan. A chocolate pot resembles a coffeepot. Usually it is smaller in size but identical in shape, it is also taller than it is wide. A little of this rich concoction went a long way. Unlike today's hot chocolate, old-fashioned cocoa was a very thick drink, and three-quarters of a demitasse cup was plenty for most people.

Dinner was the formal meal of the day, when all stops were pulled out to serve in elegant fashion, the main event of the evening. Few people today could tolerate the sheer size of a Victorian dinner, let alone spare the hours it took to prepare and eat it. The modern arrangement of silverware in a place setting: salad, fish, and dinner forks on the left, knives and soup spoon on the right, with a dessert spoon and fork above the plate is based on the pattern set in the nineteenth century. However today's most elaborate dinner is far simpler than a Victorian dinner.

China included soup tureens, sauce boats, covered oval vegetable bowls, platters in varying sizes, meat platters grooved with a tree and well designed for draining off drippings, round pudding dishes, deep oval dishes, butter plates, custard cups, oyster plates, and salad bowls. Meals often consisted of eight courses. Oysters were served first followed by two kinds of contrasting soup, clear and dark. Then a course of fish followed by roasted vegetables. Finally, entrées of a meat dish and game were served, each with accompanying side dishes of vegetables, sauces, condiments, and appetizers. The final course was dessert. It was not until the late Victorian period that a dinner service included dessert plates and coffee cups. Coffee after dinner was often served in demitasse cups. After a move to the drawing room, so the table could be cleared.

The size of formal dinnerware services decreased in the periods between 1920 and 1940. Many accessory pieces, such as bone dishes, oyster dishes, and individual salts, were no longer made in many patterns. Instead of services containing four to six platters, the number was reduced to two or three. This period also witnessed the increased importation of inexpensive Japanese table services, of which Noritake enjoyed a significant market share. The abundance of inexpensive Japanese imported dinnerware in the American market following the end of World War II contributed to the demise of some American pottery manufacturers, many who had experienced financial difficulties during the depression. Japanese dinnerware manufacturers directly challenged English and European manufacturers for dominance of the American market.

In the 1950s, with the concept of casual dining gaining popularity, dinnerware suppliers offered Melamine dinnerware, made of plastic. The patio and kitchen became the household's primary evening dining locations; the dining room, if a home had one, was reserved for holidays and special occasions. In many suburban homes built in the 1960s, the living room and dining room were combined into a single room. The impact of television on American dining habits was dramatic. Television (TV) trays and TV dinners ended the dining room gathering for dinner in many families. While fine dinnerware had been marketed in better department, jewelry, and specialty stores, the move to casual dining brought dinnerware to the catalog mail-order firms such as J. C. Penny, Sears & Roebuck, and Montgomery Ward. Eventually, stoneware dishes could be bought at the discount stores, such as K-Mart and Wal-Mart.

But, as all things old become new again, the use of china inherited from grandparents has become popular today. Setting an eclectic dining table with a mix and match of old and new allows the resurrection of surviving pieces of older porcelain mixed in with new pieces. Shopping antiques malls and flea markets is a great source of odd pieces of old and not-so-old china. The beauty of Noritake is that dinnerware almost a hundred years old is affordable and available.

Noritake after-dinner coffee or chocolate service for 6, circa 1925. $150-200.

Noritake mayonnaise or whipped cream server, circa 1930. $35-60.

Noritake luster cake plate, circa 1920. $45-60.

CHAPTER 3.

CARE AND USE OF YOUR DINNERWARE

When you select your dinnerware, remember you will probably be using it for a number of decades, so choose something versatile, something you love, and something durable. When you choose, look at all the pieces, even if you are only going to buy basic pieces in the beginning. If you love the design on the plate, be sure you love it on the teapot or sugar bowl. Buy the best china you can afford. Do not settle for your second choice because it is cheaper. You are going to have to live with this choice for a long time. Once you have purchased your china, plan to use it. With today's emphasis on casual living, having a set of everyday stoneware that is made to survive the dishwasher and microwave is a good idea. But do not put your porcelain away in the china cabinet to be used only on holidays. Use it as often as you can. Sometimes the feeling "I deserve this" can be satisfied with a cup of tea in your finest china cup.

Whether your china was inherited from your grandmother or purchased new, caring for it needs to become everyday practice. Every use establishes the link of ownership and enhances the connection you feel for the pattern and pieces you have. All china will break, but for all its look of delicacy, china is quite durable.

To provide reasonable care, start with your china's storage. Make sure the storage area can support the weight of a full set of dinnerware. Storing china on shelves too high to reach is a disaster waiting to strike. Keep dishes in cabinets from knee to shoulder height for surer handling. Also, because rapid changes in temperature can damage dinnerware, do not store your china in cabinets that are attached to an outside wall of your home. An outside wall can conduct cold in the winter. Your china can take a wide range of temperatures as long as the change is gradual. Direct sunlight acts as a bleaching agent, so do not store your dinnerware where it is exposed to direct sunlight everyday. Ideal storage areas keeps ceramic surfaces from touching each other, this includes touching by stacking or by touching the sides of pieces. Contact with another piece of china can cause chipping or damage to the surface. When stacking flat ceramic pieces on top of each other, avoid stacking more than you can comfortably pick up. Place a simple paper napkin between stacked plates to reduce wear on the surfaces. The best way to store (and display) cups is to hang them from safety cup hooks. If you are going to display large pieces by standing them up, be sure there is an adequate plate stand or a plate rail to hold the dishes upright. Wooden stands are less likely to scratch your dinnerware. Be especially careful if your china cabinet has glass shelves, which can be very slippery. If you feel as if you have to hold your breath when putting your dishes away, you probably need to devise a better storage area.

Whether you wash your china by hand or in a dishwasher is a matter of personal preference. I do both. If I am tired, I am probably better off using the dishwasher and not handling my china too much, but other times I like being alone and doing it by hand. If you choose to wash your dishes by hand, be sure to have enough space to wash and dry each piece. When glazed ceramics are wet, they can easily scratch each other, so do not stack your wet dishes. Do not load too many dishes in the dishpan. One dish rattling on top of another one is the easiest way to break both of them. Porcelain can be scratched, so be careful. Wash one dish at a time and do not scrape with a sharp knife or use a steel wool pad or other abrasive. Soak your china to remove stubborn stuck-on food. Use hot but not scalding water. I usually put a rubber mat on the bottom of the sink when I am washing dishes, but if you do not have one, put an extra dish towel on the bottom of the sink as a cushion. Wash your china separately from aluminum pots or pans. China rubbing against aluminum cookware can cause a gray streak on your china.

Dry your dinnerware with a soft cloth. Letting your china drip dry is fine as long as you have a safe place for pieces to drip. An overstacked drain rack is an invitation for an accident.

Using your dishwasher is a personal choice, but a word of caution. If your china does not specifically say it is dishwasher safe, it probably is not. But, if you are in a hurry or are tired, a correctly loaded dishwasher with mild detergent on a lower temperature occasionally probably would not hurt anything. (Don't tell my mother but I occasionally put my sterling in the dishwasher.) Know your appliance, detergent, and your dinnerware before making the decision. The main thing when using a dishwasher is not to let the pieces touch each other.

Did you know strawberries can stain your china? Guilty as charged! Borax or common salt applied with a soft cloth is one good way to remove strawberry, tea, and coffee stains. Other methods include soaking the stain in a solution of dishwashing detergent and water or pouring boiling water over the stain.

Ovens, microwaves, and freezers are not places to put fine china. Some china dinnerware is now marketed as ovenproof or suitable for the freezer. If your china has this kind of capability follow the manufacturers instructions. If you have an older pattern and do not know what the manufacturer recommended, then avoid all extreme temperatures. If you are going to err, err on the side of caution in the care of your dinnerware.

Noritake breakfast set, circa 1925. $75-100.

Noritake, four cup tea pot $75-100, tea cup and saucer $18-28 and individual salts $6-12 all monogrammed, circa 1925.

Noritake, powdered sugar shaker part of a waffle set, circa 1926. $75-100 (for a set).

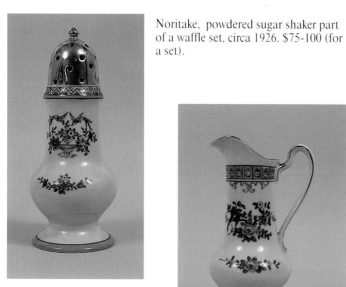

Noritake syrup pitcher with under plate , circa 1920. $25-30.

Noritake, syrup pitcher part of a waffle set, circa 1926. $75-100 (for a set).

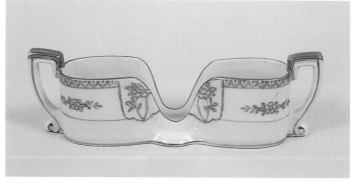

Noritake White and Gold, #175, longest running pattern, tea set for 6, circa 1911. $275-325.

Noritake butter dish (dish, strainer & dome cover), circa 1924. $50-60.

Noritake spoon holder for buffet, circa 1924. $45-60.

CHAPTER 4.

BACKSTAMPS

A backstamp is the manufacturer's mark found on the underside of a piece of china. These usually are helpful in dating and identifying the maker of a piece. Noritake did not initially mark each piece made as Noritake, as they used different symbols and logos. It was after the passage of American import laws that they added the country of origin, first as Nippon and later as Japan. By the 1930s Noritake began to name and number most of their dinnerware. Identifying early patterns is often a search leaving the buyer to accumulate clues and finally guess about the china. When I started to catalog and categorize my collection, I developed a method so that I could identify pieces that did not have a name or number.

I have included in chronological order each of the types of backstamps that I am aware of that the Noritake Company used on their dinnerware. But beware of putting too much confidence in a backstamp. Some china patterns were produced over a period of time when backstamp designs changed, so earlier pieces of the pattern carry one backstamp and later pieces a different one. Occasionally an old backstamp was reused after a new design had been introduced. So use caution in relying on backstamps.

It would be nice if when a new backstamp was created, the old one was no longer used, but this is not the way it worked. Then we also have faked backstamps. The most we can tell about backstamps is when they were registered, so all you know for sure is it was not used prior to the registration date. So the use of the backstamp to help identify a piece is just one of the many clues.

I like to think of the Noritake Company backstamps roughly in the following order.

1. The NIPPON ERA prior to use of the word "Japan" being used—the leaf, the m in wreath, the sunrise, the RC and the komaru (spider) symbol.

2. Then the long M IN WREATH period first without a banner then later with the banner for the name of the pattern.

3. In the 1930s the fancy shield and colored logos arrived which I call the M WITH THE SCROLLS & BOWS.

4. Then we jump to after the war and late 1940s with the OCCUPIED JAPAN and the NIPPON TOKI KAISHA, and ROSE CHINA.

5. 1953 brings the introduction of the N IN WREATH PRINTED with "Noritake China" printed over the symbol.

6. The early 1960s the N IN WREATH SCRIPT has "Noritake" in script over the symbol.

7. The 1970s introduce the CONTEMPORARY logo.

8. The late 1970s begins the IRELAND and early 1980s SRI LANKA and PHILLIPINES.

9. The current backstamps such as LEGACY, VERSATONE, CONTEMPORARY, EXPRESSIONS, PROGRESSION.

Company names used on backstamps of Noritake products, in addition to Noritake, are Chikaramachi, Princess China, Royale Bone China, Embassy China, Kenwood China, Albion China, and Rose China. When I first started collecting, people would say things like "you will learn how Noritake feels." I thought all china felt the same. Now after feeling thousands of pieces of china, I do recognize the thin delicate smooth "feel" of Noritake.

I have racked my brain to think of a way of identifying backstamps without numbering them. Too many people identify pieces saying Van Pattens number 27 backstamp or Alden's number 93. Well if you have not read Van Pattens book (yes there are a few who have not) you do not know what is being described. I like the way David Spain tried to limit the numbers used to identify the backstamp but he left out the backstamps that do not say Noritake. So! What to do, what to do? I have included representatives of each of the backstamps I have found on dinnerware, and I have tried to put them in chronological order. My method of identification is that I have given each backstamp a descriptive name. I have used the name in the text under each picture so you will not have to remember numbers or refer back to the section on backstamps to know which kind of backstamp. I hope you find that helpful in the identification of your Noritake. If you have any suggestions, I am always eager to discuss china and how to identify it. But remember the backstamp on my piece of a pattern may not match the backstamp you have on the identical pattern. A backstamp can be misleading sometimes so do not rely too heavily on it for identification. It is only one of the pieces of the puzzle.

1891. Maple leaf.

1908. K in circle Noritake script MIJ.

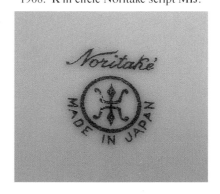

1911. R.C. with hat.

1911. R.C. handpainted nippon.

1911. Nippon under Noritake.

1912. M in wreath N/HP/Nippon.

1911. Sunrise.

1912. K in circle Nippon fancy.

1916. HOWO.

1911. R.C. in circle Nippon.

1912. R.C. with clackers NTK.

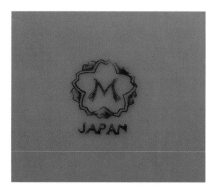
1916. Blossom M double Japan.

1911. K in circle Nippon plain.

1912 M in wreath nor/ Nippon.

1918. M in wreath N/HP/Japan.

1918. M in wreath N/HP/Japan.

1921. M Hanging Wreath.

1930. M with Crown.

1918. M in wreath N/HP/Japan.

1924. Cherry Blossom.

1931. M in shield China.

1918. M in wreath N/HP/Japan.

1925. Blossom M single Japan.

1933. M in scrolls.

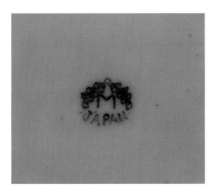

1921. M Hanging Wreath.

1928. Chikaramachi.

1933. M in scrolls.

1933. M in wreath big bow.

1935. M in wrought-iron.

1944. M on stage.

1933. M in wreath big bow.

1940. M in scroll and wreath.

1946. Rose china.

1933. M in wreath small bow 3 leaves.

1940. M in scroll and wreath.

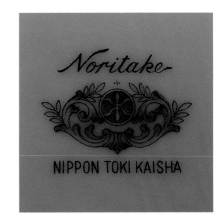

1947. K in scroll shield NTK.

1933. M in wreath small bow 3 leaves.

1944. M on stage.

1947. K in scroll shield occupied.

1949. M in wreath bow OJ.

1949. R.C. in leafy shield.

1953. N in wreath printed.

1949. M in wreath bow OJ.

1950. Noritake script.

1953. N in wreath printed.

1949. K in circle Noritake script NTK.

1952. N in scroll shield Japan.

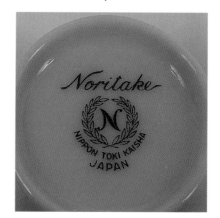

1955. N crossed stems NTK.

1949. K in circle Noritake script MIJ.

1953. N in wreath printed.

1955. Fine China stars.

17

1956. R.C. in wreath.

1962. N in wreath Ivory China.

1968. Okura.

1956. R.C. in wreath.

1963. N in wreath colorful.

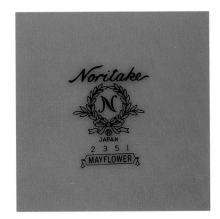

1968. N in wreath black and gold.

1961. Cook'n Serve.

1965. Progression N.

1970. Expression.

1962. N in wreath Ivory China.

1967. Lamp Bone China printed Japan.

1970. Contemporary FC Japan.

DISH-WASHER SAFE
OVEN SAFE

Noritake
Craftone

JAPAN

BLUE SKY
8760

1972. Craftone.

Keltcraft
misty isle

COLLECTION
by
Noritake
DETERGENT-SAFE
MICROWAVE & OVEN-SAFE
©
IRELAND
9138
ETERNAL BLUSH

1983. Keltcraft misty isle.

ONEIDA
BY
Noritake
SRI LANKA

1994. Oneida Sri Lanka.

Contemporary
FINE CHINA
by Noritake
SRI LANKA

LONGWOOD
2485

1974. Contemporary FC Sri Lanka.

Legendary
by
Noritake
SRI LANKA

SWEET LEILANI
3482
©

1983. Legendary Sri Lanka.

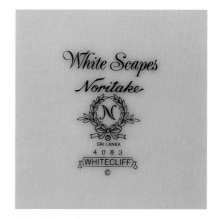

White Scapes
Noritake
N
SRI LANKA
4083
WHITECLIFF
©

1995. White Scapes.

Legacy
by
Noritake
©
PHILIPPINES

1977. Legacy Philippines.

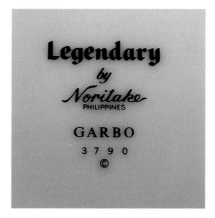

Legendary
by
Noritake
PHILIPPINES

GARBO
3790
©

1983. Legendary Philippines.

New Lineage II
BY Noritake
Bone China
N
THAILAND
4762
PALESTRA
©

1996. New Lineage II bone china.

Noritake
Ireland

IRELAND
2963
ANTICIPATION
©

1977. Ireland.

NEW DECADE
by
Noritake
DETERGENT SAFE
MICROWAVE & OVEN SAFE
©
JAPAN
9094
CAFÉ DU JOUR

1984 . New Decade wave.

1996. N in wreath ivory china.

1997. Oneida Japan.

1961. Franciscan.

1960. United Airlines.

IDENTIFICATION METHOD

(HOW TO LOOK IT UP)

First let me tell you that if you are trying to find out more information on a piece of Noritake china you currently own or are considering purchasing, and it has a name or number, you are in luck. Just turn directly to the back of this book to the Noritake name index or the Noritake number index. Look up the page your pattern is on using the indexed page numbers. When you get to the page with your pattern, you will find time frames of manufacture, price guides, and china blanks (shapes) used for that pattern. You are one of the lucky ones and have a piece that is easily identified. I hope the additional information is interesting.

What if you have a piece that is not named or numbered and you want to find it in this book? I have developed a few questions that will lead you to a specific area, which will describe your pattern. If your pattern is actually pictured here, you will have all the information about your pattern that I was able to locate.

Even with all the information I have collected about Noritake china, I am always on the lookout for old catalogs, or magazine advertisements. I am searching for information on all Noritake pieces. If you have any information about a pattern, please share it. If you have a price list from when you purchased your china, or pictures of pieces available, do not think, "Oh this is only twenty years old and not a collectible." All bits of information are valuable when trying to piece together the past. Send information (copies are welcome; send originals only if you do not want them back) that expands this research or any comments, positive or negative to: Robin Brewer, 12012 Queens Place, Huntsville, AL 35803-1822. Your input is valuable and appreciated.

My method of identifying patterns of Noritake dinnerware involves identifying elements of the design, color of the porcelain, and finally the major color of the pattern. Since the majority of Noritake china has flowers, the appearance of any other elements in addition to the flowers, such as a bird or butterfly is chosen as the identifying element. What I mean by the identifying element is: any other unique thing other than flowers that we can define and pick out of the pattern. Said another way: since almost all Noritake china has flowers, we will ignore the flowers and identify the pattern by other unique parts of the design. When the design is all flowers, then I use the color of the china on which the flowers are applied. Finally (and probably the most arbitrary) is the identification of the major color used in the design. When selecting the major color, I do not consider the white color of the underlying plate or the cream band. Usually if there is a major color on the rim band, it is the color I pick. The color order is white, gold, orange, pink, maroon, green, blue, gray, black, and mixed. I use mixed as the color when no one color seems to

dominate. If I have multiple patterns with the same elements, then I try to arrange them in chronological order, relying on the backstamp and patent numbers if available. These are the questions to ask yourself when trying to decide which chapter to look in: Is the design only lines or is the color solid? *(Ch. 6)* Is the design mainly a geometric organization of lines? *(Ch. 7)* Is the design made up of scrolls and feathers? *(Ch. 8)* Is the design of leaves and evergreens or does it contain trees? *(Ch. 9)* Does the design contain fruit? *(Ch. 10)* Are the flowers stylized? *(Ch. 11)* Are there any creatures such as birds, butterflies or fish in the design anywhere? *(Ch. 12)* If none of these questions take you off to a chapter containing your pattern, then the large category of patterns made up of flowers *(Ch. 13)* is broken down to the underlying plate. Now, on to the method of identifying your china. The next sections explain the categories other than flowers, so you can answer the design element questions. Once you have read and understand my method, you will be able to look at the table of contents to this book and flip straight to the page with your pattern.

Trying to collect all the patterns of Noritake dinnerware is like trying to collect all the little liver pills Carter made. Noritake actually re-issued patterns and have some that are so similar only the designer can tell the difference. One feature of the organization of this identification guide is that when you locate the place your pattern should be, you will see other very similar patterns. If you have inherited your grandmother's china, or bought a piece you could not pass up at a flea market, you should be able to find not only your pattern, but also matching or coordinating patterns for enlarging your set.

Example of the line only design.

Example of the geometric design.

Example of the birds or creatures design.

Example of the stylized gold only design.

Example of the geometric design.

Example of the birds or creatures design.

Example of the stylized (white on white) design.

Example of the flowers on white plate design.

Example of the feathers design.

Example of the stylized flowers design.

Example of the flowers on a white with cream band design.

Example of the flowers on a white with cream band plate design.

Example of the flowers on a white with cream band design.

Example of the fruit design.

CHAPTER 6.

LINES AND SOLIDS

The first element is simple lines or solid colors. If your Noritake has only a line around the rim or a wide colored border or is solid in color, these pieces are located in the first section. Noritake has made gold trimmed pieces since the beginning. Some have pattern names, some have different width to the trim, and some have an additional pin line. If the trim looks identical and the backstamps are different this only means the pattern was in production over a time period, which saw a change in backstamps, or pieces destined for different countries. I was surprised at the variations of this simple design. Each picture contains the following information, if available: description; name; Noritake number; design patent number; backstamp; years of production; and the name of its blank.

A solid white piece. Noritake script. 1950. Classic.

A white piece with a ribbed border. Oneida Sri Lanka. 1994.

A gold edged white piece with a gold line around the rim monogrammed with an R and signed J.B. Crosman. Sunrise. 1911- Original.

A solid white piece. N crossed stems Japan. 1973. Teaset. Domestic Japanese Market.

A gold edged white piece with thin gold line around the edge. Sunrise. 1911. Tea set.

A solid white piece with small white on white rectangles raised around the rim (demitass). N in wreath black and gold. 1968.

A gold edged white piece with a wide gold rim line (cream and mustard pot). Sunrise. 1911. Original.

A gold edged white piece with a gold line around the rim and an inner pin line of gold (cake plate). Colonial. R.C. in circle Nippon. 1911-1914. Original.

A gold edged cream piece with a double gold line around the rim outside line wider inner line a pin line.M in wreath nor/ Nippon. 1912. Original.

A gold edged white piece with a half-inch-wide gold rim line and an inner gold pin line. Handles are solid gold. Goldena. M in wreath nor/ Nippon. 1914-1918. Original.

A gold edged white piece with a gold line around the rim. Pierepoint. M in wreath nor/ Nippon. 1912-1930. Original.

A gold edged cream piece with a gold rim and sold gold handles with a monogram. Yukon (the). M in wreath nor/ Nippon. 1914. Original.

A gold edged white piece with a thin gold line around the rim. M in wreath N/HP/ Japan. 1918.

A gold edged white piece with a thin gold line around the rim (individual cream and sugar). M in wreath N/HP/Japan. 1918. Original.

A solid gold piece with a luster finish (individual salt, pepper and mustard) M in wreath N/HP/Japan. 1918.

A gold edged white piece with a solid gold line around the rim (saki cups). Noritake script. 1950-1970.

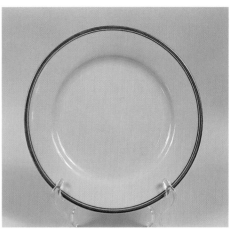

A gold edged ivory china piece with double gold line around the rim. Viceroy. 7222. N in wreath Ivory China. 1976-1987. Victorian II coupe.

A gold edge white piece with a quarter-inch gold band around the rim with another pin line right next to the rim. Coronet. M in wreath N/HP/Japan. 1921-1930 . Original.

A gold edged white piece with a wide gold rim and a gold monogram (individual salt shakers, 2 shapes). Noritake script. 1950.

A gold edged white piece designed and produced for the Danbury Mint (dinner bell). N in wreath black & gold. 1975.

A gold edged white piece with a half-inch gold line around the rim. : Gwendolyn. 5083. M in wreath big bow. 1933. Rim.

A gold edged white piece with a gold line around the rim with an inner gold pin line. K in scroll shield occupied. 1947-1949.

A gold edged white piece with a narrow pin line gold line around the rim and a inner pin line. N in wreath printed. 1953.

A gold edged white piece with a thin gold line around the rim with a double inner gold line. Gloria. 6526. N in wreath black and gold. 1974-1975. Classic.

A gold edged white piece with three gold pin lines around the rim and a inner gold pin line. Goldart. 5290. N in wreath printed. 1953.

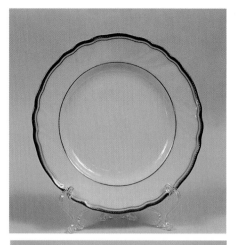

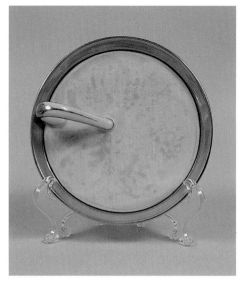

A gold edge white piece with scalloped rim with a wide and a narrow gold line around the rim and an inner pin line of gold. Salutation. 4309. Factory in shield. 1995-1998. Estate.

A gold-edged pearlized white piece with a wide orange band and inner gold line. M in wreath N/HP/Japan. 1927-1934. Azalea.

A gold edged white piece with a gold enclosed brown edge. Royale Café. 6539. N in wreath black and gold. 1968. Classic.

A gold edged orange luster piece with art deco bright orange blue and white flowers on the handles (cake plate). M in wreath N/HP/Japan. 1922. Original.

A gold edged white piece with a gold rim with a second pin line on the rim and an inner pin line of gold. Contemporary FC Philippines. 1976. Classic.

A gold edged white piece with an impressed clover leaf design (3" square, mint dish). Okura OAC art china. 1960-1998.

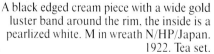

A black edged cream piece with a wide gold luster band around the rim, the inside is a pearlized white. M in wreath N/HP/Japan. 1922. Tea set.

A gold edged white piece with a wide bright yellow band outlined in gold (cream soup). M in wreath N/HP/Japan. Mushroom.

A gold edged white piece with an orange line around the edge and the glaze is a pearlized glaze. M in wreath N/HP/Japan 1927-1934. Azalea.

A gold edged white piece with solid yellow color (after dinner). M on stage. 1940 timeframe. Mushroom.

A white piece with lavender, pink, and blue lines around the edge intersected by geometric v shape. United Airlines. Noritake script. 1950.

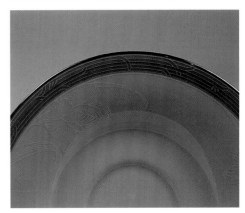

A silver edged ivory china piece with a flower etched cream on cream and is outlined with a federal blue and rose pink lines. Breathless. 7704. Fine China in wreath 1984-1992. New Traditions.

A gold edged white piece with solid yellow color no design. K in circle Noritake script NTK. 1949.

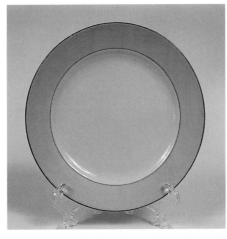

A brown edged white piece with a wide band of light pink band. K in circle Noritake script NTK. 1949.

A gold edged white piece with solid red color. M on stage. 1940 timeframe. Mushroom.

A gold edged white piece colored solid mint green(large coffee cup). 621. K in circle Noritake script MIJ. 1949.

A black edged white piece with a solid bright yellow color, the handle and rim are black. K in circle Noritake script MIJ. 1949.

A black edged blue luster piece lined with orange and outlined with black (after dinner). M in wreath HP/Nippon. 1911-1920.

A gold edged white piece with a rim edge of maroon with a gold pin line on top. Royale Claret. 6537. N in wreath black and gold. 1968. coupe.

A gold edged white piece with a wide blue border with an inner gold line (child's tea set).Sunrise. 1911-1918. Child's set.

A black edged white piece with a wide blue luster band with white etched flowers and an inner black line. M in wreath N/HP/Japan. 1921-1928.

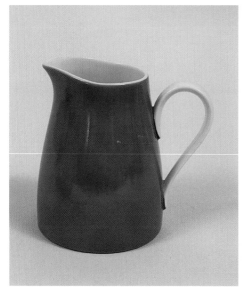

A white piece with solid green color. Noritake script. 1950.

A blue edged white with cream band piece with a large cream band outlined with blue (individual breakfast teapot). M in wreath N/HP/Japan. 1918-1928. Tea set.

A gold edged white piece with a wide blue band and an inner gold line. M in wreath N/HP/Japan. 1921-1928. Azalea.

A black edged solid blue luster piece with gold insides. M in wreath N/HP/Japan. 1921-1928. Azalea.

A gold edged white piece with a wide blue band outlined in gold (cream soup). M in wreath N/HP/Japan. 1918. Mushroom.

A silver edged white piece with a silver line around the edge and an inner silver line. N in wreath printed. 1953. LaSalle.

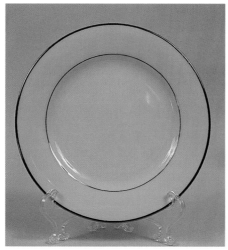

A silver edged white piece with a quarter inch silver line around the rim. Silverdale. 5594. N in wreath printed. 1955. Butterfly.

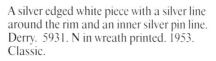

A silver edged white piece with a silver line around the rim with an inner silver pin line. Pinnacle. 2019. N in wreath black and gold. 1963-1970. Coupe.

A silver edged white piece with a silver line around the rim and an inner silver pin line. Derry. 5931. N in wreath printed. 1953. Classic.

A silver edged white piece with a double silver line around the rim with an inner silver pin line. Regency. 2219. N in wreath black and gold. 1975-1981. Commander.

A silver edged white piece which is solid white with the silver pin line edge. Fremont. 6127. N in wreath black and gold. 1975-1978. Concerto.

A silver edged white piece with a small pin line of sliver around the edge, the form has a diamond pattern around the border. Sonoma. 6353. N in wreath black and gold. 1968-1978. Butterfly form.

A silver edged white piece with a silver and bronze line around the edge. Compton. 6524. N in wreath black and gold. 1968. Concerto.

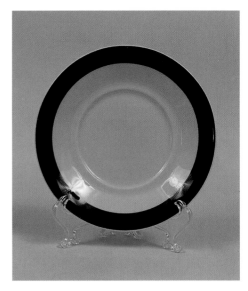

A gold edged white piece with a wide band of black. Forest Bounty. 4058. Impromptu Sri Lanka. 1995-1998. Paramount New Traditions.

A silver edged white piece with a wide gray band around the border with an inner silver line. Grayburn. 5323. N in wreath printed. 1953.

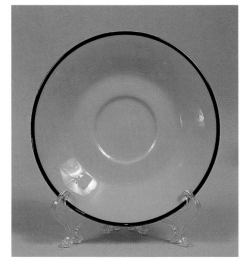

A silver edged white piece with a quarter-inch silver line around the rim. Pilgrim. 6981. N in wreath black and gold. 1963-1970. Coupe.

A silver edged white piece with a wide and narrow line of silver round the rim and an inner silver pin line. Contemporary FC Philippines. 1976. Classic.

A gold-edged white piece with a wide black band with an inner gold line on a scalloped china piece (cream soup saucer). M in wreath N/HP/Japan. Mushroom.

CHAPTER 7.

GEOMETRIC PATTERNS

If your pattern is not a simple trim line or a solid, ask yourself this question. Does the pattern consist of only geometric lines, that is, lines that do not outline a recognizable object such as leaves, flowers, or feathers?

A gold edged white with cream band piece with a gold geometric design on the border with a inner gold line (pancake server). M in wreath HP/Nippon. 1911-1920. Original.

A gold edged white piece with a gold and black geometric design of circles and dots. Angora (The). M in wreath nor/ Nippon. 1912. Original.

A gold edged white piece with a gold and black geometric design around the border. Crete (the). M in wreath N/HP/Japan. 1921-1930. Original.

A gold edged white with cream band piece with gold U's around the edge and a geometric gold design in a rectangle (pierced berry bowl). M in wreath HP/Nippon. 1911-1920. Original.

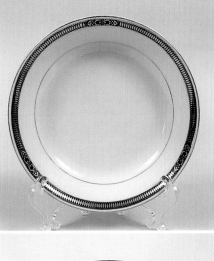

A gold edged white piece with a gold on black geometric design on the rim. Chanwood. M in wreath N/HP/Japan. 1930. Original.

A gold edged white piece with gold and brown geometric design around rim (gravy with faststand). Caliban. 3733. M in wreath big bow. 1933. Rose china.

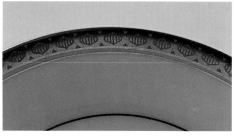

A gold edged white piece with a half-inch geometric design gold border with an inner gold pin line. Richmond. 6124. N in wreath printed. 1961-1989. LaSalle.

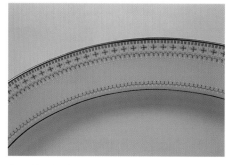

A gold edged white piece with gold geometric lines loops and crosses around the border. Barrington. 2030. N in wreath black and gold. 1975-1980. Commander.

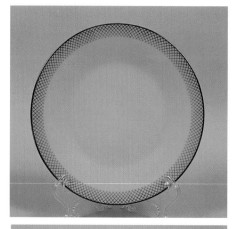

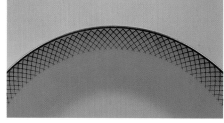

A gold edged white piece with a gold lattice work geometric border. Seville. 6521. N in wreath black and gold. 1968. Coupe.

A gold edged white piece with a gold geometric design on a diamond shaped china piece. Irmina. 6601. N in wreath black and gold. 1963-1968.

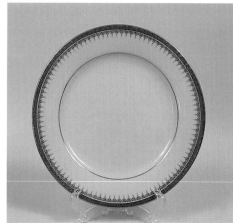

A gold edged cream piece with a gold Greek key pattern around the rim outlined with gold fleurs-de-leis and an inner gold pin line. Edinburgh. 7146. N in wreath black and gold. 1968. Rim.

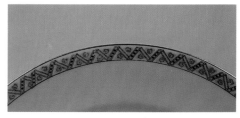

A gold edged white piece with a geometric ziz-zag design of blue lines and yellow with black dots framed with pink flowers.Metz (the). M in wreath nor/ Nippon. 1912-1913. Original.

A gold edged white piece with a geometric striped yellow and black lines design around the rim. Sunrise. 1911.

A gold edged white piece with a gold geometric design around the border (sugar bowl). Chancellor. 9751. Lamp Bone China gold/black. 1987-1990. Royal Pierpont.

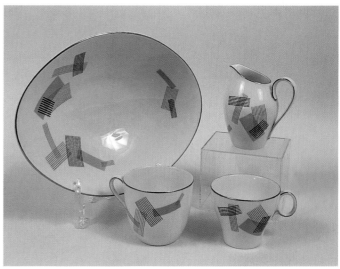

A orange edged white piece with a wide yellow band the inner band is a black geometric border (8" plate and mustard pot). M in wreath N/HP/Japan. 1921-1928.

A silver edged white piece with a pink panel covered with black and gray lines creating a geometric pattern in an offset design. N in wreath printed. 1953. Coupe.

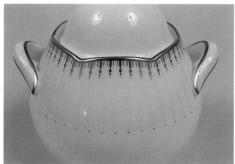

A gold edged white piece with a yellow geometric design around the rim. Maple leaf. 1890-1920. Original.

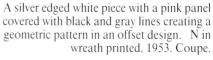

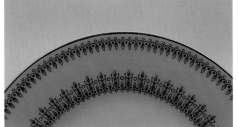

A gold edged white piece with a pink geometric design of silver loops with magenta dots around the border and inner line. Nina. 6667. N in wreath colorful. 1965. Classic.

A gold edged white piece with a green and pink geometric design in alternating squares (sugar bowl demitass). R.C. with hat. 1911. Tea set.

A gold edged white piece with green outlined in black and gold geometric design in windows around the border, some pink flowers in every other window. M in wreath HP/Nippon. 1911. Tea set.

A gold edged white with cream band piece with green loops around the rim interrupted by a geometric design of crosses in an circle with dangling lines. Argonne (the). 005859. M in wreath N/HP/Japan. 1921-1928. Original.

A brown edged white piece with a green and brown geometric design around the border (8" plate and bottom of covered vegetable). Maple leaf. 1890. Original.

A gold edged white piece with a green gold and white geometric checker board pattern around the rim. M in wreath nor/ Nippon. 1912. Original.

A white edged white piece with green and brown squares arranged in a geometric design (made for the Japanese market). N crossed stems NTK. 1955. Tea set.

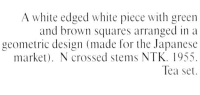

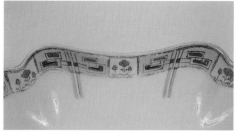

A gold edged white piece with a blue background to a green geometric design interspersed with orange buds. R.C. handpainted nippon. 1911. Original.

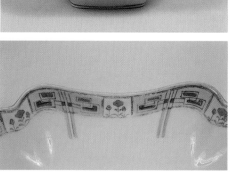

A gold edged white piece with blue and black geometric design around diamond shaped blue designs with pink background. 002746. R.C. with clackers NTK. 1912-1961.

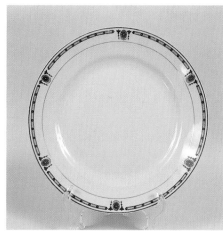

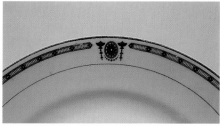

A gold edged white piece with a blue and brown geometric design with medallions of blue umbrellas interrupting the border design, a thin gold pin line inner line. M in wreath nor/ Nippon. 1912. Original.

A gold edged white piece with a border of blue gold and white checks (creamer). M in wreath nor/ Nippon. 1912. Original.

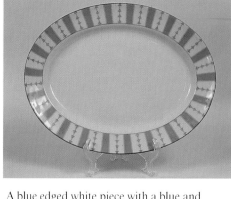

A blue edged white piece with a blue and white stripped geometric design around the rim. Yale (the). M in wreath N/HP/Nippon. 1912. Original.

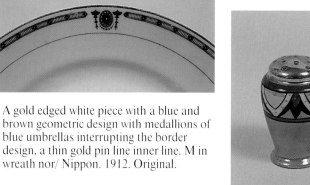

A gold edged blue luster piece with art deco red gold and black petals (salt and pepper). M in wreath N/HP/Japan. 1918.

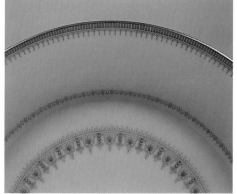

A gold edged white piece with a blue geometric border and inner line. Maya. 6213. 0196309. N in wreath printed. 1955. LaSalle.

35

A white piece with a blue Greek key design around the rim (inscribed the President Hotel Hong Kong (ashtray) N in wreath colorful. 1963.

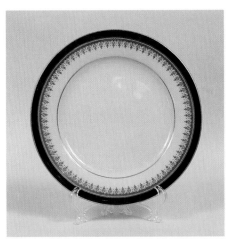

A gold edged white piece with a navy band edged with a gold geometric design with an inner gold pin line. Grand Monarch. 3595. Legacy Philippines. 1986-1998. Commander.

A silver edged white piece with a silver geometric band around the border. Richland. 6130. N in wreath printed. 1961. LaSalle.

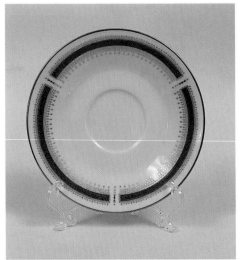

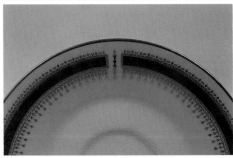

A gold edged white piece with a navy blue border edged with gold geometric lines. Blue Dawn. 6611. N in wreath black and gold. 1968.

A gold edged cream piece with a narrow border of blue, purple, emerald, and black rectangles outlined with gold, creating a geometric border. Vancover Gold. 9747. Lamp Bone China gold/black. 1986-1994. Royal Pierpont.

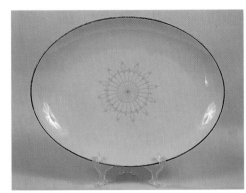

A silver edged ivory piece with a central geometric design of silver on white. Selene. 7536. N in wreath Ivory China. 1974. Champagne form.

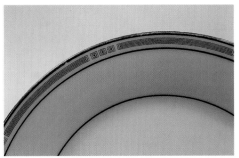

A silver edged white piece with a silver geometric design of three boxes inside each other both oblong and square. Van Orsdale. 3995. N in wreath Philippines. 1988. Remembrance II.

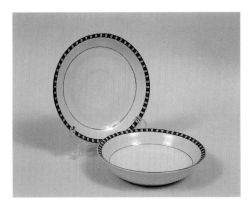

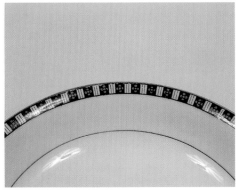

A gold edged white with cream band piece with a black and gold geometric design around the rim. Lafayette. M in wreath N/HP/Japan. 1921-1930. Original.

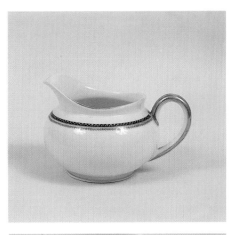

A gold edged white piece with a gold and black geometric design around the border (creamer). Blossom M single Japan. 1925. Original.

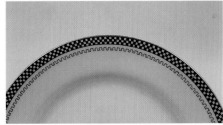

A gold edged white piece with a black and white checker board pattern around the rim, and an inner black pin line Greek key design. K in scroll shield Japan. 1947. Tea set.

A gold edged white with cream band piece with black Greek key geometric design around the rim with a skyline border. Audrey. 3078. K in scroll shield Japan. 1947. Rose china.

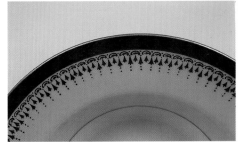

A gold edged white with cream band piece with black and gold geometric design around the border. M in wreath bow OJ. 1949. Rim.

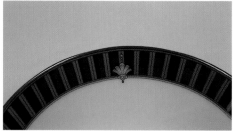

A brown edged white piece with a black
geometric pattern with black gray and brown
alternating lines with a small gray fleur-de-
lis(fruit bowl). Border Bouquet. 4025. N in
wreath black and gold. 1993-1994. Paramount.

A gold edged white piece with a wide black
band with light gray Egyptian designs on the
black the inner band is a wide gold line.
Portfolio. 7736. Fine China in wreath. 1991-
1999. New Traditions.

A silver edged white piece with silver and tan
geometric spokes surrounding the border.
Biarritz. 6006. 00187156. N in wreath
printed. 1954. Concerto.

A white piece with a black and gold geometric rope design around
the rim (restaurant china).Oneida Japan. 1997.

A gold edged white piece with a black border
to lavender and gold chain geometric design
around the rim. King's Guard. Fine China
in wreath. 1986-1989. New Traditions.

CHAPTER 8.

SCROLLS AND FEATHERS

If you still have not found your pattern, look to see if there are feathers or scrolls and no flowers or very, very few flowers in the pattern. Many of the flowered patterns also use scrolls around the flowers. This section is for patterns in which the major element is the scrolls or feathers. Again the color sequence is white, gold, orange, pink, maroon, green, blue, gray, black, and mixed.

A gold edged white piece with gold and green scrolls around a gold stylized bouquet. Gracelyn. 5856. N in wreath printed. 1953-1958. Butterfly.

A gold edged white piece with gold and gray scrolls around the border. Stanwyck. 5818. 182091. N in wreath printed. 1952. Butterfly.

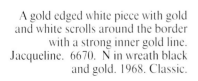

A gold edged cream piece with gold scrolls accented with light green leaves. Aldridge. 9702. Lamp Bone China gold/black. 1975-1980. Sheer ivory bone.

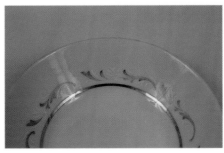

A gold edged white piece with gold and white scrolls around the border with a strong inner gold line. Jacqueline. 6670. N in wreath black and gold. 1968. Classic.

A gold edged white piece with white scrolls on a green background (stick butter dish). Thurston. 6871. N in wreath colorful. 1975-1977. LaSalle.

A gold edged white with cream band piece with a green border to a gold geometric design. Regent. M in wreath small bow 2 leaves. 1930 . Rose china.

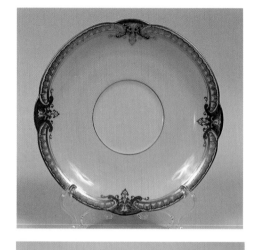

A gold edged white piece with green scrolls with blue stylized flowers. Maytone. 2359. Contemporary FC Japan. 1975-1980. Classic.

A gold edged white piece with a green border with gold scrolls an inner line of gold. Warrington. 6872. N in wreath colorful. 1975-1979. LaSalle.

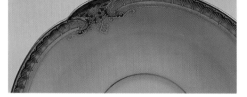

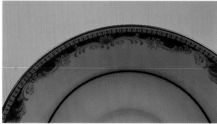

A gold edged white with cream band piece with a green background to a gold scroll design. Grenwold. M with crown. 1930.

A silver edged white piece with a dark green outlined black scroll design around the border. Monterey. 2211. N in wreath black and gold. 1975-1976. Coupe.

A gold edged white piece with a wide marbled emerald band with gold scrolls. Essex Court. 4727. Lamp Bone China gold/black. 1994-1998.

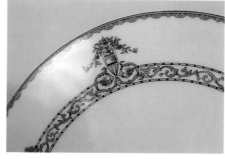

A gold edged white with cream band piece with a blue scroll border the design is a gold vase with a few tiny blue flowers and green leaves surrounded by blue scrolls (round covered vegetable). Darby. M in wreath N/HP/Japan. 1921. Original.

A white piece with a blue geometric border with blue scrolls connecting urns of gold. Amiston. 0069540. M in wreath N/HP/Japan. 1929. Original.

A gold edged white with cream band piece with a blue border of scrolls and a small blue stylized flower (bottom of round covered vegetable). M in wreath N/HP/Japan. 1921. Original.

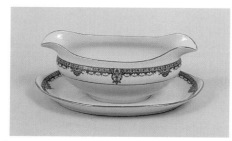

A gold edged white piece with blue and mustard scrolls and geometric designs intersected with a blue scroll outline of a blue four petal design. Reims (the). M in wreath N/HP/Japan. 1921-1930. Original.

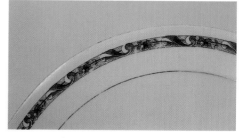

A gold edged white with cream piece with a multi-color geometric border of scrolls and arrows in a narrow band (round covered vegetable). Cherry Blossom. 1924-1931. Original.

A gold edged white with cream band piece with a wide blue border overlaid with gold scrolls and leaves (6 cup teapot). Vornay. 4794. 0089527. M in wreath big bow. 1933. Rose china.

A gold edged white piece with a blue border outlined with gold scrolls emanating from an urn. Oberlin. 2486. Contemporary FC Sri Lanka. 1975-1980. Classic.

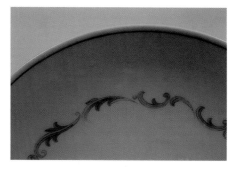

A white piece with a gray pin line around the rim and an inner line of gray and turquoise scrolls, a central design is gray leaves with gray blue bells. N in wreath printed. 1953. LaSalle.

A silver edged white piece with blue border framed with gold scrolls with blue and silver inner pen lines. Oxford. 5767. N in wreath printed. 1957. LaSalle.

A gold edged white piece with a dark blue band outlined with gold swages and scrolls. Blue shadowed flowers in a gold vase around the border. Palestra. 4762. New Lineage II bone china. 1997-1998. New Lineage.

A silver edged white piece with a gray border of scrolls. Cavalier. 6104. N in wreath printed. 1953. Rose china.

A gold edged white piece with gray and gold scrolls in a wide border design. Glennis. 5804. 0182092. N in wreath printed. 1953. Coupe.

A silver edged white piece with silver scrolls and leaves around the border. Crestmont. 6013. 0187145. N in wreath printed. 1953-1977. LaSalle.

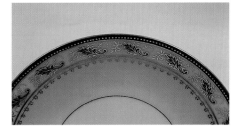

A silver edged white diamond piece with gray scrolls around the border. Camden. 6350. N in wreath printed. 1953.

A gold edged white with cream band piece with black feathers surrounded with gold scrolls (cream soup bowl). Devon. 108041. M in wreath small bow 2 leaves. 1936.

A silver edged white piece with white scrolls on a black background bordered with geometric edging. Naples. 6975. N in wreath black and gold. 1968. LaSalle.

A gold edged ivory china piece with a navy scrolls design around the border. Prelude. 7570. N in wreath Ivory China. 1975-1982. Victorian II. Rim.

A gold edged white with cream band piece with a black and gold geometric border with a gold scroll enclosed daisy. Bancroft. M in wreath N/HP/Japan. 1921-1930. Original.

A silver edged white piece with a black delicate scroll design around the border (after-dinner coffee service). Amor. 2481. Contemporary FC Sri Lanka. 1975-1976. Classic.

A gold edged white piece with brown and turquoise scrolls around the border. Esteem. 5404. N in wreath printed. 1953. LaSalle.

A gold edge white piece with brown elongated leaves or feathers around the border. Granville. 5607. N in wreath printed. 1956. LaSalle.

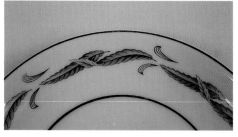

A silver edged white piece with brown feathers with a tiny pink accent and black swishes. Gaylord. 5526. N in wreath printed. 1955.

A gold edged white piece with a border of blue and gold scrolls around geometric yellow flowers with pink and blue flowers and a gold inner pin line. M in wreath N/HP/Japan. 1921-1928. Original.

A gold edged white piece with brown and turquoise scrolls. 5559. N in wreath printed. 1960. Triangle.

A white piece with green scrolls framed in blue bands interspersed with pink background under blue petals. Arleigh. 0061237.M in wreath N/HP/Japan. 1921-1928. Original.

CHAPTER 9.

LEAVES AND TREES

If your pattern does not fit either of the pervious sections, you need to ask if the pattern has just leaves or has any trees in it. If the flora can be identified as a tree it will be in this section. I call it a tree if the branch appears too thick to be a flower stem. For some patterns it is a toss up whether it is a feather or a leaf. I have tried to get these separated correctly.

A gold edged white with cream band piece with gold leaves and gold wheat around the cream border. M in wreath big bow. 1933-1935. Rim.

Above and right: A gold edged cream piece with a gold and silver leaf arrangement with orange seeds in a central design, the rim design has lines of gold that get wider then taper off on the ends. M in wreath big bow. 1933-1935. Rim.

A gold edged white piece with gold and black leaves and a double gold line on the border. 5550. N in wreath printed. 1955. Butterfly.

A gold edged white piece with gold seeds and gray leaves. Laverne. 5810. N in wreath printed. 1958. Butterfly.

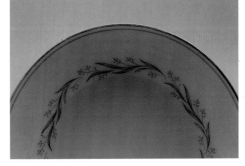

A gold edged white piece with gold leaves around the border. Laurel. 5903. 0185444. N in wreath printed. 1953. Butterfly.

A gold edged white piece with a scenic cottage and tree beside a lake with an over all yellow background. Made in Japan. 1911. Azalea.

A gold edged orange piece with a orange sunset behind a house with a large tree on the side of a lake. Chikaramachi. 1928. Tea set.

A gold edged white piece with a wide sea foam green band with a row of gold fleurs-de-lis running though it (cheese & cracker). M in wreath N/HP/Japan. 1921-1928. Original.

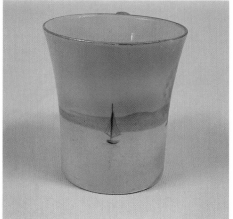

A gold edged white piece with a tree on the side of a lake with pastel water and yellow sky. Sunrise. 1911.

A black edged white piece with a wide orange band and a house with large trees on a lake. Chikaramachi. 1928. Tea set.

A gold edged white with cream band piece with a green urn and tan leaves connected in swags, the green background and tan and white leaves arranged in a geometric pattern makes up the rim design. Lorento. 3852. 0112926. M in wreath big bow. 1938. Rose china.

A white piece with a hand painted scenic design of a house beside a lake with a large tree in brown yellow and orange. Made in Japan. 1928.

A gold edged maroon piece with gold and white leaves on the maroon (exclusively for the Danbury mint). N in wreath black and gold. 1968. Classic.

A gold edged white piece with a large realistic bamboo shoot with dark green leaves in an offset pattern. Canton. 5027. M in wreath big bow. 1933-1935. Triangle.

A silver edged white piece with green and gray leaves around the border with an inner silver pin line. Lynwood. 5307. N in wreath printed. 1953.

A silver edged white piece with green pine leaves and pine cones around the border. Pinetta. 5689. N in wreath printed. 1956. Butterfly.

A gold edged white piece with green and brown leaves around the border and as a central design. Cordova. 5215. M in wreath big bow. 1933. Rim.

A silver edged white piece with green and brown bamboo leaves. Bambina. 5791. N in wreath printed. 1957. Concerto.

A brown edged white piece with green bamboo leaves in an offset pattern (snack set). R.C. in leafy shield. 1949. Concerto.

A gold edged white piece with a large offset design of gold stylized flowers with green leaves. 5471. N in wreath printed. 1954. LaSalle.

A silver edged white piece with a wide border of leaves with a background color of light mint green. 5487. N in wreath printed. 1954. LaSalle.

A gold edged white piece with a wide green band bordered with green leaves and scrolls. Chartres. 5920. N in wreath printed. 1959.

A gold edged white piece with green leaves with gold and pink stylized flowers. Claridge. 6020. 0187148. N in wreath printed. 1953. Butterfly.

A gold edged white piece with green bamboo and gold leaves.
Oriental. 6341. N in wreath printed. 1953-1968. Concerto.

A silver edged white piece with green and brown leaves around the border. Vineyard. 6449. N in wreath colorful. 1963. LaSalle.

A silver edged white piece with a grape vine of green leaves in an offset pattern. Ivyne. 6605. N in wreath colorful. 1965. Triangle.

A silver edged white piece with a offset design of grape leaves in realistic green color. Kerri. 6681. N in wreath colorful. 1965. Concerto.

A gold edged bone china piece with green ivy leaves around the border with a gold basket weave on the rim. Southern Estate. 4734. Lamp Bone China gold/black. 1994-1997. Sheer Ivory Bone.

A gold edged white piece with blue background to a scenic design with a tree at the edge of a lake. Chikaramachi. 1928. Tea set.

A gold edged ivory china piece with gold flowers and green leaves. Studio Collection. 1972.

A gold edged pearlized piece with gold trees, houses and flowers behind a gold bridge banded in blue. M in wreath N/HP/Japan. 1921-1928. Tea set.

A silver edged white piece with gray and turquoise leaves in an all over pattern. Automne. 5626. N in wreath printed. 1956. Coupe.

A gold edged blue luster piece with gold luster band and a tree on the side of a lake and no buildings or animals. M in wreath N/HP/Japan. 1921-1928. Tea set.

A gold edged white piece with a wide navy blue band with gold leaves for accents. Rangoon. 3496. Legacy Philippines. 1977. Commander.

A white piece with a gray, green, and orange leaf pattern and gray accents. K in circle Noritake script NTK. 1949.

A silver edged white piece with a gray band around the border with a central design of gray and green leaves. Lucille. 5813. 0183980. N in wreath printed. 1953.

A silver edged white piece with a wide gray band and a central three-fern design in green. Fernwood. 5444. N in wreath printed. 1954. LaSalle.

A silver edged white piece with gray leaves around the border. Graywood. 6041. N in wreath printed. 1954. Triangle.

A silver edge white piece with hand drawn leaves in a modern offset look. Capri. 5551. 0176131. N in wreath printed. 1951-1955. Concerto

A silver edged white piece with stylized gray flowers and leaves. Taryn. 5912. 0185448. N in wreath printed. 1953-1957. Butterfly.

A silver edged white piece with silver leaves around the border. Almont. 6125. N in wreath printed. 1961. Coupe.

A silver edged white piece with silver leaves around tan stylized flowers. Ardis. 5772. N in wreath printed. 1957. Butterfly.

A silver edged white piece with a gray wheat and leave design. Prosperity. 6841. N in wreath black and gold. 1968-1970. Concerto.

A gold edged white piece with brown leaves with gray leaves in an offset design. M in wreath big bow. 1950-1960. Triangle.

A gold edged luster piece with a wide blue band and a house on the side of a lake with a large tree and red sunset. M in wreath N/HP/Japan. 1921-1928.

A gold edged white piece with gold and silver wheat with gold leaves as a central design. Wheaton. 5414. N in wreath printed. 1953. Triangle.

A gold edged white piece with a large tree on the edge of a lake with a sail boat on the lake, all pastel colors. M in wreath N/HP/Japan. 1921-1928.

A gold edged white piece with brown and gray bamboo leaves in an overall design. Cho-cho-san. 6936. Fine China stars. 1955. Rim.

A white piece with a mixed color overall design with an oriental tree as the center piece. Inwood. 1871. 014763. M in wreath N/HP/Japan. 1908. Original.

CHAPTER 10.

FRUIT

If your pattern does not fit any of the previous sections, you need to ask yourself if the pattern has any fruit in it. Look closely at those urns or vases and see if it contains any fruit. Many patterns have some fruit as well as flowers, but we are looking for *any* fruit on the pattern. Even if flowers appear in the pattern, if there is *any* fruit (don't forget grapes) the pattern will appear in this chapter.

A gold edged white with cream band piece with a bowl of fruit roped off and surrounded with yellow scrolls, the border background is red with grapes, lemons and apples (oval covered casserole). Iona. M in wreath N/HP/Japan. 1921-1930. Original.

A gold edged white with cream band piece with a green border intersected with a fruit and flower arrangement surrounded with green scrolls. Surrey. M in wreath N/HP/Japan. 1921-1930. Original.

A black edged white piece with a wide yellow border intersected with a blue urn full of fruit surrounded by a pin floral swag with green leaves. M in wreath N/HP/Japan. 1921-1928. Original.

A pearlized white piece with a wide orange luster band interrupted with a vase of fruit and green leaves, the inner line is black. M in wreath N/HP/Japan. 1921-1928. Original.

A gold edged white piece with purple grapes and green leaves. Tokay. 5168. M in wreath big bow. 1950-1979. Rim.

A silver edged white piece with a large green cucumber and eggplant for decoration. N crossed stems NTK. 1955. Tea set.

A white piece with a blue luster band intersected with a vase of fruit with green leaves. M in wreath N/HP/Japan. 1921-1928. Original.

A gold edged white with cream piece with grapes and flowers in a blue scroll arrangement with a dainty yellow and black geometric border. Malvern. 0069538. M in wreath N/HP/Japan. 1929. Original.

A gold edged ivory piece with a green marble border outlined with a white lace effect, intersected with a pear and grapes. Berringer. 7335. N in wreath Ivory China. 1992-1994. Imperial Baroque.

A gold edged white with cream band piece with a blue border around a bouquet containing blue grapes pink flowers and gold leaves. Fontaine. M in wreath N/HP/Japan. 1921-1930. Original.

A gold edged white with cream piece with a blue and orange alternating semi-circle border around a blue vase with a fruit arrangement with green leaves. Sorrento. 076965. M in wreath N/HP/Japan. 1931. Original.

A blue edged white piece with blue fruit on a vine with a yellow background. October Light. 4095. Impromptu Sri Lanka. 1998. ParamouNew Traditions.

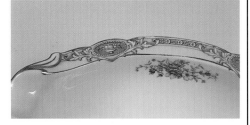

A gold edged white with cream band piece with a blue background border to a compote of gold fruit, interlaced with bouquets of pink, yellow, and blue flowers. Marvelle. 304. M in scrolls. 1933. Mushroom.

A gold edged white with cream band piece with a black border of bells and ovals intersected with black swags around a gold urn with fruit and green leaves. Lasalle. 0069535. M in wreath N/HP/Japan. 1927. Original.

A gold edged white with cream band piece with a black border of bells and ovals intersected with black swags around a gold urn with fruit and green leaves. Beverly. 0058589. M in wreath N/HP/Japan. 1927. Original.

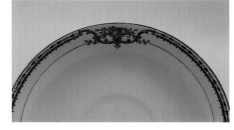

A yellow edged white with cream band piece with black geometric border intersected with a black urn full of fruit surrounded by swags of light pink flowers with green leaves. M in wreath N/HP/Japan. 1921-1928. Original.

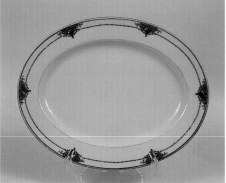

A gold edged white with cream band piece with a dark blue pin line around the edge and a mixed bouquet of fruit and flowers. Gotham. 0071437. M in wreath N/HP/Japan. 1930. Original.

A gold edged white with cream band piece with mixed color band with a fruit arrangement in a blue and black urn (double handled cream soup). Lautana. M in shield China. 1931. Original.

A gold edged white with cream band piece with mixed color band around a grouping of fruit in a gold urn surrounded by multi-colored flowers. Apollo. M in wreath N/HP/Japan. 1921-1930. Original.

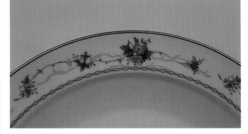

A gold edge yellow colored piece with baskets of pears and apples the inner line is a twisted green ribbon. Normandy. 8162W83. N in wreath black and gold. 1979-1985. Victorian IV.

CHAPTER 11.

CREATURES (BIRDS, BUTTERFLIES, FISH)

Look at your pattern very carefully and see if it contains any birds, butterflies, or fish. I have reserved this chapter for things that breathe, whether they look real or not. Birds and butterflies are common elements in Noritake designs. I have only found one with a fish, and I am sure there are other creatures I have not found yet.

A black edged white piece with orange panels alternating with panels of a yellow bird and blue and orange flowers with green leaves (tea set). M in wreath N/HP/Japan. 1921-1930. Tea set.

A gold edged white with cream band piece with four different butterflies on either side of a large yellow rose with green leaves (condensed milk container). R.C. handpainted nippon. 1911.

A gold edged white piece with a large yellow and blue flower with green leaves with yellow and blue butterflies (tea set). M in wreath N/HP/Japan. 1918. Tea set.

A orange edged white piece with a colorful bird and a rose design surrounded with a light orange band outlined in black. M in wreath N/HP/Japan. 1921-1930. Original.

A black edged white piece with a large orange band around the edge with a multi-colored bird and large floral arrangement (two handled bowl). M in wreath N/HP/Japan. 1921-1930.

A silver edged white piece with orange and silver fish in an all over design (coupe). 228. R.C. in wreath 1956-1960 coupe.

A gold edged white piece with a pastel pink border and butterflies around a pink flower with green leaves (child's set). Sunrise. 1911-1920. Original.

A gold edged cream piece with a green border around two birds hovering over a bouquet in a gold urn . M in wreath N/HP/ Japan. 1921-1925. Original.

A gold edged white piece with a red rose with a blue bird with a yellow breast perched on the flower. Caledonia. 7091. N in wreath black and gold. Victorian II. 1975.

A gold edged white piece with a lavender bird with a blue crop surrounded by pink roses with green leaves a wide lavender border, i.e. edged with yellow and black hatching. Chanvale. M in wreath N/HP/ Japan. 1921-1930. Mushroom.

A gold edged white piece with a wide green border intersected with a robin on a purple branch surrounded with orange flowers. M in wreath HP/Nippon. 1911-1920. Tea set.

A white piece with two green birds with brown wings facing each other. Hermitage. 6226. 0196311. N in wreath printed. 1955-1975. Concerto.

A gold edged white piece with a white bird figure in a circle surrounded with blue and gold geometric lines and horse shoes. Commodore (the). M in wreath nor/Nippon. 1912-1920. Original.

A gold edged cream piece with a green border around a design with a bird on a limb of a floral arrangement of pink and yellow flowers (after dinner service). M in wreath N/HP/Japan. 1921-1925. Azalea.

A white piece with blue oriental design of a large bird surrounded by blue flowers and blue leaves. Howo. HOWO. 1916-1921. Original.

A green edged ivory china piece with a butterfly in a garden of yellow and blue flowers with green leaves. Reverie. 7191. N in wreath Ivory China. 1975-1986. Victorian II coupe.

A gold edged cream colored piece with a multi-colored bird on a flowering bush with a wide green band intersected with flowers. M in wreath N/HP/Japan. 1921-1928. Original.

A black edged white piece with a wide blue band around the border and two birds on a limb of pink flowers. M in wreath N/HP/Japan. 1921-1930. Original.

A white piece with blue scalloped border around blue flowers with blue leaves & bllue bird. 0010733. M in wreath N/HP/Japan. 1912.

A gold edged white piece with a bird with yellow body and blue wings framed with a blue geometric lines border and blue, yellow and pink flowers. Charmeuse. 0071435. M in wreath N/HP/Japan. 1930-1933. Original.

A white piece with a royal blue phoenix bird and blue scrolls and blue hearts. M Hanging Wreath. 1921-1930. Azalea.

A gold edged white with cream band piece with a blue and gold border interspersed with a bird between two pink flowers. Cherry Blossom. 1924-1931. Original.

A gold edged white with cream band piece with a blue butterfly and pink and orange stylized flowers with blue and lavender leaves. M in wreath nor/ Nippon. 1912-1920. Original.

A gold edged white with cream band piece with a light blue border and a design of a large colorful bird among pink flowers. Cherry Blossom. 1924-1931. Original.

A cream piece with a blue bird and blue flowers. Ho-Oh. 7196. N in wreath Ivory China. 1975-1980. Victorian II coupe.

A gold edged white piece with a black and gold border with a bird with a yellow breast near blue and pink flowers. Navarre. 0069545. M in wreath N/HP/Japan. 1929-1934. Original.

CHAPTER 12.

STYLIZED DESIGN

I have sorted out the stylized flowers, those that do not look nature made. This section also includes designs such as white-on-white etched patterns with stylized (machine-made not nature-made) flowers. A good example of this is the Whiteburn pattern: if looked at from a distance of more than eighteen inches it is not immediately seen that the design is of daisies; it looks solid white. Any flower that does not look real with petals or leaves but is highly stylized reminiscent of the Art Deco era, will also be in this section. If the pattern you are trying to identify has a real looking rose, but it happens to be colored blue, it is not in this section. When I refer to real looking flowers I am talking about the design, not the color. With the exception of gold flowers, some are very real looking roses, some are hard to tell, so I put all gold floral designs in this area to keep them together, there are many gold on white and gold on cream designs.

A silver edged white piece with a white on white stylized flower design in a basket. Whitehall. 6115. N in wreath printed. 1975-1980. LaSalle.

A silver edged white piece with a white on white stylized design with gray shadows. Armand. 6315. N in wreath printed. 1963.

A silver edged white piece with stylized white on white flowers with an inner silver pen line. Buckingham. 6438. 0200495. N in wreath colorful. 1956-1986. LaSalle.

A gold edged white piece with white on white stylized daisies.
Sylvan. 6118. N in wreath printed. 1961. Concerto.

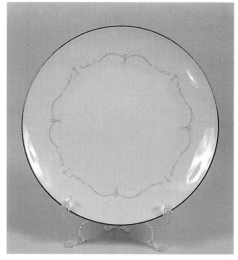

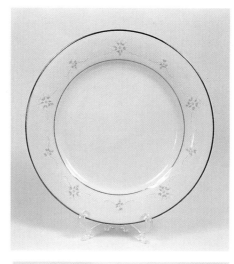

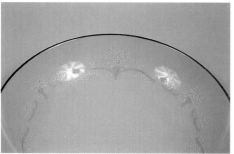

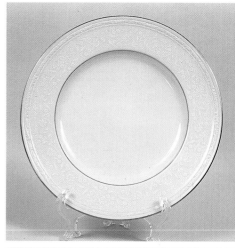

A silver edged white piece with stylized flowers connected with silver ribbon. Whitebrook. 6441. 0200484. N in wreath colorful. 1956-1978. Concerto.

A silver edged white piece with a white stylized flower with gray leaves around the border with a silver inner pen line. Monaco. 6725. N in wreath black and gold. 1968.

A silver edged white piece with white on white stylized flowers and leaves with and inner silver pin line. Misty. 2883. Contemporary FC Philippines. 1978-1989. Classic.

A silver edged white piece with stylized leaves and flowers white on white. Reina. 6450Q. N in wreath colorful. 1963. Classic.

A silver edged white piece with white stylized flowers shadowed by gray lines. Casablanca. 6842. N in wreath black and gold. 1968. Concerto.

A gold edged white piece with embossed scrolls around the edge of white on white flowers. Whitecliff. 4083. White Scapes. 1995. White Scapes.

A gold edged white with cream band piece has gold outlined daisies like flowers with gold leaves. Sunrise. 1911. Tea set.

A silver edged ivory china piece with stylized flowers white on ivory. Affection. 7192. N in wreath Ivory China. 1975-1993. Victorian II coupe.

A silver edged ivory china piece with stylized white on white scrolls. Marseille. 7550. N in wreath Ivory China. 1975-1982. Victorian II rim.

A silver edged ivory piece with stylized ivory on ivory flowers and scrolls. Sorrento. 7565. N in wreath Ivory China. 1969. Victorian II rim.

A gold edged white with cream band piece with gold stylized flowers and a central gold outlined flower. M in wreath HP/Nippon. 1911-1920. Original.

A gold edged ivory china piece with stylized white on cream flowers on a scallop edged form. Chandon. 7306. N in wreath Ivory China. 1988-1998. Imperial Baroque.

A gold edged ivory fine china piece with ivory stylized flowers. Turtle Bay. 7710. Fine China in wreath. 1985-1988. New Traditions.

A gold edged white with cream band piece with a gold flower encircled with gold scrolls. M in wreath HP/Nippon. 1911-1920. Original.

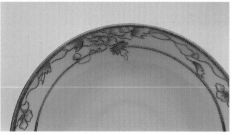

A gold edged white piece with gold framed flowers with green leaves. M in wreath HP/Nippon. 1911-1920. Original.

A gold edged white piece with gold stylized flowers in a gold encircled medallion, gold stars form a lattice work background behind gold scrolls. M in wreath HP/Nippon. 1911-1920. Tea set.

A gold edged white piece with alternating panels of cream and white around the border decorated with gold scrolls and gold roses in a medallion. K in circle Nippon plain. 1911-1920. Original.

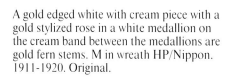

A gold edged white with cream piece with a gold stylized rose in a white medallion on the cream band between the medallions are gold fern stems. M in wreath HP/Nippon. 1911-1920. Original.

A gold edged white piece with gold stylized flowers with gold leaves connected with gold swags. K in circle Nippon plain. 1911-1920. Tea Set.

A gold edged white piece with gold roses on gold swages with gold U-shapes around the border. K in circle Nippon plain. 1911-1920. Tea set.

A gold edged white piece with gold edged flowers with gold leaves. K in circle Nippon fancy. 1911-1920. Tea set.

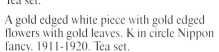

A gold edged white with cream band piece with gold scrolls surrounding a single oval with a gold stylized rose inside.White and gold. 175. 0016034 and 0043061. K in circle Nippon fancy. 1912-1999. Original. La Salle.

A gold edged white with cream band piece with a gold stylized flower with gold leaves on the cream band. M in wreath N/HP/Japan. 1921-1928. Original.

A gold edged white with cream band piece with a gold stylized flower with gold leaves.M in wreath N/HP/Japan. 1921-1928. Azalea.

A gold edged white piece with a gold border of lattice and gold edged flowers with gold leaves. M in wreath N/HP/Japan. 1921-1928. Original.

A gold edged white with cream band piece with a gold geometric border around gold stylized flowers. M in wreath N/HP/Japan. 1921-1928. Original.

A gold edged white with cream band piece with a gold framed white stylized flower with gold leaves and a small delicate pink flower on the cream band. M in wreath N/HP/Japan. 1921-1928. Azalea.

A gold edged white with cream band piece with gold scrolls around the stylized border. M in wreath N/HP/Japan. 1921-1928. Original.

A gold edged white piece with a gold scroll bordered medallion with a stylized flower in the center, the rim is cobalt blue with gold geometric design. M in wreath N/HP/Japan. 1921-1928. Azalea.

A gold edged white with cream band piece with a gold rose in a gold scroll enclosed medallion. M in wreath N/HP/Japan. 1921-1928. Azalea.

A gold edged white with cream band piece with a gold stylized flower surrounded with gold leaves and gold scrolls. M in wreath N/HP/Japan. 1921-1928. Original.

A gold edged white piece with stylized gold flowers with gold leaves and gold vase shaped intersects. (Buttertub) M in wreath N/HP/Japan. 1921-1928. Azalea.

A gold edged white with cream band piece with a stylized gold rose in a gold wreath intersecting a gold U design encircling the rim (cheese and cracker tray). M in wreath N/HP/Japan. 1921-1928. Azalea.

A gold edged white with cream band piece with stylized flowers surrounded with gold ferns and a gold net with scrolls around the rim. M in wreath N/HP/Japan. 1931. Mushroom.

A gold edged white with cream band piece with a gold arrangement in a gold vase surrounded by gold scrolls and gold U-shaped design. 0077630. M in wreath N/HP/Japan. 1931. Original.

A gold edged white with cream band piece with a gold leaf orange flower with dots of blue on each side. Raised Gold. 0042200. M in wreath N/HP/Japan. 1933. Original.

A gold edged white with cream band piece with gold stylized leaves, grapes, and stems around the rim of leaves on black. M in wreath big bow. 1950-1959. Rose China.

A gold edged white with cream band piece with gold background to stylized flowers and leaves. Goldkin. 4985. M in wreath big bow. 1950-1959. Rose China.

A gold edged white with cream band piece with stylized gold flowers in a gold vase with gold scrolls around the border a wide gold parallel lines form the inner line. Fleurgold. 0077631. M in wreath N/HP/Japan. 1931. Original.

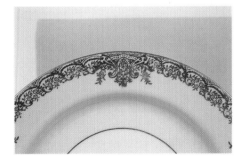

A gold edged white with cream band piece with gold stylized flowers surrounded with gold scrolls and gold leaves. Galavan. M in wreath small bow 2 leaves. 1930. Mushroom.

A gold edged white piece with gold stylized flowers in a central design with black leaves. Winton. 5521. 0176126. N in wreath printed. 1951. LaSalle.

A gold edged white with cream band piece with a gold floral arrangement in a gold urn. 4789. M in wreath bow OJ. 1949. Rose china.

A gold edged white with cream band piece with a gold bouquet with gold leaves and trim. 4986. M in wreath big bow. 1950-1959. Rose China.

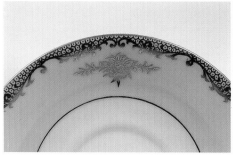

A gold edged white with cream band piece with a gold border of scrolls and a elaborate urn with three parts filled with gold flowers connected by a criss cross of gold dashes. Bancroft. 5481. N in wreath printed. 1954. LaSalle.

A gold edged white with cream band piece with a gold trim and gold flower with gold leaves on the cream band. M on stage. 1940. Mushroom.

A gold edged white piece with gold and white stylized flowers bordered with geometric designs. Highclere. 2062. N in wreath black and gold. 1968. Commander.

A gold edged white with cream band piece with stylized flower on a cream border with green and blue ribbons around geometric designs. Lazarre. M in wreath N/HP/Japan. 1921-1930. Original.

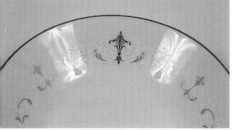

A gold edged white piece with gold accented stylized white on white flowers. Courtney. 6520. N in wreath black and gold. 1968. Coupe.

A gold edged white piece with stylized white and gold scrolls and leaves. Duetto. 6610. N in wreath black and gold. 1968. Coupe.

A gold edged ivory china piece with yellow and white stylized daisies. Fragrance. 7025. N in wreath Ivory China. 1965-1985. Victorian II rim.

A gold edged white piece with stylized gold leaves and flowers around the rim with an inner gold pin line. New Charm. 6522. N in wreath black and gold. 1968. LaSalle.

A white piece with a wide yellow band and black stylized flowers. M in wreath HP/Nippon. 1911-1920. Tea set.

A gold edged white piece with orange, yellow, and olive geometric and stylized flowers in bars around the piece. Espana. 6805. N in wreath black and gold. 1968. Triangle.

A gold edged white piece with pink stylized flowers interspersed with brown leaves. Sunrise. 1911. Tea set.

A gold edged cream piece with a border design of stylized flowers in cream on a red band. Tribute. 7165. N in wreath ivory china. 1975-1979. Victorian III.

A silver edged white piece with a stylized floral black design on a inch wide olive green band. Walden. 2028. N in wreath black and gold. 1975. Classic.

A silver edged white piece with a stylized green and gold flower with scrolls for leaves in a central design. September song. 2048. Cook'n Serve. 1975-1977.

A gold edged white piece with green leaves around stylized flowers in pink medallions. Regina. 0013674. M in wreath nor/ Nippon. 1908-1912. Original.

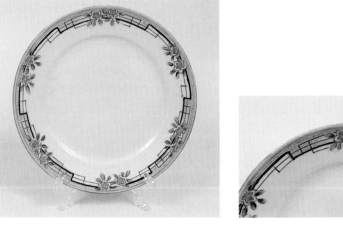

A gold edged white piece with stylized flowers white on white around the border shadowed with olive green. Eugenia. 2160. N in wreath black and gold. 1975-1980. Commander.

A gold edged white piece with a border of geometric red and black lines around pink stylized flowers with green leaves. Sunrise. 1911. Tea set.

A gold edged white piece with blue stylized branches and flowers with blue leaves. Granada. 3063. K in scroll shield Japan. 1981-1992. Nor. Ireland I.

A silver edged white piece with green and lavender flower on the border with green leaves and an inner silver pin line. Tradition. 2356. N in wreath black and gold. 1975-1977. Commander.

A green edged bone china piece with green and lavender stylized flowers and leaves. Caliph Palace. 4415. N in wreath bone gold. 1990.

A gold edged white with cream band piece with blue background and brown stylized leaves. Claire. 657. 0103007. M in wreath big bow. 1950-1955.

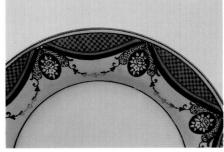

A gold edged white with cream band piece with a wide swag blue border of lattice work around black medallions with gold stylized flowers connected with gold swags. M in wreath N/HP/Japan. 1928-1933. Mushroom.

A gold edged white piece with stylized blue and gold flowers with gray and gold leaves in a bold overall design.Danielle. 5776. N in wreath printed. 1957. Coupe.

A silver edged white piece with a border design of a green background with white stylized flowers etched on the green. Vienne. 6885. N in wreath black and gold. 1975-1977. Classic.

A silver edged blue piece with stylized white on blue flowers and leaves. With a silver inner pin line. Fidelity. 8003W81. N in wreath black and gold. 1973-1982. Victorian IV.

A silver edged white piece with a stylized flower in white shadowed in pale blue. Ravel. 2213. N in wreath black and gold. 1975-1982. Classic.

A silver edged white piece with white on white stylized flowers with a blue shadow. Cache Pot. 3132. N in wreath black and gold. 1981-1983. Remembrance II.

A silver edged white piece with a blue band with silver stylized flowers on the band edged with a silver inner pen line. Blueridge. 5858. N in wreath printed. 1953-1958.

A silver edged white piece with a blue scroll design with white accent scrolls. Jenica. 3471. 0034921 Contemporary FC Japan. 1968. Commander.

A white piece with a blue band overlaid with white stylized flowers with two inner blue pin lines. Lace Shadow. 3988. N in wreath Sri Lanka. 1990-1991. Paramount.

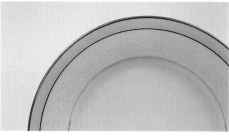

A silver edged white piece with a blue band around white on white stylized flowers and scrolls. Brandon. 6222. N in wreath printed. 1962.

A silver edged white piece with a central design of black and gray leaves toped with black star shaped seeds. Graycliff. 5861. N in wreath printed. 1954. Coupe.

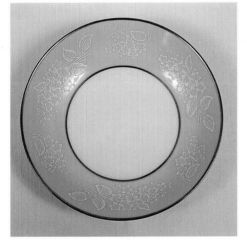

A silver edged white piece with a wide gray border with dainty etched stylized flower outlines. Damask. 5698. N in wreath colorful. 1963. Coupe.

A silver edged bone china piece with a silver band around a cream on cream stylized floral design. Hermitage. 9740. Lamp Bone China gold/black. 1985-1993. Royal Pierpont.

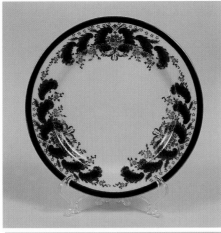

A gold edged white piece with a black border and black and gold stylized leaves and scrolls. M in wreath N/HP/Japan. 1921-1928.

A gold edged white piece with a wide black border with gold scrolls on the border. M in wreath N/HP/Japan. 1921-1928.

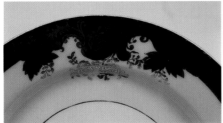

A gold edged white with cream band piece with a wide black border with gold scrolls on the border. M in wreath N/HP/Japan. 1921-1928.

A gold edged white piece with stylized gold flower inside a medallion with a black background. Black and Gold. 0020056. M in wreath N/HP/Japan. 1911-1930. Original.

A completely white piece with a small stylized dot and line floral impression in black and gold (butter pats). 1356. N in wreath printed. 1953. Concerto.

A silver edged white piece with a wide black band with black stylized flowers on the band. Mirano. 6878. N in wreath black and gold. 1968-1979. Classic.

A gold edged bone china piece with a black border with gold strips and gold stylized flowers. Spell Binder. 9733. Lamp Bone China gold/black. 1983-1993. Sheer Ivory Bone.

71

CHAPTER 13.

FLOWERS

Last but not least is the flower section. Most Noritake patterns will fall into this section, so there are three major subsections. If you have gotten this far and have not been led to another section, the next question is what color is the plate. This is the plate under the pattern. Your choices are white, white with a cream colored band around the outer rim, or another color which includes ivory china. Now it does not matter how wide the cream band is. If your plate background color around the edges is cream, you will look in the "white with a cream band" section. Once you have made the sub-selection, patterns are again ordered by the major color scheme other than the color of the plate background. So if your pattern has large pink roses on a cream band with a white center, you will go to the "white with a cream band" section and pass the white and the gold colored patterns to get to the pink ones. Sometimes deciding what is the principal color can be a problem. The last color segment in each section if for mixed colors. This is for patterns with bouquets, which have equal amounts of many colors. Many times the primary color is actually a trim around the edge not the flowers. Now give it a try and see if you can find your pattern with just a few page turns.

WHITE

A gold edged white piece with large yellow flowers with green leaves. Canterbury. 5226. M in wreath big bow. 1950-1959.

A gold edged white piece with a narrow green band around the rim with an inner gold pin line with a yellow and orange flower with green leaves (open salt). Sunrise. 1911. Tea set.

A gold edged white piece with a yellow border with blue design around a blue background to a pink rose with green leaves. Montclare. 0058595. M in wreath N/HP/Japan. 1927. Original.

A gold edged white piece with a large yellow rose bordered on both sides by pink roses with brown leaves. K in scroll shield NTK. 1947. Rose china.

A gold edged white piece with a yellow border with back trim around pink flowers with green leaves.M in wreath HP/Nippon. 1911-1920. Tea set.

A gold edged white piece with a yellow border with black and white lines around a pink flower with green leaves. Chikaramachi. 1928. Original.

A white piece with large yellow daisies in an offset pattern. Shasta. 2167. Cook 'n Serve. 1960-1970.

A gold edged white piece with an orange flower with green leaves on a bold and tan lattice design. M in wreath HP/Nippon. 1911-1920. Original.

A gold edged white piece with an orange and white dogwood floral design. 5329. N in wreath printed. 1949-1953. LaSalle.

A white piece with yellow and white daisies around the rim. Marguerite. 6730. 0209609. Cook'n Serve. 1975-1977.

A gold edged white piece with a wide yellow band framing a red flower with green leaves border by yellow and blue geometric design. M in wreath N/HP/Japan. 1920-1928. Tea set.

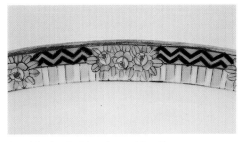

A gold edged white piece with yellow roses with light green leaves interspersed on a gold with peach striped band with black zigzags (celery set). R.C. handpainted nippon. 1911. Tea set.

A gold edged white piece with a wide orange pearlized band and central basket with yellow and blue flowers with green leaves. M in wreath N/HP/Japan. 1921-1928. Tea set.

A gold edged white piece with yellow, orange flowers with green leaves and a looped border. Aida. 2043. N in wreath black and gold. 1968-1975. Commander.

A black edged white piece with a wide orange luster band with an orange, yellow and blue flower in a black medallion with black lattice background (covered syrup server). M in wreath N/HP/Japan. 1921-1928. Original.

A gold edged white piece with a large peach rose with green leaves and silver basket weave as background. R.C. with clackers NTK. 1912-1920.

A gold edged white piece with purple and lavender flowers with green leaves and vines interrupted by gold outlined vase with gold curls. Sunrise. 1911.

A gold edged white piece with lavender violets with green leaves with a gold inner pin line. Violette. 3054. N in scroll shield Japan. 1952-1970. Tiangle.

A silver edged white piece with a wide green band and a central floral design of lavender and beige flowers with green leaves with purple edges. Shasta. 5305. N in wreath printed. 1953.

A gold edged white piece with delicate pink flowers around the border with an inner trim of blue stylized flowers on a gray band. Benton. 6204. N in wreath printed. 1962. Rim.

A gold edged white piece with lavender and blue dot rim design around lavender roses sprinkled around the edges. Melita. 6205. N in wreath printed. 1962. Rim.

A gold edged white piece with purple violets and green leaves alternating with a bud and leaf outlined in gold. Avalon. 5150. M in wreath big bow. 1950-1953. Rim.

A gold edged white piece with lavender, blue, and gold flowers with green leaves. An inner pin line in gold. Longwood. 2485. Contemporary FC Sri Lanka. 1975-1980. Classic.

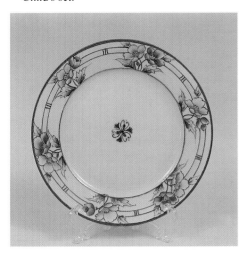

A gold edged white piece with pink roses border with gold design on a black background(childs cup). Maple leaf. 1890. Child's set.

A gold edge white piece with a large pink flower design with green leaves connected by an ivory band outlined in gold, with a central three petal gold design. Maple leaf. 1890.

A gold edge white piece with raised dots of gold framing a pink flower with green leaves. K in circle Noritake script MIJ. 1908. Original.

A gold edged white piece with pink roses along a gold line with a gold enclosed blue diamond on the rim. K in circle Noritake script MIJ. 1908. Tea set.

A gold edge white piece with pink flowers with green leaves around the border with brown stems connecting the roses, gold stripes create the rim decorations. Sunrise. 1911.

A gold edged white piece with pink flowers with green and blue leaves interrupted with gold roses and gold outline (chocolate set). M in wreath HP/Nippon. 1911-1920.

A gold edged white piece with pink flowers with lavender leaves all around the border. Sunrise. 1911.

A gold edged white piece with a wide gold border around single pink flower on a stem with green leaves (bowl with ball feet). M in wreath HP/Nippon. 1911-1920. Original.

A gold edged white piece with large pink and purple tulips with green leaves covering the whole piece (blank sold by Noritake, buyer R.K. painted it.) Nippon under Noritake. 1911-1920.

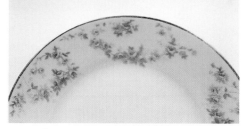

A gold edged white piece with a single pink flower occurring around the rim connected with a thin green ribbon, two thin gold pin lines occur in addition to the gold edge around the rim. M in wreath N/HP/Nippon. 1912. Original.

A gold edged white piece with garlands of tiny roses with green leaves. Bosnia (the).M in wreath N/HP/Nippon. 1912.

A gold edged white piece with a gold border with a black geometric design around a floral grouping of pink flowers with lavender leaves. M in wreath N/HP/Nippon. 1912. Original.

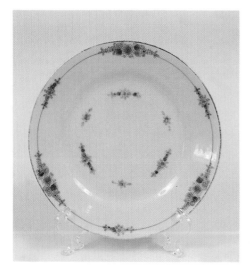

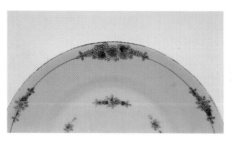

A gold edged white piece with pink flowers on the border connected with a pen line. M in wreath nor/ Nippon. 1912.

76

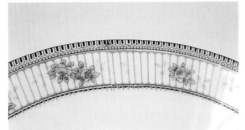

A gold edged white piece with pink flowers with black loops around the border and the flowers are separated with gold bars (covered oval casserole). Ormonde Bassett. M in wreath N/HP/Nippon. 1912-1922. Original.

A gold edged white piece with a pastel pink border decorated with a wreath of pink flowers on green leaves tied at top with a blue bow. M in wreath N/HP/Japan. 1921-1928. Original.

A gold edged white piece with pink flowers set off by gold rose boughs on a black fleurs-de-lis rim design. M in wreath N/HP/Japan. 1921-1928. Rim.

A gold edged white piece with gold bulls eyes around the rim and a single pink flower with green and lavender leaves encircled with gold scrolls (match holder). M in wreath N/HP/Japan. 1921-1928. Azalea.

A gold edged white piece with a pink and blue flower with green leaves separated by a half-inch pink band. M in wreath N/HP/Japan. 1921-1928. Original.

A gold edged white piece with a delicate band around the rim with pink roses on a cream band. Ansonia. M in wreath N/HP/Japan. 1921-1930. Original.

A gold edged white piece with large pink azalea flowers with green leaves. Azalea. 0019322, 0252622. M in wreath N/HP/Japan. 1921-1938. Azalea.

A gold edged white with cream band piece with a delicate pink flower in a black and gold geometric edged border. Chanossa. M in wreath N/HP/Japan. 1921-1930. Azalea.

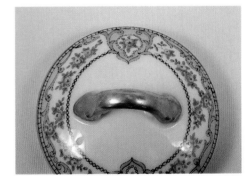

A gold edged white piece with pink roses in a gold background medallion surrounded with blue scrolls connected by black outlined gold dots. Portland. 0013673. M in wreath N/HP/Japan. 1908-1920. Original.

77

A gold edged white piece with swages of pink flowers with green leaves and a few green scrolls. 0014800. M in wreath N/HP/Japan. 1908.

A gold edged white piece with pink flowers with lavender leaves broken by black bars around a blue flower. Cherry Blossom. 1924-1931.

A silver edged white piece with an all over design of pink flowers with gray leaves. R.C. under laurel. 1926. Rim.

A gold edged white piece with a large pink, yellow, blue, and lavender floral arrangement with green leaves. China Peony. M in wreath big bow. 1950-1953. Rose china.

A gold edged white piece with pink and white flowers around the border with green and blue leaves. Roselace. 5041. M in wreath big bow. 1950-1953. Rim.

A gold edged white piece with pink and white flower around the border with green leaves and an inner old pin line. Roselane. 5147. M in wreath big bow. 1950-1953. Rose china.

A gold edged white piece with swags of dark pink roses and a gray striped border outlined with gold scrolls. Ridgewood. 5201. M in wreath big bow. 1950-1979. LaSalle.

A gold edged white piece with large pink roses with brown leaves arranged with a few white flowers. Rosilla. 5212. M in wreath big bow. 1950-1953. Coupe.

A gold edged white piece with a three bloom pink carnation with green leaves in an offset pattern. K in scroll shield NTK. 1947. Rim.

A gold edged white piece with large pink flowers and green leaves. Pink Poppy. 514. K in scroll shield Japan. 1947. Rose china.

A gold edged white piece with delicate pink flowers connected with gray scrolls. Noritake script. 1953.

A gold edged white piece with large pink roses with green leaves. 6234. M in wreath big bow. 1947-1953. Rose china.

A gold edged white piece with intermittent pink roses with green leaves. K in circle Noritake script NTK . 1949. Rose china.

A silver edged white piece with pink roses in a silver urn with green and lavender leaves. N in wreath printed. 1953.

A gold edged white piece with a pink bouquet with green leaves. K in scroll shield NTK. 1947. Rose china.

A gold edged white piece with pink roses with green and brown leaves encircle the entire rim. N in scroll shield Japan. 1952. LaSalle.

A silver edged white piece with an allover pattern of pink and silver flowers with green leaves, the inner pin line is silver. Anita. 5309. N in wreath printed. 1953. Rim.

A silver edged white piece with a pink lily design outlined with gray leaves. Kent. 5422. N in wreath printed. 1954. LaSalle.

A gold edged white piece with tiny pink flowers with brown leaves. Reverie. 5431. N in wreath printed. 1954. LaSalle.

A silver edged white piece with large white flowers with pink trim and green leaves and brown stems. Chatham. 5502. 0176133. N in wreath printed. 1951. Concerto.

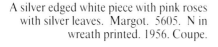

A silver edged white piece with pink roses with silver leaves. Margot. 5605. N in wreath printed. 1956. Coupe.

A gold edged white piece with a gold lattice work intermittent around the border with sprays of pink roses with green leave covering the rim. Charmaine. 5506. 0176135. N in wreath printed. 1953. Rim.

A gold edged white piece with a pink central rose with brown and black leaves an inner double pin line in gold. Daryl. 5510. N in wreath printed. 1955. Coupe.

A silver edged white piece with tiny pink and white flowers with green and yellow leaves. Arlene. 5802. N in wreath printed. 1958. Butterfly.

A silver edged white piece with small pink roses with gray leaves and gray scrolls. Windsor. 5924. 0185452. N in wreath printed. 1953.

A silver edged white piece with pink and white flowers in an offset design with green and tan leaves. Barbara. 6009. 0189202. N in wreath printed. 1954. Triangle.

A silver edged white piece with large pink roses with gray leaves in an offset design. Rosemarie. 6044. N in wreath printed. 1960. Coupe.

A silver edged white piece with a single pink rose with gray leaves and stem. Pasadena. 6311. N in wreath printed. 1963-1978. Concerto.

A white piece with a large pin rose with green gray leaves. Young Love. 118. Cook 'n Serve. 1961.

A silver edged white piece with pink roses surrounded with silver scrolls. Mayfair. 6109. N in wreath printed. 1961. Coupe.

A silver edged white piece with a pink and maroon border with swags of pink flowers with gray leaves. 590. R.C. in wreath. 1956. Rim.

A silver edged white piece with pink flowers on the border with blue leaves connected with delicate pink and blue flowers. A gray border with blue dots. Fairmont. 6102. 0194925. N in wreath colorful. 1975-1987. LaSalle.

A silver edged white piece with a single pink rosebud with greenish gray leaves in an offset design. Rosemead. 6210. N in wreath printed. 1962. Coupe.

A gold edged white piece with one large pink rose offset from the center. Roseville. 6238. N in wreath colorful. 1963-1965. Butterfly.

A gold edged white piece with a large pink rose with realistic leaves and small yellow and blue daisies. Firenze. 6674. N in wreath colorful. 1965.

A silver edged white piece with a large pink flower in an offset design with pale blue leaves. Carthage. 3330. N in wreath black and gold. 1982-1998. Remembrance II.

A silver edged white piece with a single pink rose and a single bud in pink with brown leaves in an offset design. Sweet Talk. 6513. N in wreath colorful. 1963. Coupe.

A silver edged white piece with tiny pink roses with tan leaves in an offset design. Gail. 6710. N in wreath colorful. 1968-1983. Coupe.

A silver edged white piece with large pink and lavender flowers on a gray background. River Place. 3881. N in wreath black and gold. 1988-1989. Paramount.

A silver edged white piece with a pin and blue floral border connected with green stems with green leaves. Pauline. 6586. N in wreath colorful. 1963. LaSalle.

A silver edged white piece with a rim design of pink and blue flowers with green and brown leaves, white buds appear as dots. Mayflower. 2351. N in wreath black and gold. 1968. Rim.

A silver edged white piece with pink flowers on a delicate gray band with gray leaves. Tarkington. 3695. Legendary Sri Lanka. 1986-1993. Commander.

A gray edged white piece with a large red flower in a central design with white flowers with green leaves. K in scroll shield NTK. 1947-1949.

A gold edged white piece with a maroon border framing a dainty maroon rose with brown leaves. Jean. 6724. N in wreath colorful. 1966. LaSalle.

A gold edged white piece with a green background to a gold swag border with a small pink flower (tea strainer). R.C. handpainted nippon. 1911. Tea set.

A silver edged white piece with red and blue flowers around the border. Forever. 2690. Contemporary FC Sri Lanka. 1974. Classic.

A gold edged white piece with a green Greek key design alternating with pink and yellow flowers with green leaves. Sunrise. 1911. Chocolate set.

A gold edged white piece with green and white checkerboard border design with pink and blue flowers connected by green leaves. M in wreath N/HP/Nippon. 1912. Original.

A gold edged white piece with a green checkered border, around the piece are pink roses enclosed with a half circle of gold dots (breakfast tea set). M in wreath N/HP/Japan. 1921-1928.

A gold edged white piece with a green leafy vine around the rim with occasional pink flowers, also a purple cross design. M in wreath N/HP/Nippon. 1912. Original.

A gold edged white piece with pink and blue flowers with green leaves separated by half-inch wide pastel green stripes. M in wreath N/HP/Japan. 1921-1928. Original.

A gold edged white piece with green border background to a black geometric design and a flower in a green medallion surrounded by black outlined bells. M in wreath N/HP/Japan. 1921-1928. Original.

A gold edged white piece with white flowers around the edge as well as a central design. Laurette. 5047. M in wreath big bow. 1950-1953. Rose china.

A white piece with a dainty pink, blue and yellow floral grouping surrounded with green leafy scrolls on a pale cream background outlined in blue. 0061237. M in wreath N/HP/Japan. 1921-1928. Original.

A gold edged white piece with a wide mint green band with a central design of pink purple and yellow flowers with green leaves. M on stage. 1940. Mushroom.

A gold edged white piece with a one inch wide green band around the edge intersected with a black stripped background to a pink and yellow floral grouping (cake plate). M in wreath N/HP/Japan. 1921-1928. Original.

A gold edged white piece with a large white blossom with a lavender center, large green leaves surround this central design. K in scroll shield NTK. 1947. Tea set.

A silver edged white piece with green leave and a white daisy flower. Wellesley. 6214. 0196310. N in wreath printed. 1962. Triangle.

A silver edged white piece with white daisies surrounded with green leaves. Annabelle. 6856. N in wreath black and gold. 1968-1976. Concerto.

A gold edged white piece with a large white dogwood flower and green leaves, the green leaves encircle the border. Winslow. 5406. N in wreath printed. 1954. LaSalle.

A silver edged white piece with a green leafed floral design with blue, white and pink flowers. Savannah. 2031. N in wreath black and gold. 1970-1991. Commander.

A silver edged white piece with green border behind white daisies with green leaves. Princeton. 6911. N in wreath black and gold. 1968-1985. Commander.

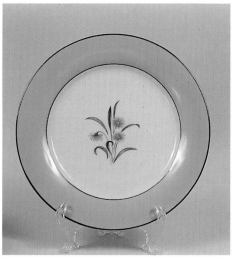

A silver edged white piece with pink flowers in the center with a wide gray band. Regina. 5442. N in wreath printed. 1975-1979. LaSalle.

A silver edged white piece with an offset design of green flowers outlined with white and a yellow center, green leaves and stems connect the flowers. Soroya. 6853. 0211113. N in wreath black and gold. 1968-1977. Concerto.

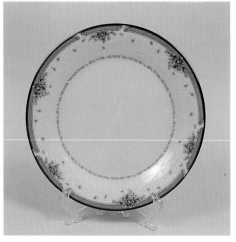

A silver edged white piece with a gray and green border overlaid with blue and pink flowers with gray leaves. Lunceford. 3884. Legendary Sri Lanka. 1988-2000. Commander.

A gold edged white piece with a green marble background for a pink floral design. Ashville. 4750. New Lineage II bone china. 1997-1998. Empire.

A gold edge white piece with a blue wreath border divided into sections with black latticework, pink, blue, and maroon flowers around the edge are connected with gold stems. Sunrise. 1911.

A gold edged white piece with a blue band with gold lattice dividing bouquets of pink flowers. Maple leaf (open salt). 1890.

A gold edged white piece with a narrow blue band around garlands of pink flowers with green leaves. M in wreath HP/Nippon. 1911–1920.

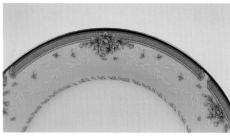

A silver edged white piece with a green border with ivory scrolls and rope edged decorated with pale pink flowers with a green leaves and white garlands in-between. Greenbrier. 4101. N in wreath Philippines. 1992-1998. Remembrance II.

A gold edged white piece with a half-inch solid blue band around the border edged by a gold striped cream design with scalloped inner edge ending in pink and yellow roses with green leaves. Maple leaf. 1890.

A gold edged white piece with a pink flower in a medallion surrounded with blue stripes in gold borders. M in wreath HP/Nippon. 1911-1920. Tea set.

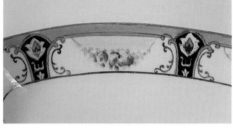

A gold edged white piece with a blue border intersected with black medallions and pink flowers with green leaves and a gold inner pin line. M in wreath N/HP/Japan. 1921-1928.

A gold edged white piece with blue flowers with green leaves. K in circle Nippon plain. 1911-1920.

A gold edged white piece with a border of blue background to gold lattice work intersected with a single pink rose with blue and green leaves. Luzon (the). M in wreath nor/ Nippon. 1912.

A gold edged white piece with a light blue border around a light pink and pastel blue flowers with lavender background and green leaves. M in wreath N/HP/Japan. 1921-1928. Original.

A gold edged white piece with a wide light blue band interspersed with a pink flower surrounded with brown scrolls. M in wreath N/HP/Japan. 1921-1928.

A gold edged white piece with pink flowers on green leaves in a medallion outlined in gold with a blue background, black with gold design panels interrupt the design. M in wreath N/HP/Japan (covered jam pot with fast stand). 1921-1928.

A brown edged white piece with a blue petal design around the rim and an intricate pink and blue flower outlined with green and blue scrolls around the edge and a central design of pink flowers. Kiva (the). M in wreath nor/ Nippon. 1912-1920.

A gold edged white piece with a blue background surrounding gold scrolls and a gold stylized flower (egg cup). M in wreath N/HP/Japan. 1921-1928.

A gold edged white piece with a wide blue border of geometric scrolls with a pink bouquet in a brown urn. Ellrose. M in wreath N/HP/Japan. 1921-1930.

A gold edged white piece with a blue triangle round pink flowers with green leaves. Magenta (the). M in wreath N/HP/Japan. 1921-1930.

A gold edged white piece with stylized white flowers splashed with color surrounded with blue scroll borders (covered jam pot). M in wreath N/HP/Japan. 1921-1928.

A gold edged white piece with blue scrolls and blue geometric border with a small red and yellow flowers with green leaves. Glenora. M in wreath N/HP/Japan. 1921-1930.

A gold edged white piece with a blue border around pink flowers bordered with blue and black medallions. Chanazure. 061239. M in wreath N/HP/Japan. 1928.

A gold edged white piece with a wide blue band on the rim and a pink flower outlined with green and pink leaves (individual chocolate pot). M in wreath N/HP/Japan. 1921-1928.

A gold edged white piece with a blue and black geometric border with blue, pink, yellow and lavender floral sprigs with green leaves. Sheridan. 0069533. M in wreath N/HP/Japan. 1929-1932. Azalea.

A gold edged white piece with a blue border design with small gold flowers and green leaves, intersected with a blue lattice design. Cherry Blossom. 1924-1931.

A gold edged white piece with blue scrolls surrounding a dainty pink, yellow, and blue flowers with green leaves (egg cup). Comiston (the). 0058599. M in wreath N/HP/Japan. 1927. Original.

A gold edged white piece with a blue and yellow geometric border around pink bouquet in a blue urn surrounded with blue scrolls with a blue inner pen line. Daventry. 0069544. M in wreath N/HP/Japan. 1929.

A gold edged white piece with a blue background under blue ribbons around the red poppies with gold centers. Chikaramachi. 1928.

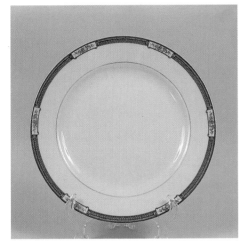

A gold edged white piece with a blue geometric half-inch band around the border intersected with a grouping of 5 roses (see Haverford). Grosvenor. 0068445. M in wreath N/HP/Japan. 1929, Mushroom.

A blue edged white luster piece with a wide blue band and large orange and purple and yellow flowers with green leaves. Chikaramachi. 1928.

A silver edged white piece with a single blue flower with green leaves. Bessie. 5788. N in wreath printed. 1957.

A silver edged white piece with a blue border around an arrangement of blue flowers in an urn with silver scrolls. Colburn. 6107. 0194926. N in wreath printed. 1961-1989. LaSalle.

A white piece with a wide baby blue band with pink yellow purple and blue flowers with green leaves on the band. The accent trim color is pastel pink. (breakfast set) M on stage. 1940. Mushroom.

A silver edged white piece with a single blue rose with gray and blue leaves. Simone. 6407. N in wreath colorful. 1963. Concerto.

A silver edged white piece with blue flowers in a central design and a wide baby blue band. Bluebell. 5558. N in wreath printed. 1955.

A gold edged white piece with blue flowers on blue and gray stems with blue leaves. Waverly. 5915. N in wreath printed. 1959.

A silver white piece with a blue rose with blue and green leaves. Sylvia. 6603. N in wreath colorful. 1965. Concerto.

A gold edged white piece with a blue border of flowers and leaves around pink and blue flowers with green leaves with a gold inner pin line. Barton. 6305. N in wreath printed. 1963. Rim.

A gold edged white piece with a blue border around an arrangement of blue flowers in a blue urn surrounded with silver scrolls. Noble. 2600. N crossed stems NTK. 1955. LaSalle.

A silver edged white piece with a repeated border design of dainty blue flowers on a stem with green leaves. Tilford. 6712. N in wreath colorful. 1967-1975. Concerto.

A silver edged white piece with garlands of blue roses with blue and silver leaves (butter pat). Mariposa. 6411. N in wreath colorful. 1963.

A gold edged white piece with blue and pink offset pansy petals floral design with green leaves (relish dish). Princess. N crossed stems NTK. 1955. Coupe.

A silver edged white piece with dainty blue bouquets with green leaves connected with garlands of green leaves. Glencoe. 6505. N in wreath colorful. 1963.

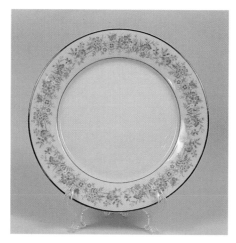

A silver edged white piece with a single blue garland of dainty roses with silver leaves. Nicolette. 6713. N in wreath colorful. 1966. Coupe.

A silver edged white piece with blue flowers around the rim with blue leaves. Milford. 2227. (lug soup) N in wreath black and gold. 1968-1985. Commander.

A silver edged white piece with a blue rim with pin and blue roses and green leaves. Lancashire. 3883. N in wreath black and gold. 1988-1996. New Lineage/Paramount.

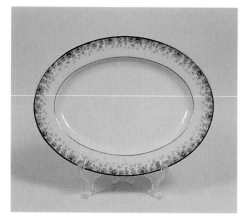

A gold edged white piece with a band of dark blue around the rim then a dainty pink floral grouping with blue and gray leaves connected with a gray and white lines. Landon. 4111. N in wreath black and gold. 1994-1998. Nor. Ireland I.

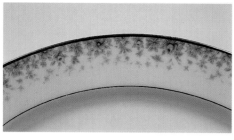

A silver edged white piece with a single blue rose offset design. Virtue. 2934. N in wreath black and gold. 1979-1996. Remembrance II.

A silver edged white piece with a dense dainty design of blue flowers with blue and gray leaves around the outer rim. Kathleen. 6722. N in wreath colorful. 1967 Rim.

A silver edged white piece with blue flowers with blue leaves and a blue geometric border, an inner pen line in silver. Blue Hill. 2482. Contemporary FC Sri Lanka. 1975-1994. Classic.

A silver edged white piece with a blue and pink floral arrangement around the border with a central blue floral design with blue leaves and dainty pink flowers with white accents. Carolyn. 2693. Contemporary FC Philippines. 1977-1996. Classic.

A silver edged white piece with pale blue and white etched flowers on the border and a pastel blue, pink and yellow floral arrangement as a central design. Anticipation. 2963. Ireland. 1981-1994. Nor. Ireland I.

A silver edged white piece with delicate blue flowers with green leaves and green and gold scrolls. Culeton. 2692. Contemporary FC Sri Lanka. 1977-1982. Classic.

A gold edged white piece with a navy band around pink and maroon flowers offset on blue stems. Legacy Philippines. 1977. Commander.

A silver edged white piece with a blue and white floral arrangement around the border with a silver inner pin line. Marywood. 2181. Contemporary FC Philippines. 1975-1996. Classic.

A silver edged white piece with a blue floral design with blue leaves a thin blue border surrounds the piece. Chadbourne. 3990. N in wreath Philippines. 1989-2000. Remembrance II.

A gold edged white piece with a wide gray rim and a central design of roses on olive brown leaves. K in scroll shield NTK. 1947. Rose china.

A gold edged white piece with pink roses inside a wide gray band. Glenrose. 5206. N in wreath printed. 1953.

A silver edged white piece with a gray border and a single design of pink flowers with gray leaves. Crest. 5421. N in wreath printed. 1954. LaSalle.

A silver edged white piece with gray border with delicate pink flowers. Petite. 5507. 0176125. N in wreath printed. 1951, Triangle.

A gold edged white piece with a blue band of geometric design around a pink bouquet of roses with green leaves connected with green leafed garlands. Love Poem. 4135. N in wreath Philippines. 1998. Nor. Ireland I.

A gold edged white piece with a large pink rose with brown leaves, the border is a gray band edged with brown leaves. Rosemont. 5048. M in wreath big bow. 1950-1953. Rose china.

A silver edged white piece with a gray band and a single pink flower with gray leaves. Lilybell. 5556. N in wreath printed. 1955. Concerto.

A silver edged white piece with a lacy gray border around dainty pink flowers surrounded with gold scrolls. Edgewood. 5807, 0182094. N in wreath printed. 1958. LaSalle.

A silver edged white piece with a silver on white design of flowers in an urn surrounded by scrolls. Ashby. 6201. N in wreath printed 1962. Rose china.

A silver edged white piece with a large single rose outlined in gray with gray leaves. Rosay. 6216. N in wreath printed. 1962-1977. Concerto.

A white edged white piece with a silver narrow pen line around the outer edge large white roses with gray and silver leaves in an offset design. Belda. 6342. N in wreath printed. 1963. Coupe.

A silver edged white piece with a gray marbled narrow border around gray and white with rose accent flowers with gray leaves connected with white ribbons. The inner line is ribbons. Kirkland. 4117. N in wreath black and gold. 1995-1998. Remembrance II.

A silver edged white piece with a lacy gray border around a pink floral arrangement with gold leaves. Garland. 5905. N in wreath printed. 1959. Coupe.

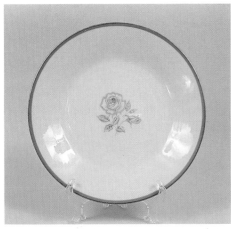

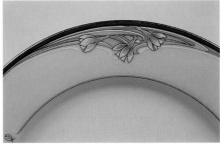

A gold edged white piece with a gray border and a single rose in gray outlined with gold. Blair Rose. 6519. N in wreath black and gold. 1968. Coupe.

A silver edged white piece with a narrow maroon band lined with gray intersected with pink flowers with gray stems and leaves. Garbo. 3790. Legendary Philippines. 1987-1990.Commander.

A gold edged white piece with black background to vase shaped inserts with red flowers and blue and green leaves. (butter tub) M in wreath N/HP/Japan. 1921-1928.

A gold edged white piece with a black band around the border with pink flowers and green leaves. Ferncroft. M in wreath nor/ Nippon. 1912.

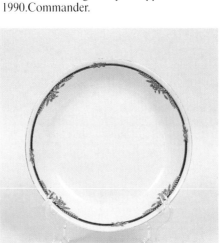

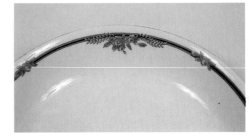

A gold edged white with cream band piece with a pink and yellow floral with black background in a medallion and black floral outlined. M in wreath N/HP/Japan. 1921-1928.

A silver edged white piece with a gray geometric border interspersed with white and gray accents flowers with gray leaves and an inner silver pin line. Sweet Leilani. 3482. Legendary Sri Lanka. 1984-1998. Commander.

A gold edged white piece with a gold scroll border around pink, yellow and blue flowers with green leaves. M in wreath N/HP/Japan. 1921-1928.

A gold edged white piece with a black and gold geometric border interrupted with a lone pink rose with green leaves. (Butter dish) Doris. 0071219. M in wreath N/HP/Japan. 1930. Original.

A silver edged white piece with a wide brown band and a centralized pink flower with brown and silver leaves. Sheridan. 5441. N in wreath printed. 1954. LaSalle.

A gold edged white piece with a mixed color border which contains yellow flowers, and blue bordersframing yellow flowers. Monterey (the). 0058595. M in wreath N/HP/Japan. 1921-1930. Original.

A Silver edged white piece with a large offset rose design in black and white, and shades of gray. Rosamor. 5851S. N in wreath colorful. 1963. LaSalle.

A gold edged white piece with flowers of lavender yellow, blue with green leaves and lavender scrolls. Knollwood. 068483. M in wreath N/HP/Japan. 1929. Original.

A gold edged white piece with large brown mums with brown leaves. Lasalle. 5142. M in wreath big bow. 1950-1953. Triangle.

A gold edged white piece with gold scrolls dividing pink, blue, flowers with green leaves. Chikaramachi. 1928.

A gold edged white piece with a central design of pink, yellow, orange, blue and purple flowers with green leaves surrounded by smaller floral groupings. Colton. 3081. K in scroll shield Japan. 1947. Classic.

A gold edged white piece with a mixed color bouquet of pink and blue with green leaves and cream edges. K in circle Nippon fancy. 1911-1920. Original.

A gold edged white piece with bright pink and yellow realistic flowers with green leaves. Phyllis. 318. M in scrolls. 1933.

A gold edged white piece with a large central floral grouping of purple, yellow, red and white flowers with green leaves. M in wreath big bow. 1933-1935.

A white piece with a central bouquet with pink, blue, yellow and white flowers with green leaves. Dresgay. 3038. K in scroll shield Japan. 1947. Rose china.

A silver edged white piece with a large central flower arrangement of blue, yellow, and red flowers with gray scrolls around the border. Sheila. 2155. N in wreath black and gold. 1975-1976. Concerto.

A gold edged white with cream band piece with mustard trim around small blue and pink flowers. Blossom M double Japan. 1916. Original.

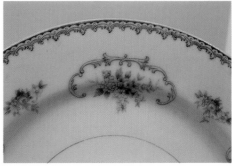

A gold edged white with cream band piece with a mustard border around a group of white, pink, and blue flowers with green leaves. Greta. M in shield China. 1931.

A gold edged white with cream band piece with a mustard yellow scroll rim design, with a pink, blue and yellow floral arrangement surrounded by mustard scrolls. M in scrolls. 1933.

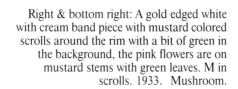

A gold edged white with cream band piece with a mustard border around a pastel floral arrangement of pink, yellow and blue flowers with green leaves all connected by gold scrolls. M in wreath N/HP/Japan. 1921-1928. Original.

Right & bottom right: A gold edged white with cream band piece with mustard colored scrolls around the rim with a bit of green in the background, the pink flowers are on mustard stems with green leaves. M in scrolls. 1933. Mushroom.

Left & above: A gold edged white with cream band piece with a mustard scroll border around floral arrangement of pink and lavender flowers with green leaves, the inner line is a fancy scroll. M in wreath N/HP/ Japan. 1921-1928. Mushroom.

A gold edged white with cream band piece with a yellow border decorated with black outlined bells and scrolls, a central floral design of pink, yellow, blue and white flowers. M in wreath N/HP/Japan. 1921-1928. Original.

A gold edged white with cream band piece with a mustard rope design on the rim outlining a pink and blue floral arrangement with gold scrolls. M in scrolls. 1933. Mushroom.

A gold edged white with cream band piece with a wide mustard border interspersed with two delicate pink roses in a medallion. Marcia. 3855. M in wreath big bow. 1933. Mushroom.

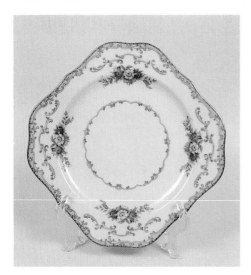

A gold edge white with cream band piece with a gold scroll enclosed yellow border with a floral bouquet. The inner line is a scroll. Alvin. 0095649. M in wreath big bow. 1933-1935.

A gold edged white with cream band piece with a mustard scroll rim design and yellow and pink and blue flowers with green leaves around the border surrounded with mustard and green tipped scrolls. Mimi. 0098141. M in wreath big bow. 1935. Mushroom.

A gold edged white with cream band piece with a fancy wide mustard trim around a white, pink and yellow flowers with mustard and gold leaves. K in scroll shield occupied. 1947. Rose china.

A gold edged white with cream band piece with a pink flower occurring around the rim connected by a lavender ribbon. M in wreath N/HP/Nippon. 1912. Original.

A gold edged white with cream band piece with a pink with blue flower band on a black background. Eleanor Bassett. M in wreath N/HP/Nippon . 1912. Original.

A gold edged white with cream band piece with a dainty pink and yellow flowers with lavender leaves (cake plate). Linwood (the). 0011657. M in wreath N/HP/Nippon. 1907-1912. Original.

A gold edged white with cream band piece with a group of pink flowers with green leaves around the rim. M in wreath N/HP/Nippon. 1912. Original.

A gold edged white with cream band piece with a group of pink flowers with yellow and blue leaves on the cream band. Lorraine (the). M in wreath N/HP/Nippon. 1912. Original.

A gold edged white with cream band piece with a pink grouping of three roses surrounded with gold "U" shaped geometric design. Sunrise. 1911. Original.

A gold edged white with cream band piece with a pink and blue flower with green leaves interspersed with a lone pink flower on the cream band. Sedan (the). 0011292. M in wreath N/HP/Nippon. 1912. Original.

A gold edged white with cream band piece with a small pink flowers in three locations bracketed with black trim. M in wreath N/HP/Japan. 1921-1928. Original.

A gold edged white piece with pink roses in gold scrolled medallions connected with pink floral decorated swags, outlined with black looped geometric border. M in wreath N/HP/Japan. 1921-1928.

A gold edged white piece with a wide yellow band around the rim and pink flowers with green leaves on swags (individual cream and sugar). M in wreath N/HP/Japan. 1921-1928. Azalea.

A gold edged white with cream band piece with a four of pink flowers with green leaves on the cream band bordered with a gold and black geometric design and a black inner pin line. Bedford. 0068443. M in wreath N/HP/Japan. 1921-1930. Rim.

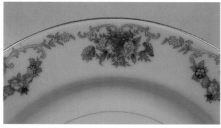

A gold edged white with cream band piece with a large group of pink flowers connected with gold scrolls on the cream band. M in scroll and wreath. 1940. Mushroom.

A gold edged white with cream band piece with a large pink rose surrounded with smaller yellow, blue and lavender flowers with green leaves. Rose china. 1946. Rose china.

A gold edged white with cream band piece with a pink and yellow flower arrangement in a gold urn surrounded with gold scrolls. K in scroll shield NTK . 1947. Rose china.

A gold edged white with cream band piece with a red border and pink flowers with green leaves in front of a black and white checker board pattern. M in wreath N/HP/Japan. 1921-1928. Original.

102

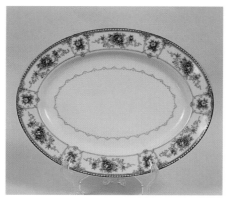

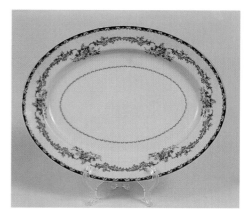

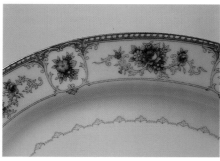

A gold edged white with cream band piece with a maroon border outlined with gold scrolls and gold daisies, the border design is pink and yellow flowers with green leaves. Laramie. M with crown. 1930. Mushroom.

A gold edged white with cream band piece with a maroon and gold rope border around a pink and blue floral group with green leaves surrounded with gold scrolls. Allure. 3706. 0097902. M in scrolls. 1935-1950. Rose china.

A gold edged white with cream band piece with a maroon and gold rim and pink, white and yellow flowers and green leaves connected with gold scrolls. Claudette. 594. 0098221. M in wreath big bow. 1935. Mushroom.

A gold edged white with cream band piece with maroon border decorated with gold scrolls and bouquets of pink, red, and purple flowers with green leaves. M in scrolls. 1933. Rim.

A gold edged white with cream band piece with a maroon and gold border around a pastel bouquet of white and pink flowers surrounded with gold scrolls. Oradell. 588. M in wreath big bow. 1933. Mushroom.

A gold edged white with cream band piece with a maroon and gold border surrounding a pink, white, blue and yellow floral arrangement with gold scrolls. Glenwood. 6500. M in scroll and wreath. 1940, Mushroom.

A gold edged white with cream band piece with a maroon border with a pink flower in a medallion surrounded by gold scrolls. K in scroll shield occupied. 1947. Rose china.

A gold edged white with cream band piece with a maroon trim outlined with gold & green scrolls around a floral multi-color bouquet with green leaves on a gold scroll loop, the inner pen line is green. K in circle Noritake script MIJ. 1949. Tea set.

A gold edged white with cream band piece with a green lattice border and pink flowers in a gold urn over gold scrolls(expresso server). M in wreath N/HP/Japan. 1921-1928.

A gold edged white with cream band piece witha green border framing gold and white flowers with gold leaves. M in wreath N/HP/Japan. 1921-1928. Tea set.

A gold edged white with cream band piece with a green background border and a swag of yellow and pink flowers. M in wreath N/HP/Japan. 1921-1928. Original.

A gold edged white with cream band piece with a green border interspersed with pink flowers with yellow and green leaves. M in wreath N/HP/Nippon. 1912. Original.

A gold edged white with cream band piece with a green border outlined with white daisies, a pink floral arrangement with green leaves decorate the rim(snack plate). M in wreath N/HP/Japan. 1921-1928.

A gold edged white with cream band piece with green clouds border outlined with gold scrolls and a floral bouquet of pink, yellow and blue flowers with green leaves. M in wreath N/HP/Japan. 1921-1928.

A cream and green luster piece with the top half in green and the bottom cream. Large orange, yellow and blue flowers with green leaves area central design. M in wreath N/HP/Japan. 1921-1928. Tea set.

A gold edged white with cream band piece with a green border interspersed with a bouquet of pink flowers with green leaves. Pendarvis. M in wreath N/HP/Japan. 1921-1930.

A gold edged white with cream band piece with green fish scales outlined with gold scrolls, with pink flowers with green leaves on the border. M in wreath N/HP/Japan. 1921-1928. Mushroom.

A gold edged white with cream band piece with a green border with white small white flowers interspersed with yellow and pink flowers with green leaves the inner line is green. M in wreath N/HP/Japan. 1921-1928.

A gold edged white with cream band piece with a green background to a yellow rose in scrolls surrounded with a black and white checked rim design, also a floral arrangement with pink and blue flowers. Fairfax. 0080461. M in wreath N/HP/Japan. 1932.

A gold edged white with cream band piece with a green border framed with gold scrolls around a pink and yellow bouquet with green leaves. Condoro. M in wreath N/HP/Japan. 1921-1930. Mushroom.

A gold edged white with cream band piece with a green background with white petals border, and a yellow with pink flowers with green leaves grouped by gold scrolls. Gloria. M in wreath small bow 2 leaves. 1930. Mushroom.

A gold edged white with cream band piece with a green and gold border around a bouquet of pink flowers in a gold urn, surrounded by green leaves. Smartnis. M in shield China. 1931.

A gold edged white with cream band piece with a green geometric rim and a large floral arrangement separated by a large green and gold scroll design, the inner border is a wide green geometric design. Marilyn. 0080467. M in wreath N/HP/Japan. 1932.

A gold edged white with cream band piece with a green border surrounding a small pink, yellow and blue flowers grouped in gold scrolls. Plaza. M in wreath small bow 2 leaves. 1930. Mushroom.

A gold edged white with cream band piece with green framed flowers interspersed with blue, pink and yellow flowers (chocolate set). Chikaramachi. 1928.

A gold edged white with cream band piece with a green and gold scroll border, and a bouquet of blue, pink and yellow flowers with green leaves. Piedmont. M in shield China. 1931. Rose china.

A gold edged white with cream band piece with a green border and a pink flower bordered with gold scrolls and green leaves. Florola. 0083374. M in shield China. 1932.

A gold edged white with cream band piece with a green and gold lattice border around a yellow, lavender and pink flowers with green leaves. M in scrolls. 1933. Mushroom.

A gold edged white with cream band piece with a green with gold scrolls border and a bouquet of white, pink and yellow flowers, an inner green scroll circle. M in scrolls. 1933. Mushroom.

A gold edged white with cream band piece with a green and gold border around a bouquet of small white, pink and blue flowers with green leaves. M in scrolls. 1933. Mushroom.

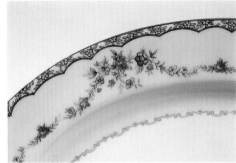

A gold edged white with cream band piece with a green leave border around floral swags of pink, yellow and blue flowers with green leaves (small platter). M in scrolls. 1933. Mushroom.

A gold edged white with cream band piece with a dainty multicolor floral arrangement surrounded with a green band with black and white dots and a yellow background. M in scrolls. 1933. Mushroom.

A gold edged white with cream band piece with white roses and green leaves on a vine. M in wreath big bow. 1948-1955. Rose china.

A gold edged white with cream band piece with a green border outlined with yellow scrolls around a multi-colored floral arrangement with blue leaves connected with gold and yellow scrolls, Charoma. 0098215. M in wreath big bow. 1948-1952. Rose china.

A gold edged white with cream band piece with a green border edged with gold and green scrolls around a floral arrangement of pink and yellow flowers with green leaves. Ingram. M in wreath small bow 3 leaves. 1948-1952. Rim.

A gold edged white with cream band piece with green and yellow lines around the rim and blue and pink flowers with yellow leaves surround with green tipped scrolls, the inner pin line is turquoise. Marlene. 0095642. M in wreath small bow 3 leaves. 1948-1952. Rim.

A gold edged white with cream band piece with a green with white scroll border interspersed with a pink flower surrounded with gold scrolls. Lynbrook. 4724. M in wreath big bow. 1948-1952. Rim.

A gold edged white with cream band piece with an olive green background to white flowers on the rim design and a multicolored floral arrangement on the border. Rose china. 1948. Rose china.

A gold edged white with cream band piece with a green border with gold scrolls and a yellow, pink and blue floral arrangement with green leaves, an inner pin line of aqua. Milroy. K in circle Noritake script MIJ. 1949. Tea set.

A gold edged white with cream band piece with a blue frame to pink flowers. M in wreath N/HP/Japan. 1921-1928. Original.

A gold edged white with cream band piece with a wide solid blue edge color and pink flowers with green leaves in a tan looped border. M in wreath N/HP/Japan. 1921-1928. Tea set.

A gold edged white with cream band piece with flowers surrounded by blue bars on the cream background, the flowers are pink roses encased in gold scrolls, the rim is gold and black design. (covered jam pot and covered creamer) M in wreath N/HP/Japan. 1921-1928. Tea set.

A gold edged white with cream band piece with a blue border around a pink, yellow and blue bouquet of flowers with green leaves. Athlone. 0080460. M in wreath N/HP/Japan. 1921-1932. Original.

A gold edged white with cream band piece with a blue flower with green leaves, blue scrolls frame a small pink flower. M in wreath N/HP/Japan. 1921-1928. Original.

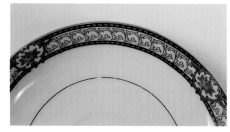

A gold edged white with cream band piece with pink flowers in a gold urn surrounded with a blue bar and yellow dot border. Cortez. M in wreath N/HP/Japan. 1921-1930. Original.

A gold edged white with cream band piece with a border of blue and orange around a bouquet of pink flowers with greenery in a gold scroll container, the inner line is green scrolls and gold leaves. Biarritz. 0078047. M in wreath N/HP/Japan. 1931. Original.

A gold edged white with cream band piece with blue scrolls around the rim outlined with black and gold dashes interrupted with a single pink rose. Chanbard. M in wreath N/HP/Japan. 1921-1928. Original.

A gold edged white with cream band piece with a blue lattice border around pink flowers with green leaves in a gold urn. Cyrano. M in wreath N/HP/Japan. 1921-1930 . Flying saucer.

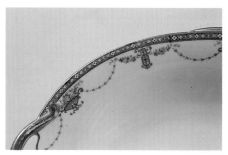

A gold edged white with cream band piece with a blue border of scrolls surrounding a pink bouquet in an urn. Camilla. 0117508. M in wreath N/HP/Japan. 1930-1939. Original.

A gold edged white with cream band piece with a blue border around pink flowers in an urn connected to a blue medallion with blue arrow heads. Chanking. M in wreath N/HP/Japan. 1921-1930. Original.

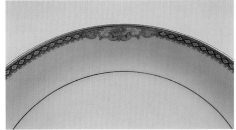

A gold edged white with cream band piece with a blue border around two pink roses. The border is a Greek key design. Deerlodge. 0069531. M in wreath N/HP/Japan. 1921-1930. Original.

A gold edged white with cream band piece with a blue border around pink and blue flowers in an urn. Grasmere. 0076567. M in wreath N/HP/Japan. 1921-1930. Original.

A gold edged white with cream band piece with a blue and mustard diamond geometric band intersected with blue scrolls around pink flowers. Meringo. M in wreath N/HP/Japan. 1921-1930. Original.

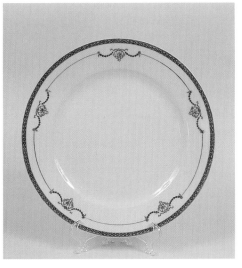

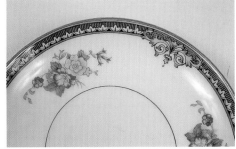

A gold edged white with cream band piece with a blue border around a pink rose framed by blue scrolls and swags. Gleneden. M in wreath N/HP/Japan. 1921-1930. Original.

A gold edged white with cream band piece with a blue rope border edged with gold scrolls and a bouquet of pink, yellow, blue and lavender flowers. Ivanhoe. 0086197. M in wreath N/HP/Japan. 1921-1930. Original.

A gold edged white with cream band piece with a blue border around light and dark pink flowers separated by gold scroll work. Pasadena. M in wreath N/HP/Japan. 1921-1930.

A gold edged white with cream band piece with a blue frame to a pink rose, framed with scrolls and gold geometric lines. Savoy. M in wreath N/HP/Japan. 1921-1930. Original.

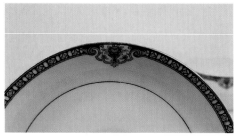

A gold edged white with cream band piece with a blue and black border framing a single red rose in an urn. Shirley. M in wreath N/HP/Japan. 1921-1930. Original.

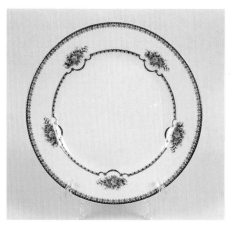

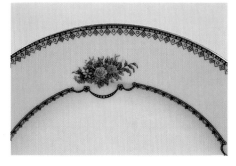

A gold edged white with cream band piece with a blue border around pink and blue bouquets. Wellsdale. M in wreath N/HP/Japan. 1921-1930. Original.

A gold edged white with cream band piece with a blue border around a single pink rose framed by swags and scrolls. Laureate. 2132. 0061235. M in wreath N/HP/Japan. 1928-1930. Original.

A gold edged white with cream band piece with blue scrolls around the rim intersected with pink roses. 0061240. M in wreath N/HP/Japan. 1928. Original.

A gold edged white with cream band piece with a blue border enclosing white leaves, intersected with pink flowers surrounded with gold scrolls. Ybry. 0076832. M in wreath N/HP/Japan. 1931. Original.

A gold edged white with cream band piece with a blue border around a bouquet of pink, yellow and blue flowers in a blue vase. Romeo. 0080459. M in wreath N/HP/Japan. 1932. Original.

A gold edged white with cream band piece with a blue and gold scrolls border to a bouquet of pink, white and lavender flowers grouped by blue scrolls. Derban. M in shield China. 1931. Mushroom.

A gold edged white with cream band piece with a blue and gold lattice border around a pink, white, blue and yellow flowers. Carmela. 4732. 0095635. M in shield China. 1935. Mushroom.

A gold edged white with cream band piece with blue and yellow border with a floral bouquet, the inner line is gold and green scrolls. Alford. M in wreath big bow. 1933-1935. Mushroom.

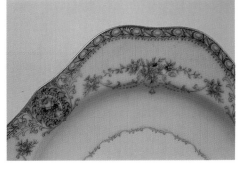

A gold edged white with cream band piece with mustard leaves and ovals around the rim and a medallion with blue border around a pink flower. Coypel. 3732. 0168374. M in wreath big bow. 1933-1935.

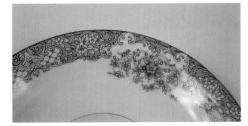

A gold edged white with cream band piece with a wide blue border of lattice work on a blue background interspersed around the border is a floral arrangement of purple, orange and blue flowers. Berenda. 4017. M in wreath big bow. 1933. Rose china.

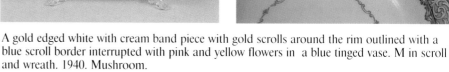

A gold edged white with cream band piece with gold scrolls around the rim outlined with a blue scroll border interrupted with pink and yellow flowers in a blue tinged vase. M in scroll and wreath. 1940. Mushroom.

A gold edged white with cream band piece with a blue background border interrupted by a pink, white, blue and orange bouquet. M in scroll and wreath. 1940. Mushroom.

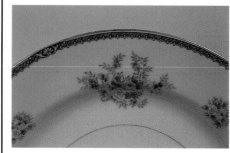

A gold edged white with cream band piece with a blue rope border around a white, yellow, orange, and blue flowers with green leaves. 1850. Rose china. 1946. Rose china.

A gold edged white with cream band piece with a blue background to white flowers outlined with gold scrolls around the border interrupted with a multi color floral arrangement. M in scroll and wreath. 1940. Flying Saucer.

A gold edged white with cream band piece with a blue rope border around a pink, white, orange, blue and yellow flowers with green leaves. K in scroll shield NTK. 1947. Rose china.

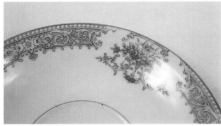

A gold edged white with cream band piece with a blue background for white scrolls around the rim interrupted by a pink floral arrangement in a gold vase. Rose china. 1946. Rose china.

A gold edged white with cream band piece with a blue border around a pink and yellow bouquet in an urn, all framed with gold scrolls. K in scroll shield occupied. 1947. Rose china.

A gold edged white with cream band piece with a blue background border, and a pink, yellow and blue group of flowers. K in scroll shield occupied. 1947. Rose china.

A gold edged white with cream band piece with a blue background to gold daises border intersected with a pink floral arrangement in a blue vase outlined with gold scrolls, vases, and leaves. K in scroll shield occupied. 1947. Rose china.

A black edged white with cream bond piece with a black geometric design around the edge and a floral design in a medallion outlined in black. M in wreath N/HP/Japan. 1921-1928.

A gold edged white with cream band piece with a black and white border with a bouquet of red roses in a black urn surrounded by black scrolls. Anaconda. M in wreath N/HP/Japan. 1921-1928. Original.

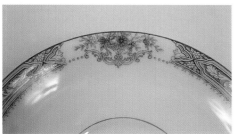

A gold edged white with cream band piece with a blue background to white leaves for a border interrupted by a pink floral arrangement with green leaves. K in scroll shield occupied. 1947. Rose china.

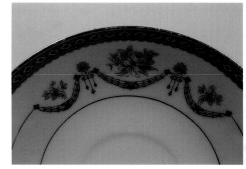

A gold edged white with cream band piece with a black background to a pink rose framed gold beading. M in wreath N/HP/Japan. 1921-1928. Original.

A gold edged white with cream band piece with a central floral arrangement and a black scalloped rim decoration. M in wreath N/HP/Japan. 1921-1928.

A gold edged white with cream band piece with a black geometric border around a pink and yellow bouquet draped with a gold and black swag. Marigold. 0071436. M in wreath N/HP/Japan. 1930. Original.

A gold edged white with cream band piece with a black and gold border around a pink and blue flower grouped with green leaves. A heart shaped black and gold scroll edged design. Castella. 0080463. M in wreath N/HP/Japan. 1932. Original.

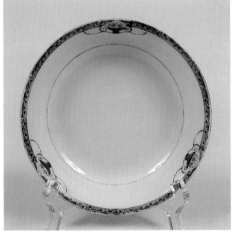

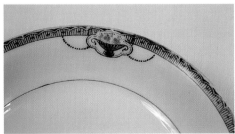

A gold edged white with cream band piece with two small pink roses in a black and gold urn surrounded by black dots, the black and yellow border is geometric with lines and dots. Cherry Blossom. 1924-1931. Original.

A gold edged white with cream band piece with a black background to white scrolls surrounding pink flowers with green leaves. M in wreath bow. OJ. 1949.

A gold edged white with cream band piece with a brown geometric half- inch border intersected with a five pink roses grouping (see Grosvenoa). Haverford. 0068445. M in wreath N/HP/Japan. 1929. Mushroom.

A gold edged white with cream band piece with a brown/tan border of daisies around the rim and a collection of pink, blue flowers with brown leaves green ferns. M in scrolls. 1933. Mushroom.

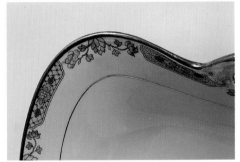

A gold edged white with cream band piece with pink, orange, and blue flower around time rim. M in wreath HP/Nippon. 1911-1920.

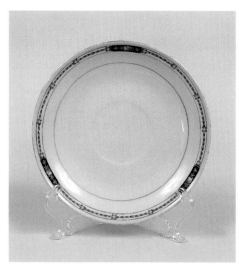

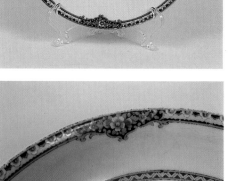

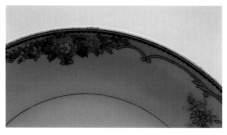

A gold edged white with cream band piece with a small border of yellow and green rope around a black background small medallion with a pink and blue flowers. Chandova. 0058438. M in wreath N/HP/Japan. 1927. Original.

A gold edged white with cream band piece with a mixed floral central design and a border yellow and blue geometric interrupted with red flower on a black background. Argosy. M in wreath N/HP/Japan. 1921-1930.

A gold edged white with cream band piece with a narrow blue, gold, and black border interspersed with pink, yellow and blue flowers with green leaves. Oxford. 0085963. M in wreath N/HP/Japan. 1930-1933. Original.

A gold edged white with cream band piece with a green and gold border, and pink, blue, and yellow flowers in an Urn atop blue scrolls with a black background inner border. Fleury. 0078052. M in wreath N/HP/Japan. 1918-1931.

A gold edged white piece with a rim design of a geometric design of green, gold and black which is interrupted by a white background to pink roses with green leaves. Kingston. M in wreath N/HP/Japan. 1921-1928.

A gold edged white with cream band piece with large pink, white, yellow and blue flowers in the center of the piece and around the edges. Wildfleur. M in wreath N/HP/Japan. 1921-1930. Mushroom.

A silver edged ivory china piece with white colored flowers and green leaves. Atlanta. 7166. N in wreath Ivory China. 1962-1979. Victorian II. Rim.

A silver edged cream piece with one large peach flower with light gray leaves. Snow Field. 7961. Contemporary FC Japan. 1984-1986. Victorian II.

A gold edged cream piece with a gold outlined white long stemmed rose. Nora. 7546. N in wreath Ivory China. 1974-1975. Champagne.

A gold edged cream piece with mixed floral bouquet around the rim and in the center. Impression. 8164W83. N in wreath black and gold. 1977-1982. Victorian IV.

A gold edged ivory china piece with peach colored flowers on green stems. Weyburne. 7248. N in wreath Ivory China. 1979-1986. Remembrance II.

A silver edged ivory piece with a dainty peach and yellow flowers with light blue leaves, boxed in with white lines. Tracery. 7258. N in wreath ivory china. 1980-1984. Remembrance II.

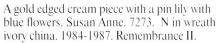

A silver edged ivory china piece with yellow border around tiny blue, yellow and pink flowers connected with a blue ribbon. Delight. 7229. N in wreath Ivory China. 1977-1983. Victorian II. Coupe.

A gold edged cream piece with a pin lily with blue flowers. Susan Anne. 7273. N in wreath ivory china. 1984-1987. Remembrance II.

119

A silver edged ivory piece with a simple silver band and border design of pink flowers with tan scrolls and green leaves and blue accent leaves. Patricia. 7551. N in wreath ivory china. 1970-1975. Victorian II.

A green edged cream piece with red scrolls and a small pink flower with green leaves the inner line is red slashes. Chikaramachi. 1928.

A silver edged ivory china piece with green leaves connecting white flowers. Cornelia. 7572. N in wreath Ivory China. 1976. Victorian II.

A silver edged ivory china piece with a maroon floral arrangement with green leaves. Adagio. 7237. N in wreath Ivory China. 1978-1994. Victorian II coupe.

A gold edged completely painted piece with a pink and white pansy with green leaves (sauce dish). M in wreath HP/Nippon. 1911-1920.

A silver edged ivory china piece with green scrolls connecting tiny white flowers. Parkridge. 7561. N in wreath Ivory China. 1975-1986. Victorian II rim.

A gold edged cream piece with large yellow, peach, pink, and lavender flowers with green leaves, the plate is scalloped around the rim. Brookhollow. 4704. Lamp Bone China printed Japan. 1990-1998. Cameo.

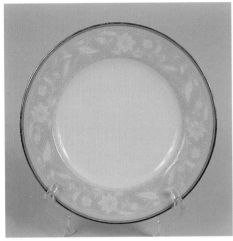

A gold edged blue piece with alternating colored flowers around the rim, the entire center of the piece is blue. K in scroll shield occupied. 1947. Rose china.

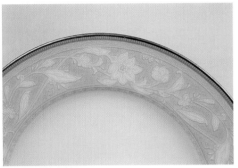

A gold edged bone china piece with a light green border topped with stylized white and pink flowers Christiana. 4746. Lamp Bone China gold/black. 1997. Empire.

A silver edged ivory piece with white flowers with green leaves (sugar bowl, lid missing). Weston. 7568. N in wreath ivory china. 1975. Champagne.

A gold edged completely painted blue piece with large pink rose with green leaves on a blue background (tea set). M in wreath N/HP/Japan. 1921-1928. Tea set.

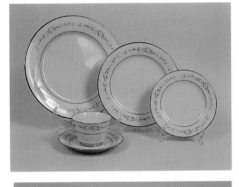

A silver edged ivory piece with dainty white flowers with green and gray leaves around the border. Heather. 7548. 0208654. N in wreath ivory china. 1975-1990. Remembrance.

A silver edged ivory china piece with a blue border around pink flowers with blue leaves. Rothschild. 7293. N in wreath Ivory China. 1986-1998. Imperial Baroque.

A gold edged blue piece with large orange, blue, white, and purple flowers around on a white rim with a solid blue center. M in wreath N/HP/Japan. 1921-1928.

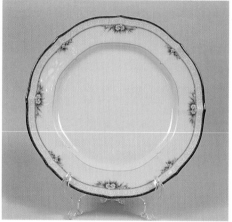

A gold edged ivory piece with a blue back-ground to a rope design around the rim with light lavender and pink flowers with green and blue leaves. Salzburg. 7299. N in wreath Ivory China. 1987-1993. Remembrance II.

A silver edged ivory piece with a blue band with cream scrolls around the shaped edge with small pink flowers around the rim with green leaves the inner line is a blue line with white dots. Allendale. 7359. N in wreath Ivory China. 1998. Imperial Baroque.

A silver edged bone china piece with blue roses with blue and silver leaves around the rim. Buenavista. 9728. Lamp Bone China gold/black. 1981-1993. Sheer Ivory Bone.

A gold edged bone china piece with blue framed pink roses that have blue leaves. Magnificence. 9736. Lamp Bone China gold/black. 1984-1996. Sheer Ivory Bone.

A silver edged ivory piece with blue flowers with blue leaves. Splendor. 7235. N in wreath ivory china. 1978-1989. Victorian II.

A silver edged cream piece with a silver with pink accent rose in a central design. Rhoda. 7542. N in wreath Ivory China. 1974. Champagne.

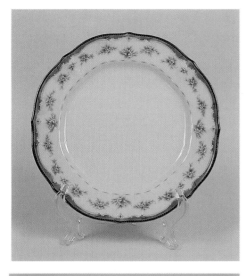

A gold edged ivory china piece with mixed color flowers with green leaves. Finale. 7213. N in wreath Ivory China. 1976-1983. Victorian II coupe.

A silver edged ivory china piece with a gray border and tiny pink flowers. Traviata. 7327. N in wreath Ivory China. 1991-1998. Imperial Baroque.

A gold edged white ivory piece with gold outlined white flowers with gray leaves. Virginia. 7564. N in wreath ivory china. 1968-1974. Champagne.

A white melamine piece with cartoon ducks in a row boat, and on a picnic. Melamine. 1960. Melamine.

A silver edged ivory china piece with a black border topped with pink and gray flowers. Etienne. 7260. N in wreath Ivory China. 1981-1996. Remembrance II.

A silver edged cream piece with a gray border and gray scrolls intersected with peach and blue and white small flowers in a gray vase. Van Buren. 9752. N in wreath Bone gold. 1987-1990. Royal Pierpont.

CHAPTER 14.

CHINA BLANKS

A china blank is the shape of a piece prior to a pattern being applied. Noritake in the early years bought blanks from other china manufacturers. This is why you can find a distinctively shaped Nippon piece with the Noritake backstamp and another one with Seyei Toki Co. Ltd. backstamp. Dinnerware can be divided into two types: those that have a rim and those without. The rim shape is called "rim" and the non-rim shape is called "coupe."

I have included blanks named by the Noritake Company, and in the earlier years I have named the blanks according to the shapes. The blanks are arranged alphabetically by name. The shape of china follows the fashion of the times. Yet a tried and true best seller might be in production for thirty years or more. The accessories are changed and the pattern lives on.

ALLAIRE SHAPE 1997–1998

This is the 1997 Allaire White Bone China blank. This blank has a mug as well as a cup and saucer and is ribbed with a top heavy design. The china itself has raised ridges on all pieces. The plates and bowl are rimmed. The finial on the coffee server and sugar bowl is a bud shape. The form is narrower at the bottom and bulbous on top.

In 1997 this blank consisted of the following pieces:

cup and saucer
Mug
plates: bread and butter, salad and dinner
bowls: fruit, rim soup.
oval platter: medium
round vegetable (salad bowl)
sugar and creamer
coffee server w/cover
gravy w/tray
salt and pepper

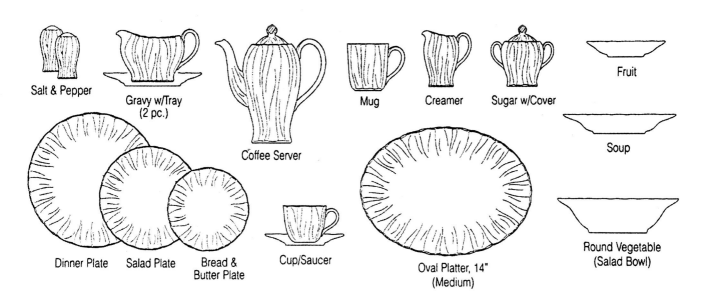

Salt & Pepper   Gravy w/Tray (2 pc.)   Coffee Server   Mug   Creamer   Sugar w/Cover   Fruit

Soup

Dinner Plate   Salad Plate   Bread & Butter Plate   Cup/Saucer   Oval Platter, 14" (Medium)   Round Vegetable (Salad Bowl)

Permitted by Noritake Co., Limited, Japan.

ARCTIC SHAPE 1992-1998

This is the 1992 Arctic China blank. This blank has a mug as well as a cup and saucer. The china itself has raised ridges on all pieces. The plates and bowl are rim shaped. The finial on the coffee server and sugar bowl is a bud shape. The form is rounded on all pieces.

In 1992 this blank consisted of the following pieces:

cup and saucer
Mug
plates: bread and butter, salad and dinner
bowls: fruit, rim soup, cereal.
oval platter: medium
round vegetable (salad bowl)
covered vegetable
sugar and creamer
coffee or tea server w/cover
gravy w/tray
salt and pepper

Gravy w/Tray (2 pc.)   Salt & Pepper   Oval Platter, 14"
(Medium)   Round Vegetable
(Salad Bowl)   Covered Vegetable

Dinner Plate   Salad Plate   Bread & Butter Plate   Cup/Saucer   Coffee/Tea Server   Sugar w/Cover   Creamer

Soup   Fruit   Cereal   Mug

Permitted by Noritake Co., Limited, Japan.

AZALEA SHAPE 1927–1934

My name for this is the Azalea blank, even though many other patterns use this shape. The sugar bowl and teapots have square open-handled lids. The syrup pitcher has a triangle open-handled lid. The jam jar, after-dinner coffee and covered candy lids all have round knobs. Handles to the vegetable bowls, covered casserole, celery, bonbon, and cake plates are open. This set appears as though every piece produced by Noritake has been painted with the same pattern even when the pieces do not match. (Numbers refer to the pieces in the line art.)

In 1932 this blank consisted of the following pieces:

2. cup and saucer
3. whipped cream set
4. tea plate set
7. sugar and cream set
8. bread and butter plate
9. fruit saucer
10. cake plate
12. salad bowl
13. dinner plate
14. Condiment
15. Teapot
16. Casserole
17. platter, 14 x 10 inches
19. soup plate
39. refreshment set
40. gravy boat
54. butter tub
55. oatmeal dish
56. platter, 12 x 9 inches
89. salt and pepper shaker
97. syrup pitcher
98. breakfast plate
99. celery or roll tray
100. Jug
101. open vegetable
119. relish dish
120. egg cup
121. pickle or lemon set
122. berry, sugar, and cream or
     Sugar and syrup for waffles
123. sugar and cream
124. bouillon cup and saucer
125. jam jar
126. individual salt-and-pepper shakers

169. teapot tile
170. Compote
171. two-compartment relish
172. Vegetable
182. after-dinner coffee pot
183. after-dinner cup and saucer
184. bonbon dish
185. grapefruit or candy bowl
186. platter, 16 x 12 inches
187. footed vase
188. nut or fruit bowl
189. spoon holder

190. vinegar bottle
191. handled mustard jar with spoon
192. match or toothpick holder
193. Dolly Varden basket
194. Relish
310. deep bowl
311. platter small
312. butter chips
313. covered candy jar
314. cheese or butter dish
315. fruit or salad plate
338. grille plate

Permitted by Noritake Co., Limited, Japan.

BONE CHINA SHAPE 1993–1999

The Bone Sheer white china which has a rim shape. The sugar bowl, covered vegetable and coffee pot have a open loop of touching petals for finials on top of a gently sloped lid. This blank has an exaggerated ear shape on all handles.

In 1985 this blank consisted of the following pieces:

cup and saucer
after dinner cup and saucer
plates: bread and butter, salad and dinner
bowls: fruit, rim soup
oval platters: small, medium, large
round vegetable: open (salad bowl)
rectangle vegetable: open
covered vegetable
sugar and creamer
coffee server w/cover
gravy w/tray
butter/relish tray
salt and pepper
handled hostess tray

Permitted by Noritake Co., Limited, Japan.

BUTTERFLY SHAPE 1955–1965

This fine Butterfly white formal china is a coupe shape. The finials to the sugar, teapot, and casserole have a two-winged butterfly look. The cups have lost the foot but are taller with a narrow bottom. Most pieces have a silver trim.

In 1965 this blank consisted of the following pieces:

cup and saucer
plates: bread and butter, salad and dinner
bowls: fruit, soup
oval platters: small, medium, and large
oval vegetable, open
round-covered vegetable (casserole)
sugar and creamer
teapot w/cover
gravy w/stand
butter/relish tray
salt and pepper

CAMEO SHAPE 1990–1998

This fine Cameo bone china blank is a ridged shape. The handles are ornate mushroom-shaped. The handle on all lids is an open square bracket. There is a distinct teapot, short and round, as well as a coffee server.

In 1990 this blank consisted of the following pieces:

cup and saucer
plates: bread and butter, salad and dinner
bowls: fruit, rim soup, and cream soup (handles)
oval platters: small, medium, and large
oval vegetable, open
round vegetable (salad bowl)
round covered vegetable (casserole)
sugar and creamer
coffee server w/cover
tea pot w/cover
gravy w/stand
butter/relish tray
salt and pepper
handled hostess tray
trays: butter, relish, sandwich
cake plate with cake server
shell dish
leaf tray

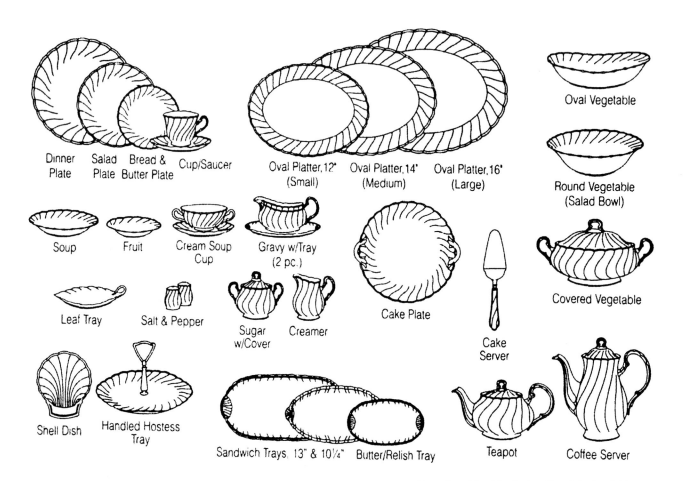

Dinner Plate   Salad Plate   Bread & Butter Plate   Cup/Saucer

Oval Platter, 12" (Small)   Oval Platter, 14" (Medium)   Oval Platter, 16" (Large)

Oval Vegetable

Round Vegetable (Salad Bowl)

Soup   Fruit   Cream Soup Cup   Gravy w/Tray (2 pc.)

Cake Plate

Covered Vegetable

Leaf Tray   Salt & Pepper   Sugar w/Cover   Creamer

Cake Server

Shell Dish   Handled Hostess Tray

Sandwich Trays, 13" & 10¼"   Butter/Relish Tray   Teapot   Coffee Server

CHAMPAGNE SHAPE 1974–1980

The Champagne ivory formal china, which has a coupe shape. The sugar bowl, covered vegetable and coffee pot have tall oval stems for finials on top of a gently sloped lid. There is a distinct teapot and coffee server and a smaller after-dinner cup and saucer for this blank. The look is sleek and simple for a very modern over-all look.

In 1976 this blank consisted of the following pieces:

cup and saucer
after-dinner cup and saucer
plates: bread and butter, salad and dinner
bowls: fruit, soup
oval platters: medium, large
oval vegetable, open
covered vegetable
round vegetable, open (salad bowl)
sugar and creamer
coffee server w/cover
teapot w/cover
gravy w/tray (no handle)
salt and pepper

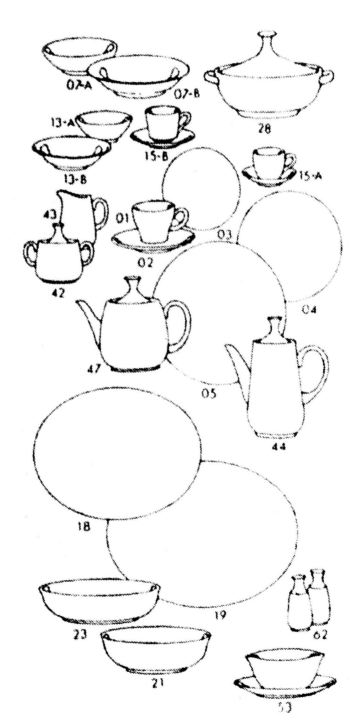

Permitted by Noritake Co., Limited, Japan.

131

CLASSIC SHAPE 1974–1998

This Classic white formal china which has a coupe shape. The sugar bowl, covered vegetable, and coffee pot have a oval stem for finials on top of a gently sloping lid. There is a distinct teapot and coffee server and a smaller after-dinner cup and saucer for this blank. The look is sleek and straight almost square, with a flat on top shape for handles.

In 1977 this blank consisted of the following pieces:

cup and saucer
after-dinner cup and saucer
plates: bread and butter, salad and dinner
bowls: fruit, soup, lug soup
oval platters: small, medium, large
oval vegetable: open
covered vegetable
divided vegetable
round vegetables: small and large
sugar and creamer
coffee server w/cover
teapot w/cover
gravy w/stand
covered butter (stick shape)
salt and pepper
pickle dish
celery dish

Permitted by Noritake Co., Limited, Japan.

COMMANDER SHAPE 1970–

The Commander white formal china has rim-shaped plates and coupe bowls. The sugar bowl, covered vegetable, and coffee pot have a tall bud-shaped finial. There is a distinct teapot and coffee server and a smaller after-dinner cup and saucer for this blank. The look is smooth and round, with a simple ear shape for handles.

In 1977 this blank consisted of the following pieces:

cup and saucer
after-dinner cup and saucer
plates: bread and butter, salad and dinner
bowls: fruit, soup, lug soup
oval platters: small, medium, large
oval vegetable: open
covered vegetable
divided vegetable
round vegetable, small
   And large
sugar and creamer
coffee server w/cover

teapot w/cover
gravy w/stand
covered butter (stick shape)
salt and pepper
pickle dish
celery dish

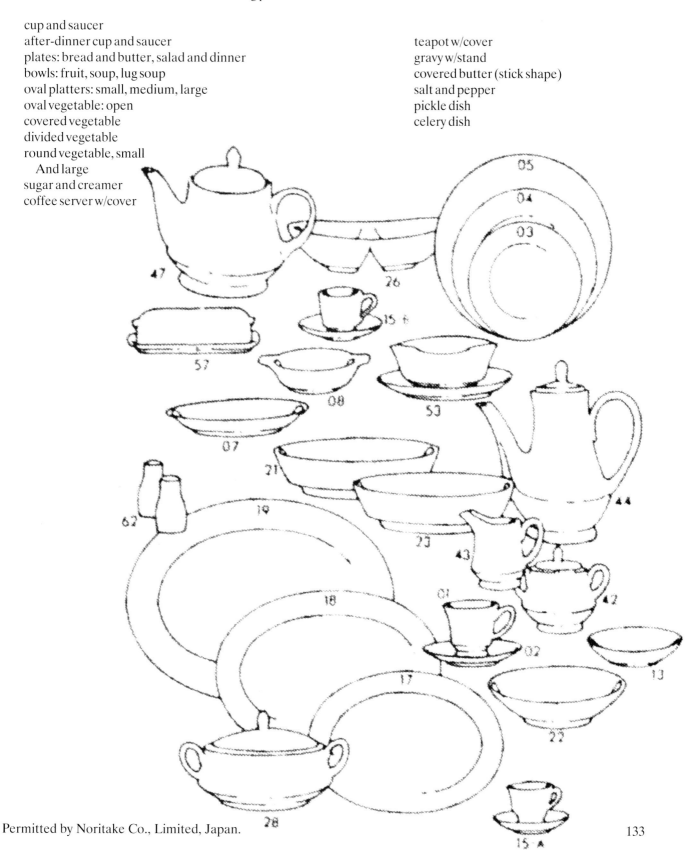

CONCERTO SHAPE 1953–1978

This fine china blank is a coupe shape. The handles are simple smooth ear-shaped. The handle on all lids is a sleek oval knob. There is a distinct teapot, short and bottom heavy, as well as a coffee server, tall slim with an hourglass shape. In 1976 this blank consisted of the following pieces:

cup and saucer
after dinner cup and saucer
plates: bread and butter, salad and dinner
bowls: fruit, soup, and lug soup (handles)
oval platters: small, medium, and large
oval vegetables: open and divided
round vegetable: small, large (salad bowl)
round covered vegetable (casserole)
sugar and creamer
coffee server w/cover
tea pot w/cover
gravy w/stand
butter w/cover
salt and pepper
pickle dish
celery dish

Permitted by Noritake Co., Limited, Japan.

134

ELEGANCE SHAPE 1980–1987

This Elegance formal china blank is a gracefully embossed shape. The handle on all lids is a swept back bud. This pattern is rounded with a wider bottom and narrower top.

In 1985 this blank consisted of the following pieces:

cup and saucer
plates: bread and butter, salad and dinner
bowls: fruit, rim soup, and cereal
oval platters: small, medium
oval vegetables: open and covered
round vegetable (salad bowl)
sugar and creamer

coffee server w/cover
gravy w/stand
salt and pepper
handled two-tier hostess tray
bud vase
candle holder

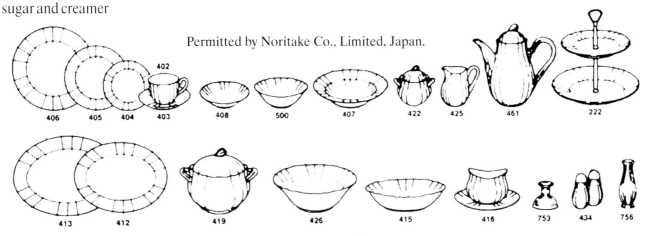

Permitted by Noritake Co., Limited, Japan.

EMBOSSED IVORY (HALLS OF IVY) 1994–

This Embossed Ivory Formal china blank is a sculptured shape. The handles are ornate in shape. The handle on all lids is a bud shape. The plates are a rim shape and the coffee server is top heavy, as is the creamer and sugar. This shape has a distinct mug as well as a cup and saucer available.

In 1998 this blank consisted of the following pieces:

cup and saucer
mug
plates: bread and butter, salad and dinner
bowls: rim fruit, rim soup,
oval platters: medium and large
oval vegetable: open
round vegetable (salad bowl)
round covered vegetable (casserole)

sugar and creamer
coffee server w/cover
gravy w/stand
butter/relish tray
salt and pepper
compote
divided hostess server
handled hostess tray

EMPIRE SHAPE 1976–

This fine bone china blank is a rim shape. The handles are simple classic ear-shaped. The handle on all lids is a round button. The coffee server is top heavy and the gravy is not attached to the tray.

In 1998 this blank consisted of the following pieces:

cup and saucer
plates: bread and butter, salad and dinner
bowls: rim fruit and rim soup
oval platters: medium
oval vegetable, open
round vegetable (salad bowl)
sugar and creamer
coffee server w/cover
gravy w/tray
butter/relish tray
salt and pepper
handled hostess tray

Fruit

Oval Vegetable

Gravy w/Tray
(2 pc.)

Creamer

Coffee Server

Round Vegetable
(Salad Bowl)

Soup

Sugar w/Cover

Salt & Pepper

Butter/Relish Tray

Handled Hostess Tray

Dinner Plate Salad Plate Bread &
Butter Plate

Cup/Saucer

Oval Platter, 14"
(Medium)

Permitted by Noritake Co., Limited, Japan.

ESTATE PORCELAIN SHAPE 1991 –

This Estate Porcelain china blank is a sculptured rim shape. The handles are very ornate in shape. The handle on all lids is a bud shape. There is a distinct teapot, short and round; soup tureen is on feet; as is a coffee server.

In 1998 this blank consisted of the following pieces:

cup and saucer
plates: bread and butter, salad and dinner
bowls: fruit, rim soup, and cream soup (handles)
oval platters: small, medium and large
oval vegetable, open
round vegetable (salad bowl)
round covered vegetable (casserole)
sugar and creamer
coffee server w/cover
teapot w/cover
gravy w/stand
butter/relish tray
salt and pepper
soup tureen, 5 quart
centerpiece (footed)
Candlestick

FLYING SAUCER SHAPE 1932–1936

My name for this is the Flying Saucer blank. The sugar bowl, teapots, covered butter, and casserole all have a pointed flying saucer look. Handles to the casserole and vegetable bowls are solid extending out a little for a better hand hold. Square fruit or salad plates are new, and double-handled cream soup bowls have been added. There is a teapot but no coffee server. The cake plate and celery tray still have cut-out handles.

In 1932 this blank consisted of the following pieces (not all pictured):

cup and saucer
plates: bread and butter, tea, breakfast, salad and dinner
bowls: fruit, soup, cream soup (handles), salad, oatmeal, deep
after-dinner cup and saucer
oval platters: small, medium, large
oval vegetables: small open, large open,
   divided, covered
sugar and creamer
teapot w/cover
gravy w/stand
covered butter
pickle dish
celery dish
salt and pepper
cake plate

Permitted by Noritake Co., Limited, Japan.

COMPARE! THEN YOU'LL RECOGNIZE THE BIG VALUE IN THIS FINE IMPORTED CHINA DINNERWARE AND EVERY PURCHASE BRINGS A *PREMIUM!*

SHARON PATTERN

IMPERIAL BAROQUE SHAPE 1988–1998

This Imperial Baroque formal china blank is a sculptured rim shape. The handles are squared off on the top. The handle on all lids is a round button shape. The coffee server and sugar and creamer are wide and straight in shape with an indented rim around the top.

In 1998 this blank consisted of the following pieces:

cup and saucer
Mug
plates: bread and butter, salad and dinner
bowls: rim fruit, rim soup
oval platter, medium
round platter, small
oval vegetable, open
round vegetable (salad bowl)
round-covered vegetable (casserole)
sugar and creamer
coffee/tea server w/cover
gravy w/tray
salt and pepper
cake plate
square centerpiece
hors d ouevre platter
round covered box
napkin rings

Gravy w/Tray (2 pc.)

Oval Platter, 14" (Medium)

Round Platter, 11½"

Cake Plate, 12"

Square Centerpiece

Soup

Fruit

Handled Hostess Tray

Salt & Pepper

Napkin Ring (Set of 4)

Round Covered Box

Mug

Dinner Plate

Salad Plate

Bread & Butter Plate

Cup/Saucer

Hors D'Ouevre Platter

Sugar w/Cover

Creamer

Coffee/Tea Server

Covered Vegetable

Oval Vegetable

Round Vegetable (Salad Bowl)

Permitted by Noritake Co., Limited, Japan.

LASALLE SHAPE 1949–1987

This is the LaSalle white formal china which is rim shape. The sugar bowl, covered vegetable, and coffee pot have a open strap for handles. There is a distinct teapot (short and wide) and coffee server (tall and sleek) and a smaller after-dinner cup and saucer for this blank. The gravy bowl is still a lot like the original shape. Cups are low tea cups on a footed base. In 1983 the white and gold pattern 175 was produced in this shape.

In 1983 this blank consisted of the following pieces:

cup and saucer
after dinner cup and saucer
plates: bread and butter, salad and dinner
bowls: fruit, rim soup, lug soup
oval platters: small, medium, large
oval vegetable: open
round vegetable (salad bowl)
covered vegetable
sugar and creamer
coffee server w/cover
teapot w/cover
gravy w/stand
butter w/cover
salt and pepper
two-tier hostess tray
napkin rings
dinner bell
candle holder

Permitted by Noritake Co., Limited, Japan.

MASTERS COLLECTION SHAPE 1988 –

This Masters Collection white bone china blank is a modern rim shape. The handles are an exaggerated ear shape. The handle on all lids is a fan shape to complement the spouts on the tea and coffee pots. The lines are very straight, the only curve in this entire collection is the spout on the gravy bowl.

In 1998 this blank consisted of the following pieces:

cup and saucer
Mug
plates: bread and butter, salad and dinner
bowls: rim fruit, rim soup, cream soup (handles)
oval platters: small, medium, and large
oval vegetable, open
round vegetable (salad bowl)
round covered vegetable (casserole)
sugar and creamer
coffee server w/cover
Teapot
gravy w/tray
butter/relish tray
salt and pepper
sandwich tray

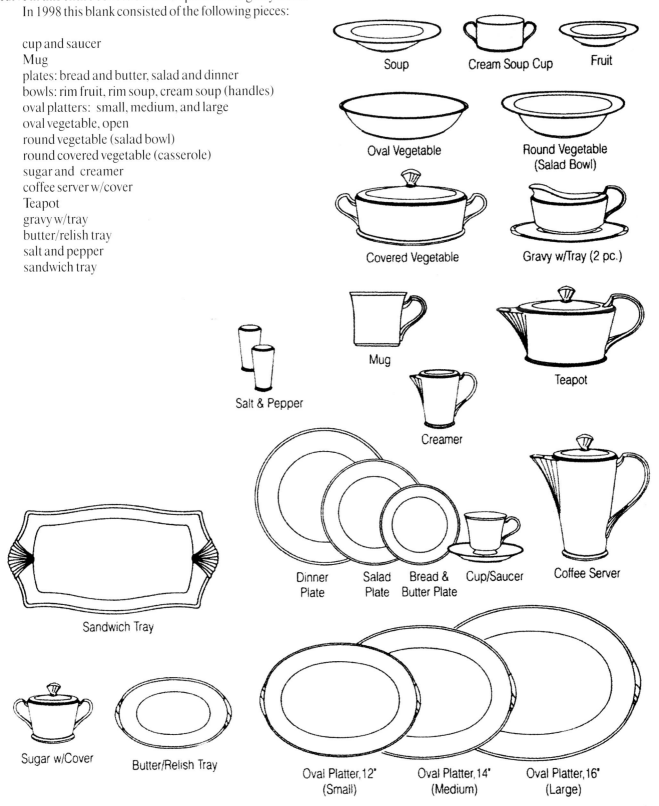

Soup   Cream Soup Cup   Fruit

Oval Vegetable   Round Vegetable (Salad Bowl)

Covered Vegetable   Gravy w/Tray (2 pc.)

Mug   Teapot

Salt & Pepper   Creamer

Sandwich Tray

Dinner Plate   Salad Plate   Bread & Butter Plate   Cup/Saucer   Coffee Server

Sugar w/Cover   Butter/Relish Tray

Oval Platter, 12" (Small)   Oval Platter, 14" (Medium)   Oval Platter, 16" (Large)

MUSHROOM SHAPE 1933–1940

    This is the Mushroom Shape for dinnerware. The distinctive cone- shaped finial to the lids and the square top to the cream and sugar handles mark this rim-shaped blank. The covered casserole has urn-shaped handles, the cups have become footed and a divided open vegetable has made its appearance.

    In 1933 this blank consisted of the following pieces:

cup and saucer
plates: bread and butter, salad and dinner
bowls: rim fruit, rim soup
oval platters: medium, large
oval vegetable, open
covered vegetable, casserole

divided vegetable
sugar and creamer
teapot w/cover
butter/relish tray
gravy bowl w/tray

NEW LINEAGE SHAPE 1996–1998

This New Lineage white bone china blank is a rim shape. The handle on all lids is a tall button shape. The coffee server and sugar and creamer are wide and straight in shape with an recessed rim around the top for the lid.

In 1998 this blank consisted of the following pieces:

cup and saucer
Mug
plates: bread and butter, salad and dinner
bowls: rim fruit, rim soup
oval platters: small, medium, large
oval vegetable, open
round vegetable (salad bowl)
covered vegetable (casserole)
sugar and creamer
coffee/tea server w/cover
gravy w/tray
butter/relish tray
salt and pepper
handled hostess tray

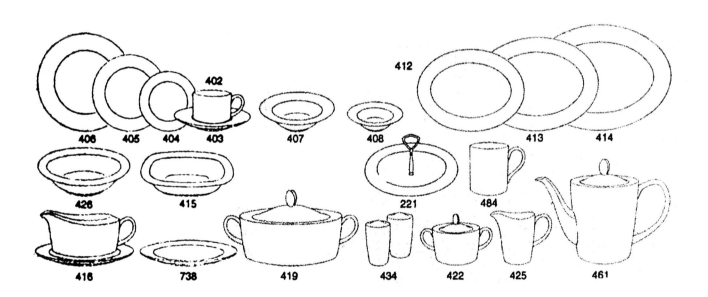

Permitted by Noritake Co., Limited, Japan.

NEW TRADITIONS SHAPE 1984–1999

The New Traditions fine china is a coupe shape. The sugar bowl, covered vegetable, and coffee pot have a square open loop for a handle. The elongated shape gives a tall appearance of delicacy. There is a distinct teapot and coffee server and a smaller espresso cup and saucer for this blank. Later versions added a handle to the gravy boat.

In 1985 this blank consisted of the following pieces:

cup and saucer
espresso cup and saucer
plates: bread and butter, salad and dinner
bowls: fruit, soup
oval platters: medium, large
round platter: large
round vegetables, deep and shallow
covered vegetable
sugar and creamer
coffee server w/cover
teapot w/cover
gravy w/stand
butter/relish tray
salt and pepper

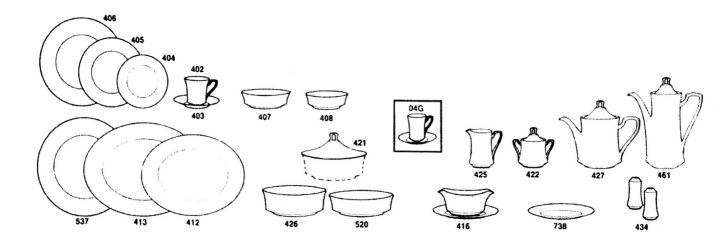

Permitted by Noritake Co., Limited, Japan.

NORITAKE IRELAND 1 SHAPE 1975–1998

The Noritake Ireland 1 china, is rim shape. The sugar bowl, covered vegetable, and coffee pot have a round bud for finials. The sides of the vegetable bowls have a lip or rim. The cups are tall like mugs. The spout of the coffee pot, teapot, and gravy boat are more like a pitcher than typical pouring spouts.

In 1985 this blank consisted of the following pieces:

cup and saucer
after-dinner cup and saucer
plates: bread and butter, salad, luncheon, soup, and   dinner
bowls: fruit, rim soup
oval platters: medium, large
round platter, medium
oval vegetable, open
round vegetables, open, covered
sugar and creamer
coffee server w/cover
teapot w/cover
Gravy
butter/relish tray
salt and pepper
two-tier hostess tray
napkin rings

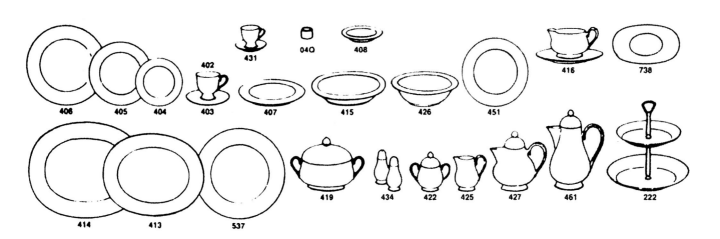

Permitted by Noritake Co., Limited, Japan.

NORITAKE IRELAND II SHAPE 1983–1986

The Noritake Ireland 2 china is embossed shape. The sugar bowl, covered vegetable and coffee pot have a round bud for finials. The elongated embossed swirls are clustered on the rim shape. There is a distinct teapot and coffee server and a smaller after-dinner cup and saucer for this blank.

In 1985 this blank consisted of the following pieces:

cup and saucer
after-dinner cup and saucer
plates: bread and butter, salad and dinner
bowls: fruit, rim soup
oval platters: medium, large
round platter: large
oval vegetable, open
round vegetable (salad bowl)
covered vegetable
sugar and creamer
coffee server w/cover
teapot w/cover
gravy w/tray
butter/relish tray
salt and pepper
two-tier hostess tray

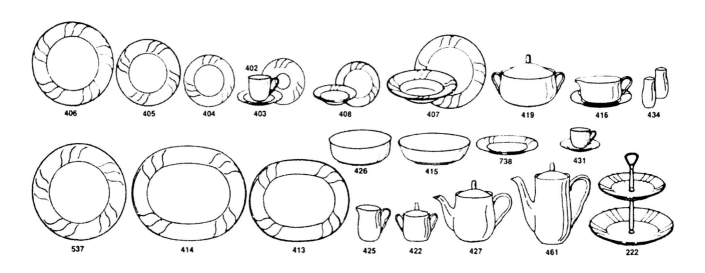

Permitted by Noritake Co., Limited, Japan.

ORIGINAL SHAPE 1914–1930

The Original china is a simple coupe shape. The sugar bowl, butter dish, and covered vegetable have a open half-oval for a handle. The cup has a low profile with a simple ear-shaped handle. The butter dish is a 7-inch plate with a pierced drainer and a round dome cover.

In 1920 this blank consisted of the following pieces (not all pictured):

> cup and saucer
> plates: bread and butter, salad and dinner
> bowls: fruit, soup
> oval platters: small 8-inch and medium 12-inch
> oval covered casserole
> oval baker: 7-inch
> sugar and creamer
> butter round 3 pieces
> sauce boat (gravy with fast stand)
> pickle dish

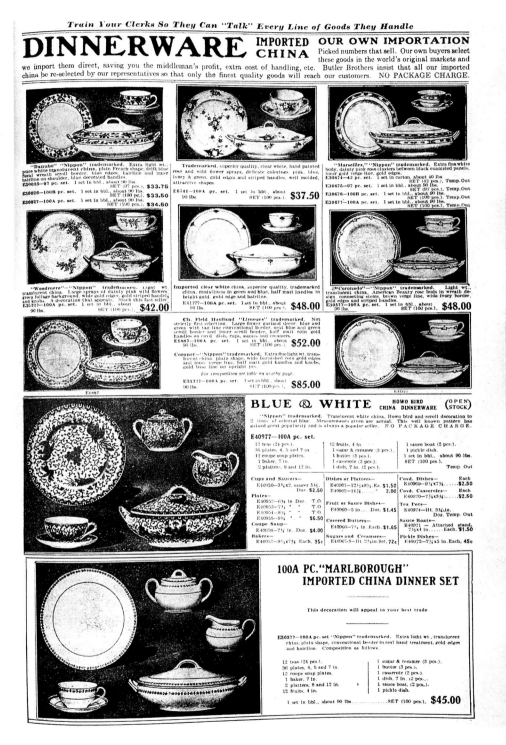

Permitted by Noritake Co., Limited, Japan.

PARAMOUNT SHAPE 1987 –

The Paramount white formal china is a rimmed plate and coupe bowl shape. The sugar bowl, covered vegetable, and coffee pot have a oval bud for finials. The overall shape has clean straight lines. There is a distinct teapot and coffee server and the gravy has no handle for this blank.

In 1998 this blank consisted of the following pieces:

cup and saucer
after-dinner cup and saucer
Mug
plates: bread and butter, salad and dinner
bowls: fruit, soup
oval platters: small, medium, large
oval vegetable, open
round vegetable (salad bowl)
covered vegetable
sugar and creamer
coffee server w/cover
teapot w/cover
gravy w/tray
salt and pepper
handled hostess tray
napkin ring
dinner bell
covered box
Candlestick
Ramekin
cheese board
Trivet
Vase

Permitted by Noritake Co., Limited, Japan.

148

PRELUDE SHAPE 1997–

This Prelude china is ribbed shape. The sugar bowl and coffee pot have a oval bud for finials. The overall look is a chubby rounded shape. The simple lines of this shape do not require a pattern.

In 1998 this blank consisted of the following pieces:

cup and saucers
Mug
plates: salad and dinner
bowl, rim soup
oval platter, large
round vegetable (salad bowl)
sugar and creamer
coffee server w/cover
salt and pepper

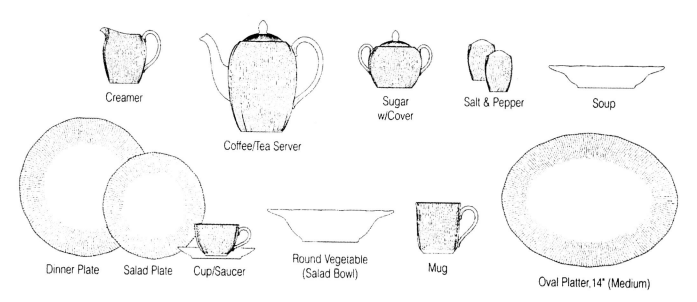

Creamer Coffee/Tea Server Sugar w/Cover Salt & Pepper Soup

Dinner Plate Salad Plate Cup/Saucer Round Vegetable (Salad Bowl) Mug Oval Platter, 14" (Medium)

Permitted by Noritake Co., Limited, Japan.

REMEMBRANCE I SHAPE 1976–1987

The Remembrance I china is a simple coupe shape. The sugar bowl, covered vegetable and coffee pot have a ribbed tall bud for finials. There is a distinct teapot and coffee server and a smaller after-dinner cup and saucer for this blank. The serving pieces are smooth and rounded with enlarged ear-shaped handles.

In 1983 this blank consisted of the following pieces:

cup and saucer
after-dinner cup and saucer
plates: bread and butter, salad and dinner
bowls: fruit, soup, and cream soup (handles)
oval platters: small, medium, large
oval vegetable, open
round vegetable (salad bowl)
covered vegetable
sugar and creamer
coffee server w/cover
teapot w/cover
gravy w/tray
butter/relish tray
salt and pepper
two-tier hostess tray
napkin rings
dinner bell
candle holder

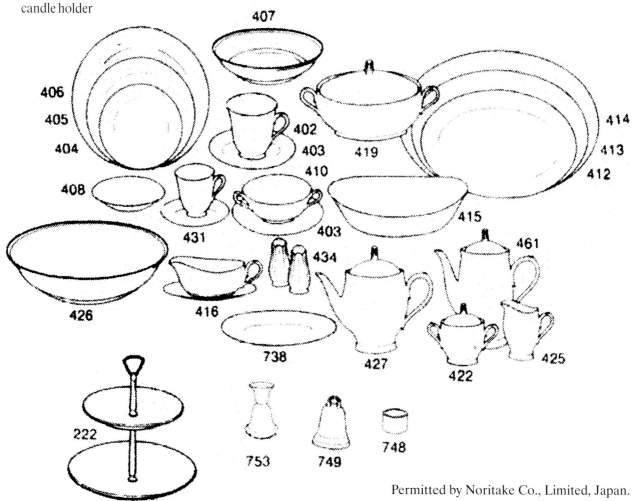

Permitted by Noritake Co., Limited, Japan.

REMEMBRANCE II SHAPE 1983–1999

The Remembrance II formal china (white and ivory) is a simple coupe shape. The sugar bowl, covered vegetable and coffee pot have a ribbed tall bud for finials. There is a distinct teapot and coffee server and a smaller after-dinner cup and saucer for this blank. These serving pieces are the same as Remembrance I shape.

In 1985 this blank consisted of the following pieces:

cup and saucer
after-dinner cup and saucer
plates: bread and butter, salad and dinner
bowls: fruit, soup, and cream soup (handles)
oval platters: small, medium, large
oval vegetable, open
round vegetable (salad bowl)
covered vegetable
sugar and creamer
coffee server w/cover
teapot w/cover
gravy w/tray
butter/relish tray
salt and pepper
two-tier hostess tray

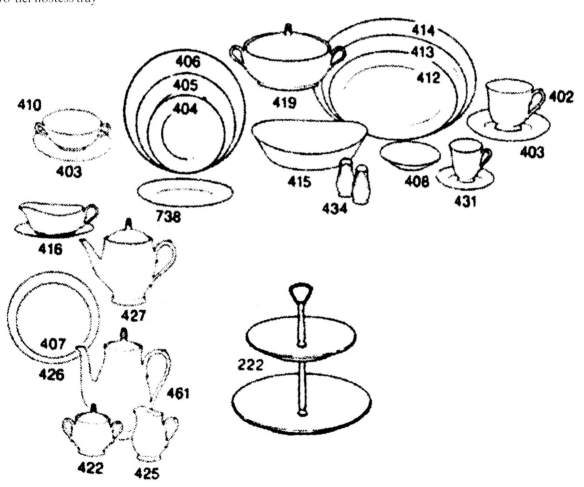

Permitted by Noritake Co., Limited, Japan.

ROSE CHINA SHAPE 1947–1953

Rose china rim shape was in use as production resumed after World War II. The covered casserole has handles that turn up and stand away from the body of the bowl. The cups are footed low tea cups, and the finials to the lids are rose buds.

In 1949 this blank consisted of the following pieces:

cup and saucer
after-dinner cup and saucer
plates: bread and butter, salad and dinner
bowls: rim fruit, rim soup
oval platters: medium, large
oval vegetable, open
covered vegetable, casserole
sugar and creamer
teapot w/cover
butter/relish tray
gravy bowl w/tray
salt and pepper

ROYAL PIERPONT SHAPE 1985–1998

This is the Royal Pierpont white formal china which has a refined elegance with gently scalloped rims. The sugar bowl, covered vegetable, and coffee pot have a round button for finials on top of a domed shaped lid. There is a distinct teapot and coffee server and a smaller after-dinner cup and saucer for this blank. The handles are a double loop. The gravy, covered casserole, soup tureen, and sugar bowl are round chubby pieces with side handles that are shaped like straps.

In 1985 this blank consisted of the following pieces:
cup and saucer
after-dinner cup and saucer
plates: bread and butter, salad and dinner
bowls: fruit, soup, and cream soup (handles)
oval platters: small, medium, large
oval vegetable, open
round vegetable (salad bowl)
covered vegetable
soup tureen
sugar and creamer
coffee server w/cover
teapot w/cover
covered gravy with saucer
butter/relish tray
salt and pepper
two-tier hostess tray

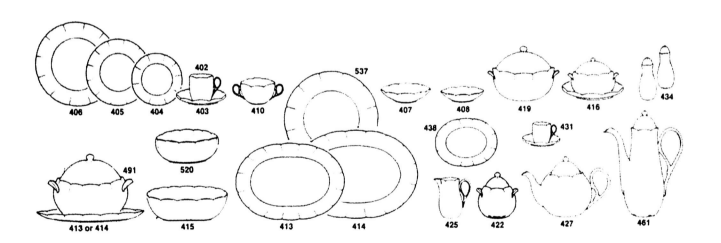

Permitted by Noritake Co., Limited, Japan.

SHEER IVORY SHAPE 1986–

This Sheer Ivory bone china blank is a rim shape. The handles are an exaggerated ear shape. The handle on all lids is an open oval loop. The coffee server and sugar and creamer are tall and straight in shape. There is a distinct teapot.

In 1998 this blank consisted of the following pieces:

cup and saucer
Mug
plates: bread and butter, salad and dinner
bowls: rim fruit, rim soup, and cream soup (handles and saucer)
oval platters: small, medium, and large
oval vegetable, open
round vegetable (salad bowl)
oval covered vegetable (casserole)
sugar and creamer
coffee server w/cover
teapot w/cover

gravy w/tray
butter/relish tray
salt and pepper
handled hostess tray
napkin rings

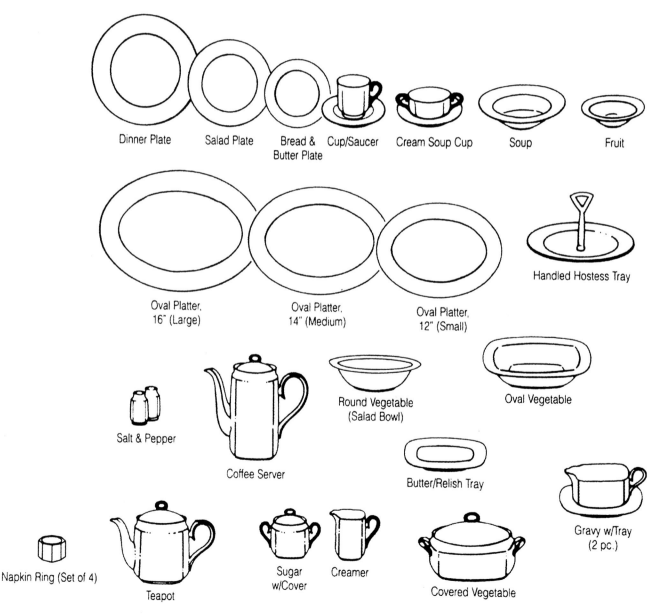

Dinner Plate   Salad Plate   Bread & Butter Plate   Cup/Saucer   Cream Soup Cup   Soup   Fruit

Oval Platter, 16" (Large)   Oval Platter, 14" (Medium)   Oval Platter, 12" (Small)   Handled Hostess Tray

Salt & Pepper   Coffee Server   Round Vegetable (Salad Bowl)   Oval Vegetable

Butter/Relish Tray   Gravy w/Tray (2 pc.)

Napkin Ring (Set of 4)   Teapot   Sugar w/Cover   Creamer   Covered Vegetable

TRIANGLE SHAPE 1960–1970

This is the Triangle Formal china shape; it has a coupe shape. The finials are like ski jumps in a triangle shape. The creamer and gravy look more like a shuttle scoop than a pitcher, very modern and sleek.

In 1960 this blank consisted of the following pieces:

cup and saucer
plates: bread and butter, salad and dinner
bowls: fruit, soup
oval platters: medium, large
oval vegetable, open
covered vegetable, casserole

sugar and creamer
teapot w/cover
butter/relish tray
gravy bowl w/tray
salt and pepper

VICTORIAN II SHAPE 1969–1987

The Victorian II ivory formal china has a rim shape. The sugar bowl, covered vegetable, and coffee pot have a lampshade-shaped knob for finials on top of a almost flat lid. There is a distinct teapot and coffee server and a smaller after-dinner cup and saucer for this blank. The look is sleek and straight, almost square, with an exaggerated ear shape for handles.

In 1976 this blank consisted of the following pieces:

cup and saucer
after-dinner cup and saucer
plates: bread and butter, salad and dinner
bowls: fruit, rim soup
oval platters: small, medium, large
oval vegetable, open
covered vegetable
sugar and creamer
coffee server w/cover
teapot w/cover
gravy w/stand
salt and pepper

Permitted by Noritake Co., Limited, Japan.

VICTORIAN III SHAPE 1973–1982

The Victorian III ivory formal china has a rim shape. This shape is different for the straight up sides of the soup and fruit bowls. The other serving pieces are identical to the Victorian II shape.

In 1977 this blank consisted of the following pieces:

cup and saucer
after-dinner cup and saucer
plates: bread and butter, salad and dinner
bowls: deep fruit, deep soup
oval platters: medium, large
oval vegetable, open
sugar and creamer
coffee server w/cover
gravy w/stand
salt and pepper

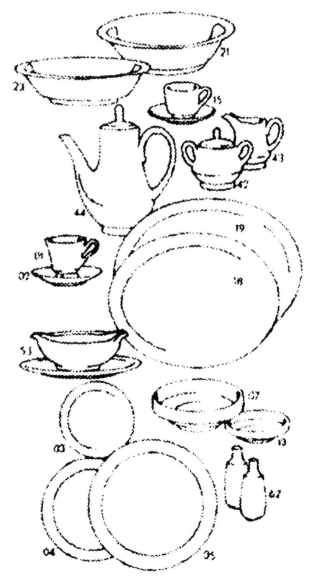

Permitted by Noritake Co., Limited, Japan.

VICTORIAN IV SHAPE 1973—

The Victorian II pastel formal china has a rim shape. Though the Victorian IV is called a form, it is more know by the fact it is colored china, the pieces are a conglomeration of Victorian II and Victorian III pieces with a new coffee server, creamer, and sugar in a ultrasleek bottom-heavy design. The gravy is a bowl as well as the carried-over Victorian III gravy boat.

In 1997 this blank consisted of the following pieces:

cup and saucer
after-dinner cup and saucer
plates: bread and butter, salad and dinner
bowls: rim fruit, rim soup, deep fruit, deep soup
oval platters: small, medium, large
oval vegetable, open

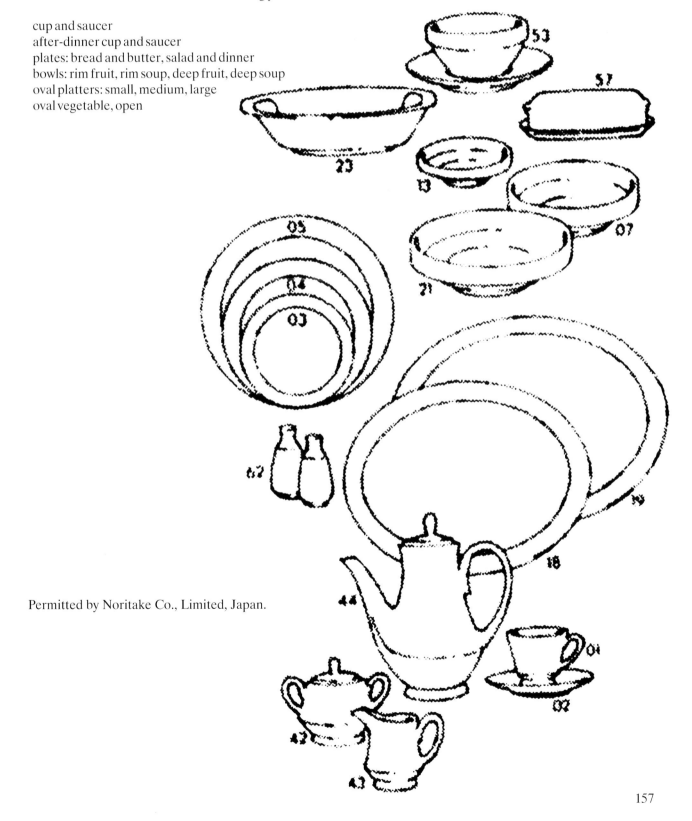

Permitted by Noritake Co., Limited, Japan.

VICTORIAN V PASTEL FORMAL CHINA 1973–1985

This is the Victorian V china blank. This blank has is produced in pastel-colored porcelain. The plates and bowl are rimmed. The butter dish is in the shape of a stick of butter, and the cup taller like a coffee cup. This blank uses the coffee server from the Victorian IV. Patterns are in golden ivory, celedon, and blue colored china.

In 1973 this blank consisted of the following pieces:

cup and saucer
plates: bread and butter, salad and dinner

bowls: fruit, rim soup.
oval platters: small, medium and large
oval vegetable, open
round vegetable (salad bowl)
sugar and creamer

coffee server w/cover
gravy w/stand
butter covered
salt and pepper
two-tier hostess tray

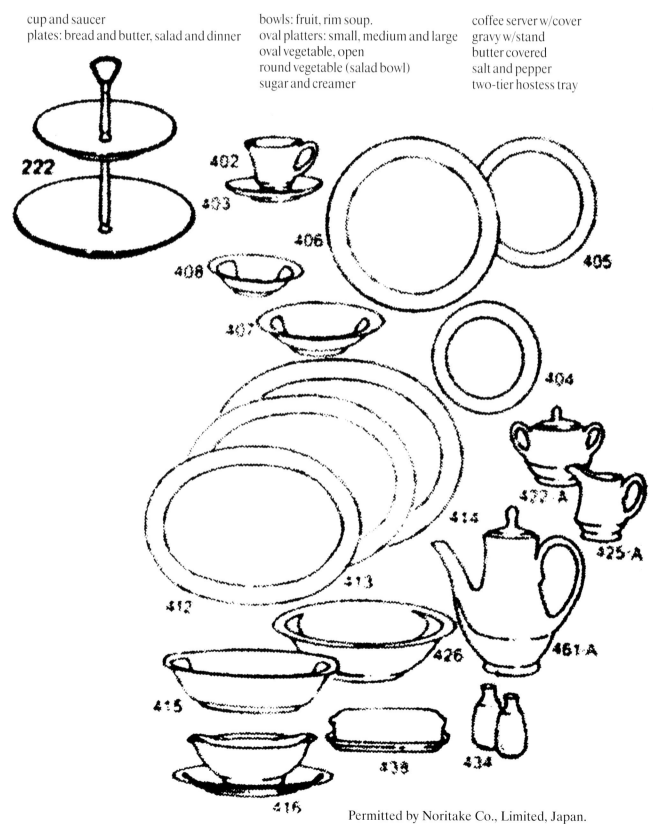

Permitted by Noritake Co., Limited, Japan.

158

WHITE IMPRESSIONS SHAPE 1995–1998

The White Impressions formal china has a scalloped rim shape. The finials are like buds on a dome-shaped lid. The handles are ear-shaped with a ridge at the bottom. The gravy has a spout and a handle.

In 1998 this blank consisted of the following pieces:

cup and saucer
plates: bread and butter, salad and dinner
bowls: fruit, soup
oval platter, medium
covered vegetable, casserole
round vegetable open (salad bowl)
sugar and creamer
coffee server w/cover
butter/relish tray
salt and pepper
handled hostess tray

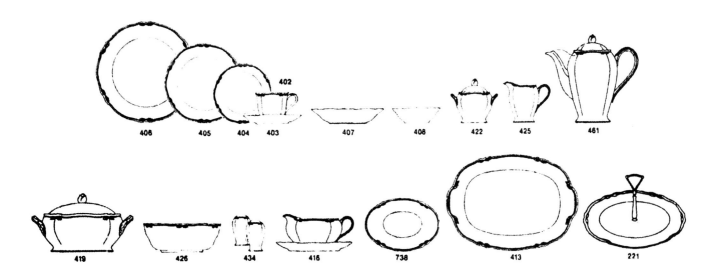

Permitted by Noritake Co., Limited, Japan.

WHITE SCAPES SHAPE 1995–1998

The White Scapes formal china, which has an embossed rim shape. The finials are like raised buttons on a gently sloping lid. The handles are ear-shaped with a ridge at the bottom. The gravy has a spout and a handle.

In 1998 this blank consisted of the following pieces:

cup and saucer
Mug
plates: bread & butter, salad and dinner
bowls: rim fruit, rim soup
oval platters: medium, large
oval vegetable, open
covered vegetable, casserole
round vegetable, open (salad bowl)
sugar and creamer
coffee server w/cover
butter/relish tray
gravy bowl w/tray
salt and pepper
handled hostess tray

Salt & Pepper

Covered Vegetable

Gravy w/Tray (2 pc.)

Mug

Oval Vegetable

Round Vegetable
(Salad Bowl)

Fruit

Soup

Butter/Relish Tray

Sugar w/Cover

Creamer

Coffee/Tea Server

Handled Hostess Tray

Cup/
Saucer

Bread & Butter Plate

Dinner Plate   Salad Plate

Oval Platter, 13½"
(Medium)

Oval Platter, 16¼"
(Large)

Permitted by Noritake Co., Limited, Japan.

160

Alphabetical Reference to
Names, Illustrations, Numbers, Designs, Backstamps, Dates, Forms, and Original Cost

The following reference is all I know of each of the Noritake patterns old and new alike, the name Noritake printed on the piece, the page on which it is illustrated in this book, the number Noritake assigned and printed on the back, the design number if it was patented, the earliest backstamp I could find on the pattern and the time frame it was produced, and the blank if I could identify one. Sometimes in the form column all I could tell was if it was a coupe shape or a rim shape. The original cost is the

suggested retail of a 5 piece place setting of the pattern during the years of production. I've included the stoneware and casual china, for completeness. For those pieces illustrated the page number follows the name in *bold italics*.

Following this Reference is a Numerical Cross-Reference, organized by pattern and/or design number. This will be useful if you have only the number. Use it to refer back to this chart.

Name, Page #	No.	Design	Backstamp	Time	Form	Cost
Abbotswood	9190		Keltcraft	1992-1994	K-RIM	43-53
Aberdale	3808		M in wreath big bow			
Aberdeen	6727		N in wreath blk/gld			
Abundance						
	B333	W17	Versatone II	1978-1982	VER2	27-40
Acacia	509	0098212	M in wreath sm. bow	1935		
Ackley	4049					
Acton	4001		M in wreath small bow			
Ada	3705					
Adagio, *120*	7237		N in wreath ivory	1978-1994	Victorian II	29-72
Adala						
Adams			M in wreath N/HP/Japan			
Adelpha	4036					
Adonis						
Adoration	3260			1982-1985	Nor. Ireland I	55-60
Adornment	7330			1991-1995	Imperial Baroque	72-85
Adrian			M in wreath N/HP/Japan			
Adrienne	3020			1980-1983	Remembrance II	30-46
Adrienne	5143			1933		
Aeolian		0076841	M in wreath N/HP/Japan	1931		
Affection, *61*	7192		N in wreath Ivory China	1975-1993	Victorian II	21-69
After Dark	3604		Sea & Sky	1986-1989	SS	46-47
After The Rain	9423		New Decade wave	1993-1994	NDC	63-66
Afton	7337			1993-1999	Imperial Baroque	82
Aida, *73*	2043		N in wreath blk/gld	1968-1975	Commander	22
Ainsworth	4104			1992-1998	Nor. Ireland I	65
Akaye						
	B350	W30	Versatone orient	1979-1982	orient	27-38
Alais (The)			M in wreath N/Nippon			
Alameda	520					
Alamosa	4228		Legendary Sri Lanka	1998	Commander	
Albany			M in wreath N/Nippon			
Alberta			M in shield China		flying saucer	
Alcona	613	0100326	M in wreath small bow	1936		
Alcott	3902			1990-1994	w/impressions	60-72
Aldea	3083			1980		
Aldridge, *39*	9702		Lamp bone china blk/gld	1975-1980	Sheer Ivory Bone	40
Alexandria	3361			1983-1985	N.Ireland II	55-65
Alexis	3721	0108369	M in wreath small bow	1936		
Alford, *113*			M in wreath small bow	1949		
Alfred						
Algonquin	3690		Legendary Sri Lanka	1985-1987	Commander	55-50
Alhambra	3331			1983-1987	Remembrance II	53-50
Alhambra	7046		Expression	1975-1977	Victorian IV	18-19
Alicia	5762	0035762	M in wreath N/HP/Japan	1920		
Allaire	4760			1997-1998	Allaire	
Allard	651		M in wreath small bow			

Name, Page #	No.	Design	Backstamp	Time	Form	Cost
Allegra	3703			1987-1989	Remembrance II	50-54
Allenby	6302					
Allendale, *122*	7359		N in Wreath ivory	1998	Imperial Baroque	71
Allerton			M in wreath N/HP/Japan			
Allison	2610		N in wreath blk/gld	1976-1986	Remembrance I	21-51
Allison	5313					
Allston						
Allure	586	0097902	M in wreath small bow	1935		
Allure, *103*	3706	0097902	M in wreath big bow	1933-1935		
Almont, *50*	6125		N in wreath printed	1961	Coupe	
Aloha	9023		Progression N	1975-1977	P1	24
Alpine Flowers						
	B966		Primastone	1977-1982	PRIMA1	28-44
Alrea			M in wreath small bow			
Alsace (The)		0058588	M in wreath N/Nippon	1927	Original	
Alsatia	4758			1997-1998	Empire	
Altadena	6437			1975-1976	Concerto	21
Althea		0089492	M in wreath small bow	1933		
Alvin, *100*		0095649	M in wreath small bow	1935		
Always	8101	W82		1975-1980	Victorian IV	25-40
Amapola	2764			1981-1983	Nor Ireland I	50
Amarillo			M in wreath N/HP/Japan			
Amaryllis	7940			1997-1998	GG	
Amazon			M in wreath big bow			
Ambrosia	7567		N in wreath ivory	1975-1978	Champagne	22-24
Amenity	7228			1977-1986	Victorian coupe II	22-56
American Flowers	7912			1990-1995	GALA	69-82
Amerita			M in wreath N/HP/Japan			
Amherst	501		K in scroll shield Japan			
Amiston, *41*		0069540	M in wreath N/HP/Japan	1929	Original	
Amor, *43*	2481		Contemporary FC Sri Lanka	1975-1976	Classic	
Amorette	5524			1955		
Anaconda, *116*			M in wreath N/HP	1921-1928	Original	
Angel D'amour	2769			1982-1985	Nor Ireland I	53-65
Angela	107		Cook'n Serve	1975-1977	CNS	19
Angora (The)		0068585	M in wreath N/HP/Japan	1929	Original	
Anita			M in wreath N/HP/Japan			
Anita, *79*	5309		N in wreath printed	1953		
Ankara	B977		Primastone	1979-1981	PRIMA1	28-30
Annabel	3872					
Annabelle, *85*	6856		N in wreath b/g	1968-1976	Concerto	21-23
Annelisa	8789			1985-1985	jfs	25
Anniversary	1979			1979-1986	Remembrance II	65-120
Annulaire					coupe	
Ansonia, *77*			M in wreath N/Nippon	1921-1930	Original	

Name, *Page #*	No.	Design	Backstamp	Time	Form	Value
Anticipation, *93*	2963		Ireland	1981-1994	Nor. Ireland I	53-72
Antigua	2163		Younger Image	1975-1976	Y/H	13
Antiquity	4304		Factory in shield	1991-1996	Estate	225-275
Apollo, *54*			M in wreath N/HP/Japan	1918		
Apple Crisp	9196		Keltcraft	1994-1994	K-RIM	61
Apple Magic	E523			1998	epoch	
Applique	3016			1980-1987	Remembrance II	35-53
April						
April Poem	4119			1995-1999	Nor. Ireland I	71
April Sky	9192		Keltcraft	1993-1994	K-RIM	50-53
Aquarius	8605		stoneware	1978-1983	CNCP1	16-36
Arabella			M in wreath N/HP/Japan		rim	
Arabesque						
Araby			M in wreath N/HP/Japan			
Arcadia	2604		N in wreath blk/gld	1976-1982	Remembrance I	22-50
Arcola						
Arctic	B972			1979-1980	PRIMA1	
Arctic Berries	4221			1998	Arctic	
Arctic Blue	4089			1998	Arctic	
Arctic Circle	4209			1997-1998	Arctic	
Arctic Gold	4001			1998	Arctic	
Arctic Green	4090			1998	Arctic	
Arctic Spring	4210			1997-1998	Arctic	
Arctic White	4000			1992-1998	Arctic	36-40
Arden	5603			1956		
Ardis	5772		N in wreath printed	1953-1957	Butterfly	
Ardmore						
Ardsley			M in shield Ivory			
Arebella	503		M in wreath small bow			
Argonne, *34*		0058597	M in wreath N/Nippon	1927	Original	
Argosy, *118*			M in wreath N/HP/Japan			
Argyle	5311		N in wreath printed	1953		
Ariana			M in wreath N/HP/Japan			
Aristocrat	7903			1973-1982	Victorian III	40-120
Aristocrat Gold	4115			1994-1998	Nor. Ireland I	117
Arizona	8677			1988-1993	SFE	50-58
Arleigh, *44*		0061237	M in wrought-iron	1921-1928		
Arlene		0095645	M in wreath small bow	1935		
Arlene, *80*	5802		N in wreath printed	1958	Butterfly	
Arlington	5221		M in wreath bow Occupied	1949	LaSalle	
Arlington Heights	4105			1992-1994	Nor Ireland I	65-72
Armand			M in wreath N/HP/Japan			
Armand, *59*	6315		N in wreath printed	1963		
Arnaud		0095654	M in wreath small bow	1935		
Arroyo						
Artic Gold						
Artic White						
Arunta						
Arvana		0089483	M in wreath small bow	1933		
Arvil			M in wreath N/HP/Japan			
Ashbury	4737			1997-1998	Bone	115
Ashby, *95*	6201		N in wreath printed	1953		
Ashford	4026		M in wreath small bow			
Ashland	7357			1998	Imperial Baroque	
Ashleigh						
Ashville, *86*	4750		New Lineage II bone china	1997-1998	Empire	85
Asian Bouquet	9301 W4		Versatone	1980-1983	VER1	30-45
Asian Song	7151			1975-1986	Victorian II	22-56
Aspen Flowers	7938			1998	IMPR	
Aspen Nights	8685			1991-1992	CNCP1	54
Aspiration	8447			1994-1994	OPT	77
Astair	9795			1990-1993	Cameo	88-100
Astor Rose						
Astorbrook	4300		Factory in shield	1991-1998	Estate	110
Astoria	2789		Contemporary FC Philip	1977-1985	Classic	29-53

Name, *Page #*	No.	Design	Backstamp	Time	Form	Value
Athena			M in wreath small bow			
Athena	6221					
Athlone, *109*		0080460	M in wreath N/HP/Japan	1932		
Atlanta		0068448	M in wreath N/HP/Japan	1929		
Atlanta, *118*	7166			1975-1979	Victorian II	22-32
Atlantic	8351		Primastone	1979-1981	PRIMA1	24-27
Atwood						
Au Naturel	9073		Progression N	1975-1983	P2	24-55
Aubery		0082450	M in wreath N/HP/Japan	1932		
Auburndale	7340			1994-1998	Imperial Baroque	85
Aubusson	3162			1982-1983	Nor. Ireland I	65
Audrey, *37*	3078		K in scroll shield Japan	1947	Rose China	
Augusta	2025		Contemporary FC Philip	1974-1975	Classic	
Augustan						
Aurora	600		M in wreath N/HP/Japan			
Austin			M in wreath N/HP/Japan			
Automne, *49*	5626		N in wreath printed	1953		
Autumn Day	8353		Primastone	1982-1987	PRIMA1	38-43
Autumn Estate	4744		New Lineage bone china	1996-1998	New Lineage	85
Autumn Rhapsody	3660			1986-1989	Nor Ireland I	53-60
Autumnwind	8630			1979-1982	PROV	25-38
Avalon	3390		Contemporary FC Philip	1983-1990	Classic	46
Avalon, *74*	5150		M in wreath big bow	1950-1953	rim	
Aventura	9144		Keltcraft misty isle	1986-1989	K-MI	37-40
Avon	5531			1955		
Avril			M in wreath N/HP/Japan			
Awareness	7741		Fine China in wreath	1993-1995	New Traditions	100-110
Azalea, *77*		0019322	Sunrise	1921-1938	Azalea	
Azalea	3885			1988-1992	Paramount	50-53
Azure	9116		Keltcraft	1982-1986	K-RIM	26-37
Azure Garden	4736			1997-1998	Sheer Ivory Bone	
Bahama	6922		Younger Image	1975-1977	Y/H	13-19
Balboa	6123					
Baldwin	7265			1982-1985	Remembrance II	53-56
Bambina, *47*	5791		N in wreath printed	1953-1957	Concerto	
Bamburg						
Bambury	3369			1983-1985	Nor Ireland II	55-65
Banana	8637		stoneware	1979-1983	CNCP1	21-36
Bancroft, *43*			M in wreath N/HP/Japan	1928	Original	
Bancroft, *66*	5481		N in wreath printed	1954		
Bantry		0086209	M in wreath N/HP/Japan	1933		
Bantry Bay		0086209	M in shield China	1933		
Barbados	6926		Younger Image	1974-1975	Y/H	13
Barbara, *80*	6009	0189202	N in wreath printed	1954		
Barcarolle	6655					
Barcelona	9152		Keltcraft misty isle	1986-1986	K-MI	37
Barenz						
Baroda		0068596	M in wreath N/HP/Japan	1929		
Baroness	6357		Contemporary FC Philip	1975-1979	Classic	22-27
Ba rrington, *32*	2030		N in wreath blk/gld	1975-1980	Commander	24-40
Barrymore	9737			1985-1998	Sheer Ivory Bone	72
Barstow	2995		Contemporary FC Philip	1979-1981	Classic	27
Barton			M in wreath small bow			
Barton, *91*	6305		N in wreath printed	1963	Rim	
Basel (The)		0068466	M in wreath N/HP/Japan	1929		
Bassano	3720		M in wreath small bow			
Bavarian Blossom	3891		Legacy Philippines	1988-1989	Commander	69
Bay Roc	8303		Primastone	1975-1976	PRIMA1	15-19
Bayard	614		M in wreath small bow			
Beaumont		0069534	M in wreath N/HP/Japan	1929		
Beaumont	5796					
Beauvais			M in shield China			
Bedford, *102*		0068443	M in wreath N/HP/Japan	1929		
Beechmont			M in wreath N/HP/Japan			
Before the Wind	B134		Sea & Sky	1985-1987	SS	33

Name, *Page #*	No.	Design	Backstamp	Time	Form	Value
Beguine	2033			1974-1975	Concerto	
Behold	7269			1982-1985	Victorian II	48-51
Belcourt	4710			1992-1994	Royal Pierpont	100-113
Belda, *95*	6342		N in wreath printed		coupe	
Belfort	6723					
Belgravia	9189		Keltcraft	1992-1995	K-COU	43-53
Bella	2697		Contemporary FC Philip	1977-1982	Classic	25-45
Bellcrest	4754			1998	Sheer Ivory Bone	
Belle						
Belle Empress	3980		Legendary Sri Lanka	1989-1998	Commander	50
Belle Femmes	3452			1984-1984	ART DECO	
Belle Rose	102					
Bellefonte		0068587	M in wreath N/HP/Japan	1929	Original	
Bellefonte		0069539	M in wreath N/HP/Japan	1929		
Bellefonte	9731			1982-1986	Sheer Ivory Bone	65-73
Bellemead						
Bellerose						
Bellfleur						
Bellodgia			M in wreath small bow			
Bellville	4219		Legendary Sri Lanka	1998	Commander	
Belmont						
Belvoir	592		M in wreath small bow			
Benedicata	6976					
Benita	3019			1980-1983	Remembrance II	30-46
Bentley	7723		Fine China in wreath	1988-1993	New Traditions	78-94
Benton, *74*	6204		N in wreath printed	1953		
Berenda, *113*	4017		M in wreath small bow			
Berkeley			M in wreath N/Nippon			
Bernice						
Berredin	9083		Progression N	1977-1981	P2	24-38
Berries'n Such	9070		Progression N	1975-1983	P2	24-55
Berringer, *53*	7335		N in wreath ivory china	1992-1994	Imperial Baroque	78-85
Berry Grove	E528			1998	epoch	
Berryvine	9211			1996-1998	HC	
Bessie, *90*	5788		N in wreath printed	1953		
Beverly, *54*		0058589	M in wreath N/Nippon	1927	Original	
Bewitch	9078		Progression N	1977-1983	P2	24-55
Biarritz, *110*		0078047	M in wreath N/HP/Japan	1931		
Biarritz, *38*	6006	0187156	N in wreath printed	1954	Concerto	
Biltmore	2581			1975-1981	Classic	
Bimini	6923		Younger Image	1975-1976	Y/H	19
Birch				1998-1999	Epoch	
Black & Gold, *71*		0020056	M in wreath N/HP/Japan	1912	Original	
Black Lace	2881			1978-1981		
Black Tango	9137		Keltcraft misty isle	1984-1987	K-MI	36-37
Blair Rose, *96*	6519		N in wreath blk/gld	1968	Coupe	
Blakely			M in wreath small bow			
Blanton			M in wreath N/HP/Japan			
Blenkheim			M in wreath N/HP/Japan			
Bleufleur B319 W30			Versatone	1979-1985	VER1	30-45
Bliss	8574		Folkstone	1976-1979	FOLK2	18-30
Bloomfield						
Blossom Mist	3787			1987-1996	Paramount	50-60
Blossom Time	7150			1975-1985	Victorian II	22-53
Blue Adobe	8678			1988-1993	SFE	50-58
Blue and Gold	7703		Fine China in wreath	1984-1987	New Traditions	60-63
Blue Bell			M in wreath N/HP/Japan		Original	
Blue Bouquet						
Blue Charm						
Blue Chintz	9014		Progression N	1974-1975	P1	24
Blue Chintz	9104		Keltcraft	1980-1987	K-COU	35-37
Blue Dawn, *36*	6611		N in wreath blk/gld	1968		
Blue Destiny	3602			1984-1987	Remembrance II	50
Blue Estate	9222			1998	HC	
Blue Glow						
Blue Haven	9004		Progression N	1975-1980	P1	24-38
Blue Hill, *93*	2482		Contemporary FC Sri Lanka	1975-1994	Classic	25-54
Blue Moon	9022		Progression N	1975-1980	P1	24-38
Blue Orchard	6695		Cook'n Serve	1975-1977	CNS-C	19
Blue Orient	3363			1983-1985	N.Ireland II	55-65
Blue Peony	7251			1979-1981	Remembrance II	
Blue Rose						
Blue Shadow	9126		Keltcraft	1983-1985	K-RIM	36-37
Blue Sky	8760		Craftone	1975-1977	CRAFT2	12-20
Blue Sky Glow	8401			1984-1985	GRMT	29
Blue Treasures	4204			1993-1994	w/impressions	69-72
Blue Willow		0011006	M in wreath N/HP/Japan	1907		
Blue Willow		0016033	M in wreath N/HP/Japan	1909		
Bluebell, *90*	5558		N in wreath printed	1955		
Blueberry	8587		Folkstone	1978-1981	FOLK2	27
Bluedawn	622	0100331	M in wreath small bow	1936		
Bluedawn	4715					
Bluelace						
Blueridge, *70*	5858		N in wreath printed	1953		
Bluetone						
Blythe	2037		Contemporary FC Philip	1975-1983	Classic	25-46
Bois Jolie	9792			1990-1991	Sheer Ivory Bone	88
Bolero			M in wreath small bow			
Bolero	2036			1974-1975	Commander	22
Boliska	2766			1981-1983	Nor. Ireland I	50
Bonaventure	3682		Legendary Sri Lanka	1985-1988	Commander	46-50
Bordeaux	3191			1982-1985	Commander	48-51
Bordeaux	5496		M in wreath N/HP/Japan	1954		
Border						
Bouquet, *38*	4025			1993-1994	Paramount	65-68
Bosnia (The), *76*			M in wreath N/Nippon	1912-1913	Original	
Boulder Ridge	8674			1988-1999	SFE	54-64
Bounty	8342		Primastone	1976-1978	PRIMA3	15-18
Bradford					coupe	
Brandon, *70*	6222		N in wreath printed	1953		
Brandywine	4057			1995-1998	Paramount	57
Brangane			M in shield China			
Breathless, *27*	7704		Fine China in wreath	1984-1992	New Traditions	60-90
Breeze	2032			1974-1975	Concerto	
Brenda	2730					
Brently	9730			1982-1987	Sheer Ivory Bone	65-82
Brewster						
Brian			M in wreath N/HP/Japan			
Briarcliff			M in wreath N/HP/Japan	1923	Original	
Briarhurst			M in wreath N/HP/Japan			
Brickhaven	4142			1997-1998	Nor Ireland I	
Bridal Rose						
	8102 W82			1975-1982	Victorian IV	25-55
Bridal Waltz	4109			1993-1998	Remembrance II	57
Briday Ribbon	4027		Legendary Sri Lanka	1994-1994	Commander	57
Bridgehampton	9753			1987-1991	Royal Pierpont	85-94
Brigette	2865			1982-1985	Nor. Ireland I	50
Bright Side	9079		Progression N	1977-1983	P2	24-55
Brighteyes	8633			1979-1982	PROV	25-38
Brighton						
Springs	9414			1988-1999	PRIMAC	60
Brightside						
Bristol B334 W18			Versatone II	1978-1982	VER2	27-40
Brittany	7195			1975-1980	Victorian III	22-37
Bromley	4156			1998	Nor Ireland I	
Brookfield	3193			1981-1986	Commander	48-51
Brookhollow, **120**						
	4704		Lamp bone china printed	1991-1998	Cameo	88
Brooklane	6112		Concerto			
Brookside	3697		Legendary Sri Lanka	1986-1987	Commander	50
Brookvale	4098		Legendary Sri Lanka	1998	Commander	
Brunswick						
Brussels	3693		Legendary Sri Lanka	1985-1988	Commander	50-55
Bryce						
Buckingham	1920					

Name, *Page #*	No.	Design	Backstamp	Time	Form	Value	Name, *Page #*	No.	Design	Backstamp	Time	Form	Value
Buckingham, *59*							Castella, *117*		0080463	M in wreath N/HP/Japan	1932		
	6438	0200495	N in wreath printed	1956-1986	LaSalle	20-51	Castillo	4075			1998	Paramount	
Buenavista, *122*							Castleberry	7960			1984-1986	Victorian II	53
	9728		Lamp bone china gld/blk	1981-1993	Sheer Ivory Bone	65-100	Cathay	6029					
Burgundy							Cathay	7179			1975-1979	Victorian III	22-32
Royale	7296			1986-1989	Imperial Baroque	60-70	Catherine						
Burlington	2081		N in wreath blk/gld				Cavalier, *42*	6104		N in wreath printed	1953		
Burma		0071854	M in wreath N/HP/Japan	1930			Cavatina	4011		M in wreath small bow			
Buttercup	8769		Craftone	1975-1980	CRAFT2	13-21	Cecile	7801		Fine China in wreath	1998	New Traditions	
Cabot	9785			1990-1998	Masters Collection	105	Celeste	5070		M with crown			
Cache Pot, *70*	3132		N in wreath blk/gld	1981-1983	Remembrance II	53	Celia	7086			1975-1977	Champagne	22-24
Cadiz	3591		Legacy Philippines	1985-1989	Commander	69	Celtic (The)			M in wreath N/HP/Japan			
Café Au Lait							Centennial						
Café du Jour	9094		New Decade wave	1986-1990	NDC	48-58	White	8679			1988-1992	CENT	50-54
Café du Soir	9091		New Decade wave	1985-1995	NDC	40-68	Cereus	615		M in wreath small bow			
Café Versailles	3762			1987-1988	Nor Ireland I	54-60	Cerulean	4726		M in wreath small bow			
Calais			M in wreath N/HP/Japan				Cervantes	7261			1981-1992	Remembrance II	53-65
Caledonia, *56*	7091			1975-1975	Victorian V		Ceylon (The)		0058581	M in wreath N/Nippon	1927	Original	
Caliban, *32*	3733		M in wreath big bow	1933	Rose China		Chadbourne, *93*						
California								3990		N in wreath/Philip.	1989-2000	Remembrance II	50-64
Dreaming	9148		Keltcraft misty isle	1986-1989	K-MI	37-40	Chadwick						
Caliph Place, *69*							Chainrose		0061230	M in wreath N/HP/Japan	1928		
	4415		N in wreath bone gold	1990-1990			Chalfont			M in wreath N/HP/Japan			
Calvert							Chalfonte	9724			1980-1985	Sheer Ivory Bone	75-88
Calypso	8757		Craftone	1975-1976	CRAFT1	10-20	Chalmette	2996		Legacy Philippines	1979-1985	Commander	40-69
Cambridge			M in wreath N/HP/Japan				Chamberlain	4705			1992-1993	Masters Coll.	113-119
Camden, *43*	6350		N in wreath printed	1953			Chambray	3192			1981-1985	Commander	48-51
Camelot	3031,6000	0117817		1939			Champagne	8161			1976-1984	Victorian IV	25-58
Camillia, *110*	3950	0117508	M in wreath N/HP/Japan	1939			Champlain	7553		N in wreath ivory	1975-1979	Victorian II	21-30
Campobello	8305		Primastone	1975-1976	PRIMA1	15-19	Chanazure, *88*		0061239	M in wreath N/HP/Japan	1928		
Canastel	3671		Legacy Philippines	1986-1989	Commander	69	Chanbard, *110*			M in wreath N/HP/Japan			
Candice	3161			1981-1985	Nor. Ireland I	53-60	Chancellor, *33*	9751			1987-1990	Royal Pierpont	90-94
Candice	5509			1953-1958	Butterfly		Chandella		0068478	M in wreath N/HP/Japan	1929		
Candlelight	7544		N in wreath ivory	1975-1976	Champagne	21-23	Chandon, *61*	7306		N in wreath ivory	1988-1998	Imperial Baroque	70
Cantara			M in shield China				Chandon						
Cantata	8224			1977-1981	Victorian IV	25-40	Platinum	7367			1998-1999	Imperial Baroque	
Canterbury, *72*	5226		M in wreath big bow	1950-1959			Chandova, *118*		0058438	M in wreath N/HP/Japan	1927		
Canterbury	9627			1982-1989	Sheer Iv. Bone	156-165	Chanesta		0068454	M in wreath N/HP/Japan	1929		
Canterbury	9705			1975-1980	Sheer Ivory Bone	40	Chanking, *110*			M in wreath N/HP/Japan	1918		
Canton, *46*	5027		M in wreath big bow	1955-1935	Triangle		Chanlake		0068457	M in wreath N/HP/Japan	1929		
Cape Town				1998	epoch		Channing	8411			1984-1986	cntp	36
Capri			M in wreath N/HP/Japan				Chanossa, *77*			M in wreath N/HP/Japan	1918		
Capri, *50*	5551	0176131	N in wreath printed	1951-1955	concerto		Chantaro		0061241	M in wreath N/HP/Japan	1928		
Caprice							Chanteuse	9308		Versatone	1982-1985	VER1	40-45
Captivate	8649			1980-1986	PROV	33-34	Chanvale, *56*			M in wreath N/HP/Japan	1918		
Cardinal	193	0098829	M in shield China	1935			Chanway			M in wreath N/HP/Japan			
Cardinal	4731						Chanwood, *31*			M in wreath N/HP/Japan	1930	Original.	
Carleton	5034		M in wreath bow Occupied	1933			Chardonnay	9156		Keltcraft	1987-1990	K-RIM	37-43
Carlisle							Chariton			M in wreath N/HP/Japan			
Carltonia		0078048	M in wreath N/HP/Japan	1933			Charleston	7148			1975-1981	Victorian II	21-35
Carlyle	7121			1975-1978	Victorian II		Charmaine			M in shield Ivory			
Carmela, *113*	4732	0095635	M in shield China	1935			Charmaine, *80*	5506	0176135	N in wreath printed	1953	rim	
Carmen		0014370	M in wreath N/Nippon	1909	Original		Charmeuse, *58*		0071435	M in wreath N/HP/Japan	1930		
Carmillia	4735	0117816		1939			Charmis			M with crown			
Carmine	3092		Legacy Philippines	1980-1986	Commander	45-80	Charoma, *108*		0098215	M in wreath small bow	1935		
Carnation	7940			1997-1998	GG		Chartres, *48*	5920		N in wreath printed	1953		
Carnegie	9772			1989-1990	Royal Pierpont	94	Chatham, *80*	5502	0176133	M in wreath N/HP/Japan	1951	Concerto	
Carole	5402		N in wreath printed	1954			Chatsworth						
Carolyn, *93*	2693		Contemporary FC Philip	1977-1996	Classic	25-54	Chaumont	6008	0187151	N in wreath printed	1954		
Carolyn	3055						Chaumont (The)			M in wreath N/HP/Japan			
Carrie	2864			1981-1985	Nor. Ireland I	50	Chavot Gold	4769			1998-1999	Masters Collection	
Carrousel							Cheer	8780		Craftone	1976-1979	CRAFT3	17-21
Carthage, *82*	3330		N in wreath blk/gld	1982-1998	Remembrance II	50	Chelsea		0071432	M in wreath N/HP/Japan	1930		
Casablanca, *60*							Chelsea Morn	3686		Legendary Sri Lanka	1986-1989	Commander	50
	6842		N in wreath blk/gld	1970	coupe		Cheramy		0087197	M in wreath sm bow 2 leaf	1933		
Cascade							Cheri						
Casino			M in wreath N/HP/Japan				Cherish	8222 W80			1975-1980	Victorian IV	25-40
Casino	8625			1979-1982	cas2	24-38	Cherita						

Name, *Page #*	No.	Design	Backstamp	Time	Form	Value
Cheryl	5917					
Chestnut Hill	7045		Expression	1975-1977	Victorian IV	18-19
Chevonia						
Chevonia	6003		M in scroll & wreath			
China Peony						
China Song	8165			1978-1983	Victorian IV	32-58
Chineblue		0076842	M in shield China	1931		
Chintz	2404			1975-1980	Commander	22-37
Cho-cho-san, *51*						
	6936		Fine China Stars	1955	Rim	
Choral Island	8410			1984-1984	cntp	
Chorus	2681		Contemporary FC Philip	1976-1981	Classic	
Christiana, *121*	4746		Lamp bone china gld/blk	1997-1997	Empire	85
Christine	3290			1982-1986	Commander	51
Christmas						
Baroque	7358			1998	Imperial	
Christy's						
World	9145		Keltcraft misty isle	1986-1989	K-MI	37-40
Churchill	9750			1987-1991	Sheer Ivory Bone	82-88
Cielito Lindo	2151		Cook'n Serve	1975-1977	CNS-R	13-19
Cimarron		1003006	M in shield china		Flying saucer	
Circle Bay	8415			1985-1986	cntp	29
Ciro	3744	0108378	M in wreath small bow	1936		
City Skies	4741		New Lineage bone china	1996-1998	New Lineage	85
Claire, *69*	657	0103007	M in wreath large bow	1950-1955		
Claridge, *48*	6020	0187148	N in wreath printed	1953	Butterfly	
Clarinda	2111			1975-1978	Concerto	21-23
Classic White	3330		Contemporary FC Philip	1975-1982	Classic	25-36
Claudette, *103*	594	0098221	M in wreath large bow	1935		
Claudette	8791			1985-1985	jfs	25
Claudia	583		M in wreath small bow			
Clear Day	9080		Progression N	1977-1983	P2	24-55
Clearlake	7914			1990-1994	GALA	63-72
Clematis	7940			1997-1998	GG	
Clemson	4227		Legendary Sri Lanka	1998	Commander	
Cleo	3415					
Cleone			M in wreath small bow			
Clermont						
Clinging Vine	B954		Primastone	1975-1977	PRIMA3	20-23
Clinton			M in wreath N/HP/Japan			
Clintonia			M in wreath N/HP/Japan			
Clovis	5855		N in wreath printed			
Club Stripe	4056			1995-1998	Paramount	57
Cobina						
Colbrook			M in wreath N/HP/Japan			
Colburn, *90*	6107	0194926	N in wreath printed	1976-1989	LaSalle	20-54
Colby			M in wreath N/HP/Japan			
Colby	5032					
Colmar						
Colonial, *24*			R.C. in circle Nippon	1911-1912		
Colonial Times	8340		Primastone	1976-1980	PRIMA1	17-27
Colony	5932			1974-1975	Butterfly	
Colton, *98*	3081		K in scroll shield Japan	1947		
Columbine	3803		M in scrolls			
Comiston, *89*		0058500	M in wreath N/HP/Japan	1927		
Commander						
White	3600			1976-1985	Commander	21-40
Commemor-						
ation	9798			1991-1992	Masters Coll.	175-188
Commodore , *57*			M in wreath N/Nippon		Original	
Compton, *30*	6524		N in wreath blk/gld		Concerto	
Concert	2803			1978-1983	Remembrance I	27-53
Concord	6207					
Condoro, *105*			M in wreath N/HP/Japan	1918		
Coniston (The)		0058599	M in wreath N/HP/Japan	1927		
Connie	7085			1975-1977	Champagne	22-24
Conservatory	7915			1992-1995	GALA	73-82
Constance						
Contemplation	8428			1985-1986	GRMT	36
Contentment	2880		Contemporary FC Philip	1978-1983	Classic	
Contessa	1485			1989-1991	w/impressions	94
Contrast	9569			1975-1980	Sheer Ivory Bone	36
Copley			M in wreath N/HP/Japan			
Copper Bud	7911			1990-1994	GALA	63-72
Coquet	2981		Contemporary FC Philip	1979-1986	Classic	27-46
Coram	7910			1990-1995	GALA	69-79
Cordell						
Cordon	2217			1975-1978	Commander	22
Cordova			M in wreath N/HP/Japan			
Cordova, *47*	5215		M in wreath big bow	1933		
Coreopsis	7940			1997-1998	GG	
Corinne						
Corinth						
Corinthia		0087198	M in wreath N/HP/Japan	1933		
Corithia						
Corliss						
Cornelia, *120*	7572		N in wreath ivory	1976	Victorian II	
Cornwall		0071425	M in wreath N/HP/Japan	1930		
Corona						
Coronado				1919-1922	Original	
Coronet, *25*			M in wreath N/HP/Japan	1921-1930	Original	
Corsage						
Cortege	7211			1976-1982	Victorian coupe II	22-50
Cortez, *110*			M in wreath N/HP/Japan			
Cortland	9178		Keltcraft	1992-1998	K-COU	43
Cosmos	8508		Folkstone	1975-1976	FOLK1	12
Costa Mesa	9146		Keltcraft	1986-1987	K-RIM	37
Cote Basque	3692		Legendary Sri Lanka	1985-1988	Commander	55-50
Cotillion	2802			1978-1983	Remembrance I	29-53
Counterpoint	8316		Primastone	1973-1977	PRIMA2	15-19
Countess	7223			1976-1987	Victorian coupe II	21-51
Country Diary	1906		Country Diary	1982-1991	K-DIARY	36-50
Country						
Fences	7920			1995-1999	IMPR	56
Country						
Ridge	E2007			1998	epoch	
Country Side	6899					
Country White	8659			1982-1986	PROV	33-34
Countrywood	9226		Keltcraft	1998	K-COU	
County Fair	8554		Folkstone	1975-1978	FOLK2	17-20
Courtney, *67*	6520		N in wreath blk/gld	1908	Coupe	
Cousteau	9782			1990-1995	Sheer Ivory Bone	88-107
Covent Garden	3786			1987-1990	Paramount	50
Coventry			M in wreath N/HP/Japan			
Coventry	2797		Legacy Philippines	1978-1985	Commander	32-69
Covina	9791			1990-1998	Sheer Ivory Bone	88
Coypel, *113*	3732	0108374	M in wreath big bow	1936		
Cragmoor			M in wreath N/HP/Japan			
Cranbrook						
Crandon			M in wreath N/HP/Japan		Mushroom	
Crazy Quilt						
	B308 W10		Versatone	1977-1981	VER1	23-30
Crest, *94*	5421		N in wreath printed	1954	LaSalle	
Crestmont, *42*	6013	0187145	N in wreath printed	1953-1977	LaSalle	20-23
Crestwood						
Crete (The), *31*			M in wreath N/Nippon	1918	Original	
Cromwell						
Crossways	7922			1995-1999	IMPR	50
Crown Flower	7324			1989-1996	Imperial Baroque	70-85
Crownpointe	4740		New Lineage bone china	1996-1998	New Lineage	85
Croydon		0076568	M in wreath N/HP/Japan	1931		
Croydon	5908					
Crystal						
Bouquet	4043		Legendary Sri Lanka	1994-1995	Commander	57
Culebra	6921		Younger Image	1974-1975	Y/H	13
Culeton, *93*	2692		Contemporary FC Sri Lanka	1977-1982	Classic	25-45

Name, *Page #*	No.	Design	Backstamp	Time	Form	Value
Cumberland	2225			1975-1998	Commander	21
Custard				1998-1999	epoch	
Cyclamen						
Cycle Brown	8658		stoneware	1982-1985	CNCP1	36
Cycle Frost	8660		stoneware	1984-1985	CNCP1	36
Cynara						
Cynthia	655		M in wreath small bow			
Cyrano, *110*			M in wreath N/HP/Japan	1918		
Cyril			M in wreath N/HP/Japan			
D'Azure	3091		Legacy Philippines	1980-1986	Commander	55-80
Daffodil	7940			1997-1998	GG	
Daisygarland	9101		Keltcraft	1980-1985	K-COU	35-36
Dallas						
Dalton			M in wreath N/HP/Japan			
Damask, *71*	5698		N in wreath blk/gld		coupe	
Damask Bouquet	9435			1995-1995	PRIMAC	75
Danbue				1919-1920		
Danielle, *69*	5776		N in wreath printed		coupe	
Daphne						
Darby, *41*			M in wreath N/HP/Japan			
Dardanelle			M in wreath N/HP/Japan			
Darlene	7035			1975-1976	Champagne	22
Darnell	4154			1998	Nor. Ireland I	
Daryl, *80*	5510		N in wreath printed	1953		
Datonia			M in wreath N/HP/Japan			
Daventry, *89*		0069544	M in wreath N/HP/Japan	1929		
Dawn	5930		N in wreath printed	1959-1986	LaSalle	18-46
Dawn Blush	9411		New Decade wave	1988-1990	NDC	48-58
Dazure						
Dearborn	4218		Legendary Sri Lanka	1998	Commander	
Dearest	2034		Contemporary FC Philip	1974-1979	Classic	22-27
Deauville			M in wreath N/HP/Japan			
Debonain	5426		N in wreath printed	1954	Rose China	
Debut	7210			1976-1982	Victorian coupe II	22-50
Decamps	3708					
Decision	8320		Primastone	1973-1977	PRIMA2	13-19
Deco Magic	3450			1984-1984	ART DECO	
Deco Spirit	3454			1984-1984	ART DECO	
Dee	2212			1975-1978	Concerto	21
Deerbrook	9150		Keltcraft misty isle	1986-1987	K-MI	37-43
Deerfield	9159		Keltcraft misty isle	1987-1995	K-MI	37-55
Deerlodge, *111*		0069531	M in wreath N/HP/Japan	1929		
Delacroix	4759			1997-1998	Empire	
Delburne						
Delevan	2580		Contemporary FC Philip	1975-1982	Classic	25-45
Delhi		0071424	M in wreath N/HP/Japan	1930		
Delia						
Delight, *119*	7229			1977-1983	Victorian II coupe	22-56
Della robia						
Delmonte		0071426	M in wreath N/HP/Japan	1930	Original	
Delphina			M in wreath N/HP/Japan			
Delrose			M in shield China			
Delta			M in wreath small bow			
Denise						
Derban, *113*			M in shield China	1931		
Derby			M in wreath N/Nippon			
Derry, *29*	5931		N in wreath printed	1953		
Desert Fire	8682			1990-1993	SFE	54-58
Desert Flowers	8341		Primastone	1975-1985	PRIMA1	15-41
Destination	8691			1992-1998	OPT	58
Devon, *43*		0108041	M in wreath N/HP/Japan	1936		
Devotion	7271			1983-1992	Victorian II	56-65
Diaden	6663		N in wreath colorful			
Diamond Head	2236		Younger Image	1975-1977	Y/H	13-19
Diamond Trac	4722			1993-1994	Bone	88-92
Diana			M in wreath N/HP/Japan			
Diana	2611		N in wreath blk/gld	1976-1986	Remembrance I	21-51
Diana	5522			1955		
Dignatio						
Dignity	7901			1972-1973	Victorian II	
Dina			M in wreath small bow			
Dogwood						
Dolores						
Dominica	6925		Younger Image	1974-1975	Y/H	13
Dominique	8788			1985-1985	jfs	25
Donegal	2179		Contemporary FC Philip	1975-1982	Classic	25
Donna						
Doranne						
Dorian			M in shield China		Rim	
Doris, *97*		0071219	M in wreath N/HP/Japan	1930	Original	
Dorrance			M in wreath N/HP/Japan			
Dorsay			M in wreath N/HP/Japan			
Dorset						
Dover	5633			1956		
Dream Street	3483		Legendary Sri Lanka	1985-1988	Commander	46
Dreamer	9122		Keltcraft	1983-1985	K-RIM	36-37
Dreamspun	4721			1993-1994	Bone	88-92
Dresala	3033					
Dresalda	3849		M in wreath small bow			
Dresdena			M in shield China			
Dresdlina			M on stage			
Dresdoll	4716		M on stage	1940		
Dresgay, *98*	3038		K in scroll shield Japan	1947	Rose China	
Dresita	4733		M in wreath bow Occupied			
Dreslina			M in wreath N/HP/Japan			
Duane						
Duetto, *67*	6610		N in wreath blk/gld	1968	Coupe	
Dulcy	5153		M in wreath bow Occupied	1975		
Duluth			M in wreath N/HP/Japan			
Durango	8647		stoneware	1981-1983	CNCP1	33-36
Dureer	3725		M in wreath small bow			
Durer			M in wreath N/HP/Japan			
Durga						
Dusk				1998-1999	epoch	
Dutch Tile	7913			1990-1994	GALA	63-72
Dutch Treat	9120		Keltcraft	1983-1985	K-RIM	36-37
Dutch Weave	9305		Versatone	1983-1984	VER1	30-45
Dynasty						
Early Spring	2362		Contemporary FC Philip	1975-1985	Classic	25-46
Eastfair	9171		Keltcraft	1988-1998	K-RIM	37
Easthampton	3491		Legendary Sri Lanka	1984-1993	Commander	46-50
Eastwind	8349		Primastone	1978-1982	PRIMA1	21-33
Edana						
Eden	3391		Contemporary FC Philip	1983-1986	Classic	46
Edenderry	2772			1981-1985	Nor Ireland I	53-60
Edenrose	6343					
Edgemont	5216					
Edgemoor	4771			1998	Allaire	
Edgerow	4078		Legendary Sri Lanka	1997-1998	Commander	57
Edgewater	7728		Fine China in wreath	1988-1991	New Traditions	78-82
Edgewood, *95*	5807	0182094	N in wreath printed	1953-1958	LaSalle	
Edinburgh, *32*	7146		N in wreath blk/sld	1968	Rim	
Edwardian Rose	7353			1998	Imperial Baroque	
Effingham	3018			1980-1984	Remembrance II	90
Egg						
El Parador	9408		New Decade wave	1988-1989	NDC	48-50
Elaine		0089484	M in wreath N/HP/Japan	1933		
Elaine		0089484	M in wreath small bow	1933		
Elation	B955		Primastone	1975-1977	PRIMA4	20-23
Elegance in						
Elegance in Blue	B133		Elegance in blue	1980-1987	Elegance	53-56
Elegante	9708			1975-1980	Sheer Ivory Bone	40
Elenor Bassett, *101*			M in wreath N/Nippon	1912-1913	Original	

Name, Page #	No.	Design	Backstamp	Time	Form	Value
Elevation	4024			1992-1994	Paramount	53-60
Elite			M in wreath N/HP/Japan	1924	Original	
Elizabeth						
Ellington	3691		Legendary Sri Lanka	1985-1996	Commander	55-57
Elloree	2169		Cook'n Serve	1975-1977	CNS-R	19
Ellrose, 88			M in wreath N/HP/Japan	1918		
Elmdale						
Elmhurst						
Elmonte		0080754	Cherry Blossom	1932		
Elms Court	4720			1993-1994	Bone	88-92
Elmsford	3204			1982-1985	Elegance	55-58
Elnora			M in wreath small bow			
Eloise			M in wreath N/HP/Japan			
Elroy			M in wreath N/HP/Japan			
Eltovar		0083377	M in shield China	1932		
Elvira	608	0098835	M in wreath small bow	1935	Rose China	
Elysee	6914			1975-1978	Commander	24-26
Elysian			M in wreath N/HP/Japan			
Embassy			M in scrolls			
Embassy	6380					
Embassy Suite	9756			1988-1998	Masters Collection	105
Embrace	2755			1977-1983	Remembrance I	40-58
Emerald Crest	4130			1998	N.Ireland I	
Eminence	6905		Contemporary FC Philip	1975-1979	Classic	21-30
Empire	2682			1976-1980		
Empire	4916					
Enchanteur	7701		Fine China in wreath	1984-1987	New Traditions	60-73
Enchantment	2754			1977-1981	Remembrance I	21-35
Engagement						
	8009 W81			1975-1984	Victorian IV	25-58
English						
Flowers	7360			1998	Imperial Baroque	
Engravings	4203			1992-1994	w/impressions	65-72
Enhancement	4035		Legendary Sri Lanka	1994-1998	Commander	57
Envoy	6325		N in wreath printed	1975-1986	LaSalle	18-46
Epic	2680			1976-1981		
Equator	8506		Folkstone	1975-1982	FOLK1	12-33
Erie			M in wreath N/HP/Japan			
Eroica	2041			1975-1981	Commander	30-60
Esmond			M in shield China			
Espana, 67	6805		N in wreath blk/gld			
Esperanza	6924		Younger Image	1975-1977	Y/H	13-19
Esplanade			M in wreath N/HP/Japan		Original	
Esquire						
Essay	8575		Folkstone	1976-1980	FOLK2	18-30
Essence	2606		N in wreath blk/gld	1976-1984	Remembrance I	
Essex	2224			1975-1980	Commander	21-35
Essex Court, 41	4727		Lamp in wreath blk/gld	1994-1998	Bone	113
Esteem, 44	5404		N in wreath printed	1953	LaSalle	
Estelle		0083367	M in wreath N/HP/Japan	1932		
Estrellita						
Eternal Blush	9138		Keltcraft misty isle	1984-1995	K-MI	36-53
Etienne, 123	7260		N in wreath ivory	1981-1996	Remembrance II	53-72
Eugenia, 68	2160		N in wreath blk/gld	1975-1980	Commander	24-40
Eureka	502		M in wreath small bow			
Evangeline	9154		Keltcraft	1987-1988	K-RIM	37
Evendale	B316		Versatone	1978-1982	VER1	27-40
Evening Gown	7738		Fine China in wreath	1992-1995	New Traditions	90-100
Evening Mood	3788			1987-1992	Paramount	50-53
Evening						
Sonnet	3701			1987-1988	Remembrance II	50-54
Everett	2586			1977-1981		
Evermore	9735			1984-1991	Sheer Ivory Bone	73-82
Exeter	604	0098834	M in wreath small bow	1935		
Fabian	684		M in wreath small bow			
Fair Wind	9422			1993-1994	PRIMAC	69-72
Fairbanks	9707			1975-1980	Sheer Ivory Bone	34
Fairburn	3461			1984-1986	N.Ireland II	53-65
Fairchild	7345			1995-1998	Imperial Baroque	88
Fairday	9130		Keltcraft misty isle	1983-1987	K-MI	36-37
Fairfax, 105		0080461	M in wreath N/HP/Japan	1932		
Fairfax	3190			1981-1985	Commander	48-51
Fairfield	2612		N in wreath blk/gld	1977	Remembrance I	
Fairmont		0080755	M in wreath N/HP/Japan	1932		
Fairmont, 81	6102	0194925	N in wreath printed	1975-1987	LaSalle	20-51
Fairview	7263			1982-1987	Remembrance II	48-51
Fallriver	B331 W15		Versatone II	1978-1982	VER2	27-40
Fallsong	8634			1980-1982	PROV	25-38
Fanfare	8621		stoneware	1978-1990	CNCP1	16-43
Fantasia	7532					
Fantasia	B979		Primastone	1983-1986	PRIMA1	47
Fantasy	8317		Primastone	1973-1977	PRIMA2	15-19
Farentino	4713			1993-1993	Masters Collection	119
Farland		0086200	M in wreath N/HP/Japan	1933		
Farney	610		M in wreath small bow			
Fascination	2998		Contemporary FC Philip	1979-1985	Classic	27-46
Faustina			M in wreath small bow			
Favorita		0078057	M in wreath N/HP/Japan	1931		
Fay	6874			1974	LaSalle	
Felicia			M in wreath N/HP/Japan			
Felicity	9028					
Fellicia	6977					
Fernand	581	0097901	M in wreath small bow	1935		
Ferncliff						
Ferncroft, 96			M in wreath N/Nippon	1912-1913		
Fernwood, 50	5444		N in wreath printed	1953	LaSalle	
Festival	8650			1980-1986	PROV	33-34
Fidelity, 70						
	8003 W81		N in wreath blk/gld	1973-1982	Victorian IV	25-55
Fiesta	483		M in wreath small bow			
Fiesta Flowers	4226			1998	Paramount	
Figaro	2042			1974-1975	Commander	22
Finale, 123	7213		N in wreath ivory	1976-1983	Victorian Coupe II	24-58
Firedance	2401			1975-1979	Commander	22-32
Firenze, 82	6674		N in wreath colorful			
First Blush	2605		N in wreath blk/gld	1976-1982	Remembrance I	21-48
Fitzgerald	4712			1993-1998	Masters Collection	187
Fjord	B951		Primastone	1975-1986	PRIMA1	15-41
Flamengo (The)			M in wreath N/Nippon			
Flanders	2038			1975-1976	Commander	22
Fleurette		0076831	M in wreath N/HP/Japan	1931		
Fleurette	2226			1975-1977	Commander	21-23
Fleurgold, 65		0077631	M in wreath N/HP/Japan	1931	Original	
Fleury, 118		0078052	M in wreath N/HP/Japan	1932		
Flirtation	7227			1977-1981	Victorian coupe II	22-37
Floating						
Garden	9302		Versatone	1980-1983	VER1	30-45
Flodena		0085202		1933		
Flomar			M in wreath N/HP/Japan			
Floral Dream	3451			1984-1984	ART DECO	
Floral Embrace	4311		Factory in shield	1994-1995	Estate	125-130
Floral Frost	B980		Primastone	1984-1986	PRIMA1	46
Floral Song	7918			1993-1995	GALA	75-79
Floral Sonnet	9216			1997-1998	HC	65
Floralee	8346		Primastone	1978-1982	PRIMA1	21-33
Floralia			M in wreath N/HP/Japan			
Floramay			M in wreath small bow			
Floreal		0076839	M in wreath N/HP/Japan	1931		
Florence	5528			1955		
Florencia		0058591	M in wreath N/HP/Japan	1927		
Floria						
Floriam Bassette			M in wreath N/HP/Japan			
Florida			M in wreath N/HP/Japan			
Florida	9402		New Decade wave	1987-1990	2000	48-58
Floris	2480			1975-1976		
Floris	5088					

Name, Page #	No.	Design	Backstamp	Time	Form	Value
Florola, 107		0083374	M in shield China	1932		
Flourish	2608		N in wreath blk/gld	1976-1983	Remembrance I	21-51
Flower Maid	7257			1980-1983	Remembrance II	37-53
Flower Power	8775		Craftone	1975-1979	CRAFT2	13-21
Flower Time	9072		Progression N	1975-1983	P2	24-55
Floweree			M in wreath N/HP/Japan			
Foam White	B138		Sea & Sky	1985-1989	SS	33-40
Fondale	605		M in wreath small bow			
Fontaine, 53			M in wreath N/HP/Japan	1921-1930		
Fontana						
Fordyce			M in wreath N/HP/Japan			
Forest Bounty, 30						
	4058			1995-1998	Paramount	57
Forever, 83	2690		Contemporary	1974-1930		
Formosa (The)			M in wreath N/Nippon			
Foxboro	4302		Factory in shield	1991-1998	Estate	225
Fragments	8445			1994-1994	OPT	77
Francine						
Fragrance, 67	7025		N in wreath ivory	1975-1985	Victorian II	22-56
Free Flight	B981		Primastone	1985-1986	PRIMA1	46
Freemont						
Fremont, 29	6127		N in wreath blk/gld	1975-1978	Concerto	18-20
French Charm	3901			1991-1998	w/impressions	63
Frey	B960		Primastone	1976-1979	PRIMA3	15-21
Frolic	2352			1975-1984	Commander	21-51
Frost Flower						
B332	W16		Versatone II	1978-1982	VER2	27-40
Fruit Parfait	7919			1993-1995	GALA	75-82
Fruit Passion	7921			1995-1995	IMPR	56
Fruitful	B952		Primastone	1975-1977	PRIMA4	20-23
Fruitmania				1998	epoch	
Gaiety	8318		Primastone	1973-1977	PRIMA2	15-19
Gail, 82	6710		N in wreath colorful			
Gainford		0097893		1935		
Gainsboro			M in wreath N/HP/Japan		Original	
Galatea		0095632	M in wreath N/HP/Japan	1935		
Galavan, 65		0097894	M in wreath sm bow 2 leaf	1935		
Galaxy	6527		Contemporary FC Philip	1974-1975	Classic	
Gallery	7246			1979-1991	Remembrance II	32-60
Garbo, 96	3790		Legendary Sri Lanka	1987-1990	Commander	46-50
Garden Empress	9741			1985-1995	Royal Pierpont	77-113
Gardena						
Garfield		0098845		1935		
Garland		0095633		1935		
Garland, 95	5905		N in wreath printed	1953		
Garland	D167		M in wreath sm bow 2 leaf			
Garnet	5656			1956		
Garnet Rose						
Garvin						
Gastonia		0098827	M with crown	1935		
Gateway	4103			1991-1992	Remembrance II	50-53
Gaylord, 44	5526		N in wreath	1955		
Gelee	3723		M in wreath small bow			
Geneva	6910			1975-1976	Commander	21-23
Georgetown	9084		Progression N	1977-1981	P2	24-38
Georgette	305		M in scroll & wreath	1949		
Georgian	6440			1975-1977	Concerto	21-23
Georgiana			M in wreath sm bow 2 leaf			
Geri	7026			1975-1978	Victorian II	22-24
Gerome	3743		M in wreath big bow	1933		
Gerome	3843		M in wreath bow Occupied		Flying Saucer	
Gilda			M in wreath N/HP/Japan			
Gilded Age	7354			1998	Imperial Baroque	
Gilded Blossoms	4134			1998-1999	Nor. Ireland I	
Gina						
Gingerbread	8584		Folkstone	1978-1981	FOLK2	22
Girado		0086205	M in shield China	1933		
Glacier						
Glenaire						
Glenbawn	2866			1981-1983	Nor. Ireland I	40-50
Glenbrook						
Glencoe, 91	6505		N in wreath colorful	1963	Coupe	
Glendale	5038					
Glendola			M in wreath small bow			
Glendola		0095648	M in shield China	1935		
Glendon						
Gleneden, 111			M in wreath N/HP/Japan	1918		
Glengarry	3806			1988-1990	w/impressions	60
Glenmore		0095634	M in wreath sm bow 2 leaf	1935		
Glennis, 42	5804	0182092	N in wreath printed	1953	coupe	
Glenora, 88			M in wreath N/HP/Japan	1928	Original	
Glenrose, 94	5206		N in wreath printed	1953		
Glenwood	5770	0181393	N in wreath printed	1953		
Glenwood, 103	6500		M in scroll & wreath	1940		
Glimmer B301	W10		Versatone	1977-1984	VER1	23-45
Gloria			M in wreath sm bow 2 leaf	1930		
Gloria, 106		0095641	M in wreath small bow	1935		
Gloria, 25	6526		N in wreath blk/gld	1974-1975	Classic	
Gold & Platinum	7713		Fine China in wreath	1985-1993	New Traditions	60-112
Gold & Sable	9758			1988-1998	Masters Collection	105
Goldart, 25	5290		N in wreath printed	1953		
Goldcoast						
Goldconda			M in shield China			
Goldcourt						
Goldcrest	470		M in wreath sm bow 2 leaf			
Goldcroft						
Golden Cove	7719		Fine China in wreath	1986-1999	New Traditions	63
Golden Dawn	8163			1979-1984	Victorian IV	25-58
Golden Lily	7733		Fine China in wreath	1990-1998	New Traditions	82
Golden Mastery	4745			1998	Masters Collection	
Golden Myth	4116			1994-1998	Nor. Ireland I	93
Golden Orchard	4049			1995-1995	Commander	57
Golden Serenade	7714		Fine China in wreath	1985-1988	New Traditions	53-64
Golden Tide	7739		Fine China in wreath	1992-1999	New Traditions	90
Golden Tribute	9769			1988-1996	Masters Coll.	85-100
Golden Twilight	4110		Legacy Philippines	1993-1998	Commander	110
Goldena, 24			M in wreath N/Nippon	1918	Original	
Goldenglo			M in wreath N/HP/Japan			
Goldenrose	3981		M in wreath sm bow 2 leaf			
Goldette	7286		Remembrance II			
Goldfleur	3983					
Goldhill	6613		N in wreath printed		LaSalle	
Goldier						
Goldinthia		0087195	M in wreath sm bow 2 leaf	1933		
Goldivy						
Goldkin, 65	4985		M in wreath big bow	1950-1959	Rose China	
Goldkin	5675			1956		
Goldlane	5084		M in wreath big bow	1933	Rose China	
Goldlane	6612					
Goldlea						
Goldlinda			M in wreath N/HP/Japan			
Goldlustra			M with crown			
Goldmere						
Goldmount(M)				1933		
Goldora	882		M in shield China		flying saucer	
Goldray			M in wreath N/HP/Japan			
Goldream	469		M in wreath sm bow 2 leaf			
Goldridge						
Goldrina	4070					

Name, Page #	No.	Design	Backstamp	Time	Form	Value
Hyde Park	6720				coupe	
Ice Flower	B976		Primastone	1979-1986	PRIMA1	28-47
Ice Rose	9113		Keltcraft	1982-1985	K-RIM	35-37
Icon	9784			1990-1993	Masters Coll.	105-119
Idalia			M in wreath small bow			
Ignition	8694			1992-1998	OPT	45
Image	8315		Primastone	1973-1977	PRIMA2	15-19
Imperial Blossom	7294			1986-1995	Imperial Baroque	60-85
Imperial Garden	9720			1980-1986	Sheer Ivory Bone	65-82
Imperial Gate	9778			1989-1992	Sheer Ivory Bone	85-94
Imperial Gold	7361			1998	Imperial Baroque	
Imperial Jade	4118			1995-1998	Nor. Ireland I	65
Imperial Platinum	7366			1998	Imperial Baroque	
Impetuous	4708			1992-1997	Sheer Ivory Bone	94-107
Impression, 119						
	8164		N in wreath blk/gld	1977-1982	Victorian IV	25-55
Inca	8505		Folkstone	1975-1981	FOLK1	15-21
Indigo Waltz	4050			1992-1998	Paramount	64
Ingram, 108			M in wreath big bow	1933		
Ingrid						
Innocence	8011			1977-1981	Victorian V	25
Inspiration	2607		N in wreath blk/gld	1976-1984	Remembrance I	24-58
Inspire	2939			1979-1982	Remembrance II	30-48
Integrity	4023			1993-1995	Paramount	57-60
Intuition	4022			1992-1993	Paramount	53-57
Inverness	6716		Contemporary FC Philip	1975-1981	Classic	21-35
Inwood, 51	1871	0014763	M in wreath N/HP/Japan	1909-1930	Original	
Iona, 52			M in wreath N/HP/Japan	1921-1930	Original	
Iona	2180			1975-1978	Commander	22
Irelafnd						
Irene			M in shield China			
Iris			M with crown			
Iris	7940			1997-1998	GG	75
Irmina, 32	6601			1963-1968	Concerto	
Isabella	6531					
Isolde	7019			1975-1978	Victorian II	22-24
Ivanhoe, 111		0086197	M in wreath N/HP/Japan	1933		
Ivanhoe	7264			1982-1987	Remembrance II	55-58
Ivory & Azure	7279			1984-1987	Remembrance II	56-53
Ivory & Ebony	7274			1984-1996	Remembrance II	56-72
Ivory & Mist	7280			1984-1988	Remembrance II	53-60
Ivory & Sienna	7281			1984-1987	Remembrance II	56-53
Ivy Lane	9180		Keltcraft	1991-1998	K-COU	43
Ivyne, 48	6605		N in wreath blk/gld	1966	Triangle	
Jacqueline, 39	6670		N in wreath blk/gld	1968	Classic	
Jacquin		0094549	M in shield China	1934		
Jadestone	7047		Expression	1975-1977	Victorian IV	18-19
Jana						
Janette	6604					
Jania						
Janice			M in shield China			
Jasmine	585		M in wreath small bow			
Jean, 83	6724		N in wreath colorful	1966	LaSalle	
Jenica, 70	3471	0034921	Contemporary Fc Japan	1968	Commander	
Jenna	3760			1987-1993	Nor Ireland I	54-69
Jennifer	2215			1975-1977	Commander	22-24
Jill	7052			1975-1976	Champagne	22
Joan	584		M in wreath small bow			
Joanne	6466					
Joely	7805		Fine China in wreath	1998	New Traditions	
Joliet			M in wreath small bow			
Josephine	6240					
Josette						
Joy	227					
Joy	8777		Craftone	1975-1979	CRAFT2	13-21
Joyce	5174					
Juanita		0076834	M in wreath N/HP/Japan	1931		
Jubilation	2756			1977-1981	Remembrance I	40
Julie	9110		Keltcraft	1982-1990	K-RIM	35-43
Juliet						
June	6448					
June Buds	8552		Folkstone	1975-1977	FOLK2	18-20
Junenight	8631			1980-1982	PROV	25-38
Juno	716	0103057	M in wreath small bow	1936		
Kachina	8458			1995-1998	SFE	44
Karen	2671			1979-1980		
Kashmir						
Kashmir	9303		Versatone	1980-1984	VER1	30-45
Kathleen, 92	6722		N in wreath colorful	1967	Rim	
Katmandu	3670		Legacy Philippines	1986-1992	Commander	69-82
Kelvin	3905		M in wreath small bow			
Kendal	6903		Contemporary FC Philip	1975-1978	Classic	21-23
Keniworth	2026			1974-1975	Commander	22
Kenmare	2773			1981-1982	Nor Ireland I	50
Kennesaw	2170		Cook'n Serve	1975-1976	CNS	
Kenosha			M in wreath N/HP/Japan			
Kensington	2029			1974-1975	Commander	22
Kensington Palace	3696		Legendary Sri Lanka	1986-1989	Commander	50
Kent, 80	5422		N in wreath printed	1954	LaSalle	
Kent	CAB30					
Kenwick	4217		Legendary Sri Lanka	1998	Commander	
Kenwood		0089482	M in shield China	1933	Scolloped edges	
Kerri, 49	6681		N in wreath colorful	1965	Concerto	
Kerrie	8347		Primastone	1978-1982	PRIMA1	21-33
Kerry Spring	9133		Keltcraft	1984-1990	K-RIM	37-43
Keyboard			M in wreath N/HP/Japan			
Khira	7804		Fine China in wreath	1998	New Traditions	
Kiev	9759			1988-1990	Sheer Ivory Bone	85-88
Kilkee	9109		Keltcraft	1981-1993	K-COU	35-50
Killian	4763			1997-1998	Empire	85
Kimberly	9703			1975-1980	Sheer Ivory Bone	55
King's Guard, 38						
	7716		Fine China in wreath	1986-1989	New Traditions	63-82
Kingston, 118			M in wreath NHP Japan	1921-1928	Original	
Kipling	4141		N in wreath blk/gld	1998	Nor Ireland I	
Kirkland, 95	4117			1995-1998	Remembrance II	62
Kiseto	B353		Versatone orient	1979-1983	orient	27-41
Kiva (The), 87			M in wreath N/Nippon		Original	
Knickerbocker	8355		Primastone	1985-1987	PRIMA1	40-46
Knightsbridge	3688		Legendary Sri Lanka	1986-1989	Commander	50
Knollwood, 97		0068483	M in wreath N/HP/Japan	1929	Original	
Knottinghill	4714			1993-1998	Cameo	100
Kontiki	2231		Younger Image	1975-1977	Y/H	13-19
Kristen						
L'amor						
La Madeleine	4307		Factory in shield	1992-1995	Estate	188-220
La Prada	4703			1991-1998	Cameo	88
Lace Shadow, 70						
	3988		N in wreath Sri Lanka	1990-1991	Paramount	50
Lace White	3847			1980-1985	Remembrance II	25-40
Lacewood	3803			1988-1993	w/impressions	60-69
Ladura			M in shield China			
Lady Eve	9777			1989-1994	Royal Pierpont	94-113
Lady Quentin	4730			1994	Sheer Ivory Bone	113
Lady Quentin	4730			1995-1995	Sheer Ivory Bone	115
Lafayette, 37		0058598	M in wreath N/HP/Japan	1927	Original	
Lafleur		0071432	M in wreath N/HP/Japan	1930		
Lake Worth	3699		Legacy Philippines	1986-1996	Commander	69-93
Lamarre	6859		N in wreath printed	1974-1975	LaSalle	
Lamelle	4715			1993-1994	Bone	88-107
Lamita	6881		Contemporary FC Philip	1975-1977	Classic	24
Lanare		0089485	M in shield China	1933		

Name, *Page #*	No.	Design	Backstamp	Time	Form	Value
Lancashire			M in wreath N/HP/Japan			
Lancashire, *92*	3883		N in wreath blk/gld	1988-1996	Paramount	50-60
Landon, *92*	4111		N in wreath blk/gld	1994-1998	Nor Ireland I	71
Laramie, *103*	3754		M in wreath small bow		Scolloped edges	
Laredo				1998	epoch	
Lares			M in wreath small bow			
Larine						
Larkspur	7048		Expression	1975-1977	Victorian IV	18-19
Larue			M in wreath small bow			
Larue	6913			1975-1979	Commander	22-32
LaSalle, *54*		0069535	M in wreath N/HP/Japan	1929		
LaSalle, *97*	5142		M in wreath big bow	1950-1953	Triangle	
Laura	2694		Contemporary FC Philip	1977-1981	Classic	25-27
Laureate, *112*	2132	0061235	M in wreath N/HP/Japan	1928-1930	Original	
Laureate	5651			1956		
Laurel, *45*	5903	0185444	N in wreath printed	1953	Butterfly	
Laurelton			M in wreath N/HP/Japan	1922-1924	Original	
Laurette, *84*	5047		M in wreath big bow	1950-1958		
Lauritz	4005		M in wreath small bow			
Lausanne			M in shield China			
Lautana, *54*			M in shield China			
Lavegas	620		M in wreath small bow			
Laverne, *45*	5810		N in wreath printed	1953	Butterfly	
Laveta	513		K in scroll shield Japan			
Lavin	3814					
Lazarre, *67*			M in wreath N/HP/Japan	1921-1930	Original	
Le Parc	9421			1992-1998	PRIMAC	65
Lebrun			M in wreath N/HP/Japan			
Lehigh						
Leilahi	2206			1975		
Lemonade Sky	9424		New Decade wave	1993-1994	NDC	66-93
Lemonique	9202		Keltcraft	1995-1995	K-RIM	55
Leomore	6676		N in wreath printed			
Leona			M in wreath small bow			
Leonore						
Leroy			M in wreath N/HP/Japan			
Leslie	678		M in wreath small bow			
Lexine			M in wreath N/HP/Japan			
Lexington						
Lila						
Lilac	3914		M in wreath small bow			
Lilac	8527		Folkstone	1973-1977	FOLK2	18-20
Lilac Glow	8402			1984-1985	GRMT	29
Lilac Time	2483			1975-1980		
Lillian						
Lily	8589		Folkstone	1978-1979	FOLK2	27-30
Lily Pond	8406			1984-1985	GRMT	36
Lilybell, *95*	5556		N in wreath printed	1955	Concerto	
Limerick	3064		K in scroll shield Japan	1981-1992	Nor Ireland I	53-65
Lincoln		0068469	M in wreath N/HP/Japan	1929		
Linda	0507		M in wreath N/HP/Japan			
Linden	525	0098217	M in wreath small bow	1935	flying saucer	
Lindrose						
Lindsay	9153		Keltcraft	1987-1988	K-RIM	37
Lindsey	8426			1987-1987	cntp	
Lineage	B306 W12		Versatone	1977-1984	VER1	23-45
Linfield						
Linsay						
Linton	7552		N in wreath ivory	1975-1979	Victorian II	21-30
Linwood, *101*		0011657	M in wreath N/Nippon	1907-1912	Original	
Lisette						
Lisle	3292			1982-1986	Commander	48-51
Lismore		0098836	M in wreath small bow	1935		
Lismore	609	0098836	M in wreath small bow	1935		
Little Daisy	8409			1984-1984	cntp	
Locarno			M in wreath N/HP/Japan			
Lockleigh	4061		White Scapes	1996-1998	w/scapes	50
Lolita	631		M in wreath small bow			
Long Ago	2757			1977-1983	Remembrance I	37-53
Longwood, *75*	2485		Contemporary FC Sri Lanka	1975-1980	Classic	
Lorelei	7541		N in wreath ivory	1975-1980	Champagne	21-35
Lorene	5764			1975-1979		
Lorento, *46*	3852	0112926	M in wreath big bow	1938		
Lorina			M in wreath small bow		Mushroom	
Lorraine	2798		Legacy Philippines	1978-1982	Commander	32-45
Lorraine, *101*			M in wreath N/Nippon	1912-1913	Original	
Lotus			M in wreath N/HP/Japan			
Louise	5204			1953		
Louvaine		0061231	M in wreath N/HP/Japan	1928		
Love Bird	8327		Primastone	1975-1978	PRIMA1	17-18
Love Poem, *94*	4135		N in wreath Philippines	1998	Nor Ireland I	
Love Song						
	8002 W81			1973-1983	Victorian IV	25-58
Loyalo		0098214	M in wreath small bow	1935		
Lucerne	6880		Contemporary FC Philip	1975-1977	Classic	30-34
Lucia						
Lucille, *50*	5813	0183980	N in wreath printed	1953		
Lucine			M in wreath N/HP/Japan			
Luise						
Lunceford, *86*	3884		Legendary Sri Lanka	1988-2000	Commander	50-57
Luray		0095638	M in wreath small bow	1935		
Lurline	4007		M in wreath small bow			
Luxoria		0091602		1934		
Luxoria		0091602	M with crown	1934		
Luzon, *87*			M in wreath N/Nippon	1914-1918	Original	
Lylewood	9760			1988-1995	Sheer Ivory Bone	85-113
Lynbrook	3903		M in wreath small bow			
Lynbrook, *108*	4724		M in wreath big bow	1933		
Lyndenwood	4707			1992-1998	Sheer Ivory Bone	94
Lyndhurst	9762			1988-1991	Royal Pierpont	90-94
Lynnbrook	2790		Contemporary FC Philip	1977-1982	Classic	27-45
Lynne						
Lynrose			M in wreath small bow			
Lynwood, *47*	5307		N in wreath printed	1953		
Lyric			M in wreath N/HP/Japan			
Lyric	9570			1975-1976	Sheer Ivory Bone	36
Macon	6717		Contemporary FC Philip	1975-1977	Classic	22-20
Madera	5106		M in wreath big bow			
Madera Blue	8476		stoneware	1975-1998	CNCP1	
Madera Ivory	8474		stoneware	1998	CNCP1	
Madera Peach	8478		stoneware	1998	CNCP1	
Madera Sea Foam	8477		stoneware	1998	CNCP1	
Madera Spruce	8475		stoneware	1998	CNCP1	
Madrigal	8352		Primastone	1981-1983	PRIMA1	27-41
Magenta, *88*			M in wreath N/Nippon	1918	Original	
Magnificence	9736			1984-1996	Sheer Ivory Bone	70-107
Magnolia	3918		M in wreath small bow			
Mahogany	8756		Craftone	1975-1977	CRAFT1	10-20
Mai-Tai	2234		Younger Image	1975-1977	Y/H	13-19
Maison Fleur	4301		Factory in shield	1991-1998	Estate	110
Majestic		0058596	M in wreath N/HP/Japan	1927		
Malabar	8308		Primastone	1975-1977	PRIMA1	13-19
Malaga	8301		Primastone	1975-1977	PRIMA1	15-19
Malay (The)		0013857	M in wreath N/Nippon	1908	Original	
Malibu	3700		M in wreath small bow			
Malibu	5823		N in wreath printed	1953		
Mallard	8652			1981-1986	PROV	38-41
Malvern, *53*		0069538	M in wreath N/HP/Japan	1929	Original	
Malverne	3501			1985-1996	Remembrance II	50-60
Mandalay	3393		Legacy Philippines	1983-1987	Commander	69-70
Mandarin Garden	9743		M in wreath N/Nippon	1985-1993	Sheer Ivory Bone	73-100
Mantigo	8167			1980-1985	Victorian V	40-53
Maple Shade	9187		Keltcraft	1992-1994	K-RIM	43-53

Name, _Page #_	No.	Design	Backstamp	Time	Form	Value
Maplewood	109		Cook'n Serve	1975	CNS	
Marble						
Canyon	9418		New Decade wave	1989-1994	NDC	58-66
Marblehill	3460			1984-1985	Nor. Ireland II	65
Marcell		0086199	M in wreath N/HP/Japan	1933		
Marcia, _100_	3855		M in wreath big bow	1933		
Marcisite		0087196	M in wreath N/HP/Japan	1933		
Marcola			M in shield China			
Mardi Gras	9019		Progression N	1975-1979	P1	24-38
Margaret	6243					
Margarita	5049		M in wreath big bow			
Margate			M in wreath N/HP/Japan		Original	
Margo			M in wreath sm bow 2 leaf			
Margot, _80_	5605		M in wreath bow Occupied	1956		
Marguerite, _73_	6730	0209009	Cook'n Serve	1975-1977	CNS-C	19
Marguerite			M in wreath N/Nippon			
Mandarin						
Mariana		0076972	M in wreath N/HP/Japan	1931		
Marie			M in shield China			
Marie Claire	8790			1985-1985	jfs	25
Mariel	3802			1988-1989	Remembrance II	50
Marigold, _116_		0071436	M in wreath N/HP/Japan	1930		
Marilyn, _106_		0080467	M in wreath N/HP/Japan	1932		
Marine Buffet	9434		New Decade wave	1995-1995	NDC	63
Mariposa	319		M in scroll & wreath			
Mariposa, _91_	6411		N in wreath, colorful	1963		
Marlboro			M in shield China			
Marlborough				1920		
Marlene, _108_		0095642	M in wreath small bow	1935		
Marne (The)			M in wreath N/Nippon		Original	
Marquerte			M in wreath N/HP/Nippon	1912-1913		
Marquis	7540		N in wreath ivory	1974	Champagne	
Marseilles, _61_	7550		N in wreath ivory	1975-1982	Victorian II	21-48
Marsellies			M in wreath N/HP/Japan	1919-1920		
Marshmallow	8585		Folkstone	1978-1981	FOLK2	22
Marvelle, _54_	304		M in scrolls	1933		
Marywood, _93_	2181		Contemporary FC Philip	1975-1996	Classic	25-54
Matchmaker						
	B304 W11		Versatone	1977-1984	VER1	23-45
Maureen	6728			1975-1979		
Mavis	5543			1955		
May Breeze	9410		New Decade wave	1988-1991	NDC	48-58
May Garden	2355			1975-1983	Commander	21-51
May Song	8553		Folkstone	1975-1978	FOLK2	18-20
Maya, _35_	6213	0196309	N in wreath printed	1955	LaSalle	
Mayfair, _81_	6109		N in wreath printed	1961	Coupe	
Mayfield						
Mayfield	7280		M in wreath sm bow 2 leaf		Form	
Mayflower		0076582	M in wreath N/HP/Japan	1931		
Mayflower, _82_	2351		N in wreath blk/gld	1975-1983	Commander	21-51
Maytone, _40_	2359		Contemporary FC Philip	1975-1980	Classic	25-27
Mayville		0069541	M in wreath N/HP/Japan	1929	Original	
McKenzie	4112			1994-1995	Nor Ireland I	72-75
Meadow	7250			1979-1983	Remembrance II	32-56
Meadow Spray	9204		Keltcraft	1995-1995	K-RIM	55
Meadowcrest	4034		Legendary Sri Lanka	1993-1994	Commander	54-57
Meadowside	4114			1994-1995	Remembrance II	60-62
Medallion	8225			1978-1983	Victorian IV	32-58
Medean	712		M in wreath small bow			
Mediterranean	2039			1975-1976	Commander	24
Medley	8771		Craftone	1975-1978	CRAFT3	13-16
Medusa			M in wreath sm bow 2 leaf			
Melissa	3080		Contemporary FC Philip	1980-1992	Classic	30-50
Melita, _74_	6205		N in wreath printed	1962	Rim	
Melody	7212			1976-1981	Victorian coupe II	22-37
Melrose	370		M in wreath small bow			
Melrose	6002			1976-1979		
Memorabilia	7916			1992-1994	GALA	73-79
Memorable	2936			1979-1981		
Memory	2882		Contemporary FC Philip	1978-1985	Classic	25-46
Mendelson	4723			1995-1999	Masters Collection	198
Mendocino	9149		Keltcraft misty isle	1986-1992	K-MI	37-43
Mendon	8687			1991-1991	CENT	65
Mentone						
Merida	515					
Merina Gold	7802		Fine China in wreath	1998	New Traditions	
Merina						
Platinum	7803		Fine China in wreath	1998	New Traditions	
Meringo, _111_			M in wreath N/HP/Japan			
Merlin		0108380	M in wreath sm bow 2 leaf	1936		
Merry						
Mushroom	B970			1979-1980	PRIMA1	
Mesa	6370					
Metarie	4108			1993-1994	Remembrance II	57-60
Metronome	8691			1992-1994	OPT	58-64
Metz (The), _33_			M in wreath N/Nippon	1912-1913	Original	
Mi Amor	4717			1993-1998	Masters Collection	119
Michelle						
Midnight Fest	9206		Keltcraft	1995-1995	K-RIM	55
Midnight						
Majesty	7295			1986-1990	Imperial Baroque	60-70
Midsummer	8762		Craftone	1975-1977	CRAFT2	12-20
Mignon			M with crown			
Mikado (The)			R.C. with hat		Original	
Milford		0089486	M in shield China	1933		
Milford, _92_	2227		N in wreath blk/gld	1968-1985	Commander	21-51
Mimi, _100_		0098141	M in wreath small bow	1935		
Minaret		0078049	M in wreath N/HP/Japan	1931		
Minerva		0069542	M in wreath N/HP/Japan	1929		
Ming	2931			1979-1982	Remembrance II	30-48
Ming Garden	9066		Progression N	1975-1980	P1	24-38
Ming Treasure	7304			1988-1989	Imperial Baroque	70
Mirabelle	3843	0114075	M in wreath small bow	1939		
Mirano, _71_	6878		Contemporary FC Philip	1975-1979	Classic	24-35
Misty, _60_	2883		Contemporary FC Philip	1978-1989	Classic	25-46
Miyoshi	7194			1975-1986	Victorian coupe II	24-56
Mo-Bay	2162		Younger Image	1975-1977	Y/H	13-19
Modesta		0069546	M in wreath N/HP/Japan	1930		
Modjeska		0076837	M in wreath N/HP/Japan	1931	Azalea	
Momentum	7734		Fine China in wreath	1991-1999	New Traditions	85
Monaco, _60_	6725		N in wreath blk/gld	1968		
Monarch		0086216		1933		
Monica			M in wreath N/HP/Japan			
Montblanc	7527		N in wreath ivory	1974	Champagne	
Montclare, _72_		0058595	M in wreath N/HP/Japan	1927		
Montebelle		0080466	M in wreath N/HP/Japan	1932	Mushroom	
Montego				1998	epoch	
Montego Bay	9155		Keltcraft	1987-1988	K-RIM	37
Monteleone	7569		N in wreath ivory	1975-1984	Victorian II	22-56
Monterey, _40_	2211		N in wreath blk/gld	1921-1938	Concerto	21
Monterey, _97_		0058595	R.C. hand painted Nippon	1927	Original	
Moon Valley	7044		Expression	1975-1977	Victorian IV	18-19
Moonbeam	7149			1975-1982	Victorian II	22-48
Moonflight	B971		Primastone	1978-1986	PRIMA1	25-47
Moonlight						
Rose	7288			1986-1989	Remembrance II	53-60
Moor	8604		stoneware	1978-1981	CNCP1	16-21
Morning Jewel	2767			1981-1990	Nor Ireland I	53-60
Morning						
Melody	9158		Keltcraft misty isle	1987-1993	K-MI	37-50
Morning Poem	4100			1991-1992	Remembrance II	50-53
Morning Song	8763		Craftone	1975-1977	CRAFT2	12
Morro Bay	9419		New Decade wave	1989-1990	NDC	58
Moselle	723		M in wreath small bow			
Mountain						
Flowers	8343		Primastone	1976-1983	PRIMA1	17-41

Name, *Page #*	No.	Design	Backstamp	Time	Form	Value
Mountain						
View	8653			1981-1986	PROV	38-41
Muriel	611	0098838	M in wreath big bow	1935		
Murmur	3017			1980-1982	Remembrance II	35-48
Musetta	3702		M in wreath small bow			
Mushroom						
Magic	8408		1984-1985	GRMT	36	
Mystic Ridge	8690			1991-1992	CNCP1	43-46
Nadine	8035		M in wreath small bow			
Namiki	108					
Nanarosa	682	0098218	M in wreath small bow	1935		
Nanarosa	4902		M in wreath big bow	1933		
Nancy	3402		Rose China with N			
Nanette	683		M in wreath small bow			
Nanking	2860			1981-1985	Nor Ireland I	53-65
Nantes	2553			1975-1984	Commander	22-51
Naomi	674		M in wreath small bow			
Naomi	4901					
Napa Valley	8336		Primastone	1975-1978	PRIMA3	17-18
Naples, *43*	6975		N in wreath blk/gld	1968	LaSalle	
Nashua			M in wreath N/HP/Japan			
Natalie	5815		N in wreath printed	1953		
Nature's						
Bounty	9199		Keltcraft	1994-1998	K-COU	53
Navarre, *58*		0069545	M in wreath N/HP/Japan	1929-1934	Original	
Nerrisa						
(Nerissa)	673	0103009	M in wreath small bow	1936		
New Apple						
Blossom	E941N			1998	epoch	
New Castle	9309		Versatone	1982-1985	VER1	40-45
New Charm, *67*						
	6522		N in wreath blk/gld	1968	LaSalle	
New Delight	7709		Fine China in wreath	1985-1985	New Traditions	60
New Destiny	3687		Legendary Sri Lanka	1986-1989	Commander	50
New Drama	3453			1984-1984	ART DECO	
New Hope	9134		Keltcraft	1984-1987	K-RIM	37
New Morn	3455			1984-1984	ART DECO	
New Orleans	9401		New Decade wave	1987-1990	2000	48-58
New Sante Fe	8510		Folkstone	1975-1981	FOLK1	15-22
New Stockholm						
	E701N			1998	epoch	
New Sweet						
Dreams	E940N			1998	epoch	
New West	8696			1992-1998	SFE	44
New Yorker	9400		New Decade wave	1987-1990	2000	48-58
Newburg	4092			1998		
Newbury	3601			1985-1998	Remembrance II	50
Nicolette, *92*	6713		N in wreath	1967		
Nicosia	6882		N in wreath blk/gld	1975-1976	Concerto	21
Night Jewel	7731		Fine China in wreath	1989-1994	New Traditions	82
Night Life	3603		Sea & Sky	1986-1989	SS	46-47
Nightsong	7268			1982-1989	Remembrance II	55-60
Nile	6719					
Nile Glow	8404			1985-1985	GRMT	29
Nimbus	8628		stoneware	1979-1986	CNCP1	16-36
Nina, *34*	6667		N in wreath colorful	1965	Classic	
Ninon	6609		N in wreath printed		concerto	
Noble	2600					
Noblesse	7902			1973-1983	Victorian coupe II	40-120
NO NAME, 58		0010733	N in wreath N/HP/Japan	1912		
NO NAME		0013680	M in wreath N/Nippon	1908		
NO NAME, 78		0014800	M in wreath/HP/Japam	1909	Original	
NO NAME		0026979	M in wreath N/HP/Japam	1915		
NO NAME		0027462	R.C. with clackers		Original	
NO NAME		0044318	M in wreath N/HP/Japan	1923		
NO NAME		0061229	M in wreath N/HP/Japan	1928		
NO NAME, 112		0061240	M in wreath N/HP/Japan	1928	Original	
NO NAME, 65		0077630	M in wreath N/HP/Japan	1931	Original	
NO NAME		0098846		1935		
NO NAME		0098846	M in wreath small bow	1935		
NO NAME		0101207	M in wreath small bow	1936		
NO NAME		0101270		1936		
NO NAME, 56	228		RC in wreath	1956-1960	coupe	
NO NAME, 81	590		RC in wreath	1956	rim	
NO NAME, 71	1356		N in wreath printed			
NO NAME	1357		N in wreath printed	1976	Remembrance I	21
NO NAME	1359			1959	Triangle	
NO NAME	1802		K in scroll shield NTK		Mushroom	
NO NAME, 66	4789		M in wreath bow Occupied	1949		
NO NAME, 66	4986		M in wreath big bow	1933		
NO NAME	5020		M in wreath small bow			
NO NAME	5295					
NO NAME, 73	5329		M in wreath bow Occupied	1949	LaSalle	
NO NAME, 47	5471		N in wreath printed	1954	LaSalle	
NO NAME, 47	5487		N in wreath printed	1954	LaSalle	
NO NAME	5528		N in wreath printed	1953		
NO NAME, 69	5548		N in wreath printed		Triangle	
NO NAME, 45	5550		N in wreath printed	1955	Butterfly	
NO NAME	5559		N in wreath printed	1953		
NO NAME	5564			1955		
NO NAME	5612		K in scroll shield NTK	1956		
NO NAME, 79	6234		M in wreath big bow	1933		
Nora, *119*	7546		N in wreath ivory	1975	Champagne	
Nordich		0081857	M in wreath N/HP/Japan	1932	Original	
Norma	518		M in wreath N/HP/Japan			
Norma	7016			1975-1983	Victorian II	22-56
Normandy, *54*	8162		N in wreath blk/gld	1979-1985	Victorian IV	25-58
Norway	E2003			1998	epoch	
Norwich	6042		M in wreath bow Occupied	1950	Rose China	
Norwood	6011					
Nouveau	2402		Contemporary FC Philip	1975-1980	Classic	21-35
Nuana	5129		M in wreath big bow	1933		
Nutmeg	9117		Keltcraft	1982-1987	K-RIM	26-37
Oak Hill	8412			1984-1984	cntp	
Oakbrook	E520			1998	epoch	
Oakleigh	4082		White Scapes	1996-1998	w/scapes	50
Oakmont	3808			1988-1993	w/impressions	60-69
Oberlin, *42*	2486		Contemporary FC Sri Lanka	1975-1980		
Oberon	661		M in wreath small bow			
Ocean Melody	9417		New Decade wave	1989-1994	NDC	58-66
Oceanic	8509		Folkstone	1975-1976	FOLK1	12
Oceanica	8623		Folkstone	1979-1981	FOLK2	24
October Fest	8555		Folkstone	1975-1981	FOLK2	18-30
October Light, *53*						
	4095		Impromtu Sri Lanka	1998	Paramount	
Odin	B961		Primastone	1976-1982	PRIMA1	15-33
Ole	9043		Progression N	1975-1977	P1	24
Olive Wreath	8684			1990-1992	CENT	65
Olympia	680		M in wreath small bow			
Ontario	3763			1988-1998	Nor Ireland I	60
Ooello			M in wreath sm bow 2 leaf			
Options						
(Black)	8440			1993-1995	OPT	46-49
Options						
(Green)	8442			1993-1995	OPT	46-49
Options						
(Yellow)	8441			1993-1995	OPT	46-49
Opulence	9799			1991-1998	Masters Collection	175
Oradell, *103*	588		M in wreath big bow	1933-1935	Mushroom	
Orange County	2168		Cook'n Serve	1975-1976	CNS	
Orchard Spring	9224			1997-1998	HC	
Ordway			M in wreath N/HP/Japan	1933		
Orient Point	7298			1987-1991	Remembrance II	54-60
Oriental, *48*	6341		N in wreath printed	1953-1968	Concerto	
Oriental Blue	1922				Original	
Oriental Dream	9102		Keltcraft	1980-1985	K-COU	35-37

Name	Page #	No.	Design	Backstamp	Time	Form	Value
Oriental Garden		8528		Folkstone	1973-1978	FOLK2	17-20
Orinda		8540		Folkstone	1974-1981	FOLK2	18-30
Ormond				M in wreath N/HP/Japan	1922	Original	
Ormonde Bassett	77						
			0014369	M in wreath N/HP/Japan	1909	Original	
Ormonde Russfit				M in wreath N/HP/Japan		Original	
Outlook		B305 W10		Versatone	1977-1985	VER1	23-45
Overture		9086		Progression N	1978-1983	P2	24-55
Oxford	118		0085963	M in wreath N/HP/Japan	1935	Original	
Oxford	42	5767		N in wreath printed	1953	LaSalle	
Oxford Lane		4020			1992-1994	Commander	54-57
Pacific Grove		9147		Keltcraft	1986-1987	K-RIM	37
Pacific Hill		4220			1997-1998	Prelude	50
Pacific Majesty		9771			1988-1998	Masters Collection	105
Pacific Winds		9420		New Decade wave	1992-1995	NDC	60-68
Pacifica		8307		Primastone	1975-1977	PRIMA1	13-19
Pagoda (The)				M in wreath N/Nippon			
Painted Desert		8603		stoneware	1978-1992	CNCP1	16-46
Paisley			0069543	M in wreath N/HP/Japan	1929		
Palace Guard		4308		Factory in shield	1992-1994	Estate	188-212
Palais Royal		9773			1989-1998	Royal Pierpont	94
Palestra	42	4762		New Lineage	1997-1998	Empire	
Palos Verde		9020		Progression N	1975-1980	P1	24-38
Pansy		7940			1997-1998	GG	
Paradise		8223 W80			1975-1985	Victorian IV	25-58
Paradise Tribute		4042			1994-1999	Paramount	68
Paragon			0074083	M in wreath N/HP/Japan	1930		
Parchment		B329 W30		Versatone	1979-1985	VER1	25-43
Paris		9727			1980-1996	Sheer Ivory Bone	60-98
Paris Opera		4718			1993-1993	Masters Collection	119
Parisian Border				M in wreath N/HP/Japan	1924	Original	
Parisian Lace		3680		Legendary Sri Lanka	1985-1990	Commander	50
Park Suite		4102			1991-1999	Remembrance II	50
Parkhill		9734			1983-1990	Sheer Ivory Bone	70-73
Parkridge	120	7561		N in wreath ivory	1975-1986	Victorian II	21-51
Parkside		B309		Versatone	1978-1982	VER1	27-40
Parnell		302		M in scrolls		Rose China	
Partners		9127		Keltcraft	1983-1990	K-RIM	36-43
Pasadena	111			M in wreath N/HP/Japan	1918		
Pasadena	81	6311		N in wreath printed	1963-1978	Concerto	21-23
Pastelle				M in wreath N/HP/Japan			
Pastoral		2049		Cook'n Serve	1975-1976	CNS	
Patches		B302 W10		Versatone	1977-1981	VER1	23-30
Patience		2964			1981-1991	Nor Ireland I	53-63
Patrice		6901			1975-1976	Concerto	21
Patricia	120	7551		N in wreath ivory	1975	Victorian II	
Patrician				M in wreath N/HP/Japan			
Paula		2158			1975-1982	Commander	21-48
Pauline	82	6586		N in wreath colorful	1963-1968	LaSalle	
Peachtree Manor		9175		Country Diary	1989-1990	K-DIARY	50
Pearl White		9006		Progression N	1975-1980	P1	24-38
Pekin				M in wreath N/HP/Japan			
Peking		2229			1975-1983	Commander	21-53
Pembroke		2892		Contemporary FC Philip	1978-1983	Classic	25-46
Pendarvis	105			M in wreath N/HP/Japan			
Penelope			0076837	M in wreath N/HP/Japan	1931		
Penelope		4781		M in wreath N/HP/Nippon			
Penrosa		3886					
Penzance		8358		Primastone	1988-1993	PRIMA1	43-58
Peonia		8010 W81			1975-1982	Victorian IV	25-55
Peony		5053		M in wreath big bow			
Peonytime		9100		Keltcraft	1980-1985	K-COU	35-37
Perdita			0078054	M in wreath N/HP/Japan	1931		
Perdita		6873		N in wreath printed	1974-1975	LaSalle	
Perseus			0078053	M in wreath N/HP/Japan	1931		
Persia		2403			1975-1979	Classic	22-32
Petal Perfect		9140		Keltcraft misty isle	1985-1987	K-MI	37
Petals Plus		9071		Progression N	1975-1981	P2	24-38
Petite	94	5507	0176125	N in wreath printed	1951-1953		
Pheasant				M in wreath N/HP/Japan		Original	
Philharmonic		4706			1992-1995	Sheer Ivory Bone	94-113
Phoebe		659	0103008	M in wreath small bow	1936		
Phoenix Bird				M hanging wreath			
Phyllis	98	318		M in scrolls	1933		
Picnic		8755		Craftone	1975-1977	CRAFT1	10-20
Piedmont	106			M in shield China	1931		
Pierepoint	24			M in wreath N/HP/Japan	1918		
Pilgrim	30	6981		N in wreath blk/gld	1970		
Pinetta	47	5689		N in wreath printed	1956	Butterfly	
Pink Poppy	79	514		K in scroll shield/Japan	1947	Rose China	
Pinnacle	29	2019			1963-1970	Coupe	
Pizzicato		8582		Folkstone	1977-1979	FOLK2	30
Platinum Lights		7292			1984-1990	Remembrance II	53-60
Platinum Serenade		7715		Fine China in wreath	1985-1988	New Traditions	53-64
Plaza	106			M in wreath sm bow 2 leaf	1930		
Pleasure		8344		Primastone	1978-1989	PRIMA1	21-50
Pledge		2938			1979-1982	Remembrance II	30-48
Plenty		8573		Folkstone	1976-1979	FOLK2	18-30
Plum Orchid		9098		New Decade wave	1986-1989	NDC	40-50
Poetry		2997		Contemporary FC Philip	1979-1985	Classic	27-46
Polar		8606		stoneware	1978-1982	CNCP1	16-33
Polka		8758		Craftone	1975-1977	CRAFT2	12-20
Polonaise		2045		N in wreath blk/gld	1975-1986	Commander	30-90
Pomegranate		8636		stoneware	1980-1982	CNCP1	21-33
Ponchartrain		7024			1975-1976	Victorian II	22
Portfolio	38	7736		Fine China in wreath	1991-1999	New Traditions	85
Portland	77		0013673	M in wreath N/Nippon	1908-1920	Original	
Potpourri		8786		Craftone	1975-1980	CRAFT2	13-21
Prairie Song		8676			1988-1989	SFE	50-54
Prelude	43	7570		N in wreath ivory	1975-1982	Victorian II	22-53
Premier				M in wreath N/HP/Japan			
Prescott		3880		Legendary Sri Lanka	1988-1996	Commander	46-57
Primadonna		6608					
Primary		8319		Primastone	1973-1977	PRIMA2	13-19
Primavera		7017			1974-1975	Champagne	21
Primula		7940			1997-1998	GG	
Princess	91			N in wreath x stems NTK	1953	coupe	
Princeton				M in wreath N/Nippon			
Princeton	85	6911		N in wreath blk/gld	1968-1985	Commander	21-53
Promise Me		8221 W80			1973-1982	Victorian IV	25-55
Prosperity	50	6841		N in wreath blk/gld	1970	Concerto	
Providence		8572		Folkstone	1976-1979	FOLK2	18-29
Pueblo		8588		Folkstone	1978-1981	FOLK2	27-30
Pueblo Moon		8457			1995-1999	SFE	44
Purity Gold		4725			1994-1999	Bone	83
Purity White		4726			1994-1999	Bone	83
Pursuit		9170		Keltcraft	1988-1998	K-RIM	50
Quadrangle		8306		Primastone	1975-1977	PRIMA1	15-19
Queen's Guard		7712		Fine China in wreath	1985-1989	New Traditions	63-82
Queen's Splendor		9746			1986-1989	Royal Pierpont	78-94
Queenanne		4018		M in wreath small bow			
Queens Mark		4310		Factory in shield	1994-1998	Estate	125
Quentin		3202			1982-1983	Elegance	55-58
Radcliffe				M in wreath N/HP/Japan			
Radiant		8322		Primastone	1973-1977	PRIMA2	13-19
Ragtime		8761		Craftone	1975-1977	CRAFT2	12-20
Rainbow			0117791		1939		
Rainbow End		8405			1984-1986	GRMT	36

Name, *Page #*	No.	Design	Backstamp	Time	Form	Value
Sand Ring	8418			1984-1984	cntp	
Sandhurst	9742			1985-1998	Royal Pierpont	77
Sandra	3062		K in scroll shield Japan			
Sanford	5860		N in wreath printed			
Santa Barbara	9405		New Decade wave	1987-1990	2000	48-58
Santa Rosa	9111		Keltcraft	1982-1985	K-RIM	35-37
Santiago	9307 W41		Versatone	1981-1985	VER1	40-45
Sapphire Cathedral	9787			1990-1992	Sheer Ivory Bone	88-94
Satin Gown	7730		Fine China in wreath	1989-1999	New Traditions	82
Savannah, *85*	2031		N in wreath blk/gld	1970-1991	Commander	21-54
Savoia	4003		M in wreath small bow			
Savona		0068470	M in wreath N/HP/Japan	1929		
Savoy, *112*			M in wreath N/HP/Japan	1918-1924	Original	
Savoy	3340 3/340			1975-1978	Concerto	
Savoy	5825			1975-1979		
Scala	2761			1982-1983	Nor Ireland I	50
Scandia				1998-1999	epoch	
Scarborough	7272			1983-1987	Remembrance II	53
Scenic(tree in meadow)			M in wreath N/HP/Japan	1927-1934	Azalea	
Scheherazade	2044			1975-1983	Commander	30-90
Sea Gems	B137		Sea & Sky	1985-1989	SS	33-40
Sea Mist	8310		Primastone	1975-1977	PRIMA1	13-19
Seabreeze	B336 W20		Versatone II	1978-1982	VER2	25-38
Seafoam	8624			1979-1982	cas2	24-38
Séance	3791		Legendary Sri Lanka	1987-1996	Commander	46-54
Seaview	B978		Primastone	1983-1986	PRIMA1	47
Secret Love	3481		Legendary Sri Lanka	1984-1988	Commander	46
Sedalia		0080553	M in wreath N/HP/Japan	1932		
Sedan	D1441					
Sedan, *102*		0011292	M in wreath N/Nippon	1907-1912	Original	
Sedgwick	2023			1974-1975	Concerto	
Segovia	2216			1975-1984	Commander	22-56
Selene, *36*	7536		N in wreath ivory	1974	Champagne	
Selika			M in wreath sm bow 2 leaf			
September Song, *68*	2048		Cook'n Serve	1975-1977	CNS-C	19
Serena	3840					
Serene Garden	7164			1975-1982	Victorian III	22-53
Serenity	2218			1975-1977	Commander	23
Sestina	9761			1988-1993	Sheer Ivory Bone	85-100
Severy		0081603	M in wreath N/HP/Japan	1932		
Sevilla	2795		Legacy Philippines	1978-1982	Commander	27-45
Seville		0058584	M in wreath N/Nippon	1927		
Seville	6521		N in wreath blk/gld	1968	Coupe	
Sezanne	6851			1975-1977	Concerto	21-23
Shahzada	3090		Legacy Philippines	1980-1983	Commander	75-120
Shamrock	9108		Keltcraft	1981-1983	K-COU	35-36
Shangri-La	2363			1975-1980	Commander	22-37
Shannon Spring	9200		Keltcraft	1979-1998	K-COU	53
Sharon			M in shield China	1975-1979	flying saucer	
Sharon	3057		K in scroll shield Japan			
Sharon	6883		Contemporary FC Philip	1975-1977	Classic	24-26
Sharon's Dream	3580		Legendary Sri Lanka	1985-1988	Commander	46
Shasta, *73*	2167		Cook'n Serve	1974-1975	CNS	
Shasta, *74*	5305		N in wreath printed	1953		
Sheila, *98*	2155		N in wreath blk/gld	1975-1976	Concerto	22
Shelburne	5316		N in wreath printed			
Shelby	3623		M in wreath small bow			
Shelton	4739		New Lineage bone china	1996-1998	New Lineage	85
Shenandoah	8581		Folkstone	1977-1977	FOLK2	20
Shenandoah	9054		Progression N	1974-1975	P1	24
Shenandoah	9729			1981-1998	Sheer Ivory Bone	65
Sheridan, *89*		0069533	M in wreath N/HP/Japan	1929-1932	Azalea	
Sheridan, *97*	5441		N in wreath printed	1929-1953		
Sherwood	9129		Keltcraft misty isle	1983-1984	K-MI	36
Shila		0071854	M in wreath N/HP/Japan	1930		
Shirley, *112*			M in wreath N/HP/Japan	1918		
Shrewsbury	3490		Legendary Sri Lanka	1984-1991	Commander	46
Sienna Sunset	4036			1994-1994	Paramount	68
Sierra	3871					
Sierra	8648		stoneware	1981-1983	CNCP1	33-36
Sierra Twilight	8667		stoneware	1986-1995	CNCP1	36-55
Silk Garland	3792		Legendary Sri Lanka	1988-2000	Commander	46-57
Silk Ribbons	3996			1990-1998	Remembrance II	50
Silk Road	8502		Folkstone	1975-1977	FOLK1	15-18
Silphium	7940			1997-1998	GG	
Silverdale	5594		N in wreath printed	1955		
Silverkey	5941		N in wreath printed	1953		
Silvester	6340					
Simone, *90*	6407		N in wreath colorful	1963	Concerto	
Simplicity in Blue	B132		Simplicity in blue	1980-1986	Elegance	53-56
Sinclair	4738		New Lineage bone china	1996-1999	New Lineage	85
Slate	9118		Keltcraft	1982-1986	K-RIM	26-28
Smartnis, *106*		0053569	M in shield China	1926	flying saucer	
Smithfield	3203			1982-1987	Elegance	55-58
Snow Field, *119*	7961		Contemporary FC Japan	1984-1986	Victorian II	53
Snow Petal	3986		Legendary Sri Lanka	1990-1992	Commander	50-54
Snowcap	8639			1980-1982	PROV	22-33
Snowden	6354		N in wreath printed			
Snowflake	8523		Folkstone	1973-1977	FOLK2	18-20
Snowville	6453					
Society Orchid	9097		New Decade wave	1986-1988	NDC	40-48
Society Satin	7722		Fine China in wreath	1987-1991	New Traditions	73-85
Softly	B962		Primastone	1977-1979	PRIMA3	30
Solemn Amber	7320			1989-1992	Imperial Baroque	150
Solemn Emerald	7322			1989-1998	Imperial Baroque	150
Solemn Sapphire	7321			1989-1991	Imperial Baroque	150
Somerset			M in shield China			
Somerset	5317		N in wreath printed	1953		
Sometsuke	B352		Versatone orient	1979-1983	Orient	27-41
Sonata	3360			1983-1986	Nor Ireland II	53-65
Sonoda	4907					
Sonoma, *29*	6353		N in wreath printed	1968-1978	Butterfly	
Sonoma	B964		Primastone	1977-1980	PRIMA3	30
Sonoma Gardens	7936			1998	IMPR	
Sonora	3940	0117814	M in wreath small bow	1939		
Sorcerer	8620		stoneware	1978-1991	CNCP1	16-43
Soroya, *85*	6853		N in wreath	1968-1977	Concerto	21-23
Sorrento, *53*		0076965	M in wreath N/HP/Japan	1931	Original	
Sorrento, *61*	7565		N in wreath ivory	1969	Victorian II	
South Pacific	8503		Folkstone	1975-1977	FOLK1	15-18
Southern Estate, *49*	4734		Lamp bone china gld/blk	1994-1997	Sheer Ivory Bone	92
Southern Glow	9005		Progression N	1974-1975	P1	24
Southern Lace	7301			1987-2000	Imperial Baroque	64-88
Southgate	9725 W32			1980-1985	Sheer Ivory Bone	75-88
Southhaven	4757			1998	Sheer Ivory Bone	
Southmoor	3801			1988-1989	Remembrance II	50
Southwood	9191		Keltcraft misty isle	1992-1995	K-MI	43-53
Spectrum	2983		Contemporary FC Philip	1983-1998	Classic	40
Spell Binder, *71*	9733		Lamp bone china gld/blk	1983-1993	Sheer Ivory Bone	85-100
Spice Blossoms	E527			1998	epoch	
Spinnaker	8304		Primastone	1975-1977	PRIMA1	15-19
Splendor, *122*	7235		N in wreath ivory	1978-1989	Victorian II	29-53

Name, *Page #*	No.	Design	Backstamp	Time	Form	Value
Sports Page	4080			1987-1998	Paramount	74
Spring Blush	9092		New Decade wave	1985-1991	NDC	40-58
Spring Debut	9197		Keltcraft	1994-1994	K-RIM	53
Spring Garden	2551			1975-1982	Commander	22-48
Spring Meadow	2484			1976-1984		
Spring Orchid	9165		Keltcraft	1988-1989	K-COU	37-40
Spring Rhapsody	3661			1975-1987	Nor Ireland I	53
Spring Song	2354			1975-1981	Commander	21-35
Spring Venture	7282			1985-1989	Remembrance II	53-60
Springfield	2932			1979-1986	Remembrance II	30-53
Springlike	8632			1980-1982	PROV	25-38
Springlow	2935			1979-1981		
Springtide	8783		Craftone	1976-1979	CRAFT3	17-21
Springtime	3417			1975-1979	Remembrance II	
Squirewood	4013			1991-1998	Paramount	50
St Regis	1919					
Stanford	5220		M in wreath small bow			
Stanford Court	9748			1986-1998	Sheer IvoryBone	73
Stanleigh			M in wreath N/HP/Japan		Original	
Stanton	5407		N in wreath printed	1953		
Stanwyck	3913		M in wreath small bow			
Stanwyck, *39*	5818	0182091	M in wreath bow Occupied	1949-1953		
Stardust	2603		N in wreath blk/gld	1976-1984	Remembrance I	22-53
Stenmark	4747			1997-1998	Empire	85
Stepping High	9181		Keltcraft	1991-1992	K-COU	43
Sterling Cove	7720		Fine China in wreath	1986-1999	New Traditions	63
Sterling Tide	7740		Fine China in wreath	1992-1999	New Traditions	90
Sterling Tribute	9770		1988-1998	Masters Collection		85
Stockbridge	3462			1984-1985	Nor Ireland I	53
Stoneleigh	4062		White Scapes	1996-1998	w/scapes	50
Stratford	3709					
Strawberry Delight	8671			1987-1993	CENT	48-57
String of Pearls	6480		Legendary Sri Lanka	1984-1988	Commander	46
Suddenly	7297			1987-1989	Remembrance II	54—60
Sue	2157			1975-1977	Commander	21
Suffolk	7549		N in wreath ivory	1974	Victorian II	
Sumiye	B351 W10		Versatone orient	1979-1983	orient	27-41
Summer Blossom	9306 W		Versatone	1981-1983	VER1	40-45
Summer Dreams	9090		New Decade wave	1985-1987	NDC	40-48
Summer Dreams	B351 W10		Versatone	1979-1980	VER1	30
Summer Estate	9212			1996-1998	HC	65
Summer Eve	7163			1975-1981	Victorian III	22-37
Summer Gold	4742		New Lineage bone china	1996-1998	New Lineage	85
Summer Hill	E530			1998	epoch	
Summer Magic	9205		Keltcraft	1995-1995	K-RIM	55
Summer Rain	9185		Keltcraft misty isle	1992-1994	K-MI	43-53
Summer Waves	4096			1995-1998	Paramount	65
Summer Breeze	8629			1980-1982	PROV	25-38
Summerfield	3095		Contemporary FC Philip	1980-1984	Classic	27-46
Summerlike	8556		Folkstone	1975-1978	FOLK2	18-20
Summerville	2152		Cook'n Serve	1975-1976	CNS	
Sundance	8302		Primastone	1975-1977	PRIMA1	15-19
Sunglow	9042		Progression N	1975-1979	P1	24-33
Sunnyside	9003		Progression N	1975-1980	P1	24-38
Sunrise Glow	8403			1984-1985	GRMT	29
Sunset Mesa	8663		stoneware	1985-1995	CNCP1	36-55
Sunswept	9781			1990-1996	Sheer Ivory Bone	88-107
Superba		0076593	M in wreath N/HP/Japan	1931		
Surf Blue	8754		Craftone	1975-1977	CRAFT1	10-20
Surprise	B338		Versatone II	1979-1982	VER2	30-40

Name, *Page #*	No.	Design	Backstamp	Time	Form	Value
Surrey, *52*			M in wreath N/HP/Japan	1918		
Susan Anne, *119*						
	7273		N in wreath ivory	1984-1987	Remembrance II	53
Sutherland	6726					
Sutton Court	3681		Legendary Sri Lanka	1985-1988	Commander	46-50
Swan Lake	3205			1982-1985	Elegance	48-51
Swansea	685		M in wreath small bow			
Swansia	6854			1975	Concerto	
Sweet Leilani, *96*						
	3482		Legendary Sri Lanka	1984-1998	Commander	46-57
Sweet Marie	3430			1984-1986	Remembrance II	50
Sweet Pea	7940			1997-1998	GG	75
Sweet Surprise	7702		Fine China in wreath	1984-1995	New Traditions	60-100
Sweet Talk, *82*	6513		N in wreath colorful	1963-1965	Coupe	
Sweet Violet	2753			1977-1982	Remembrance I	40-55
Sylvan, *59*	6118		N in wreath printed	1961	Concerto	1953
Sylvania			M in wreath N/HP/Japan			
Sylvesta			M in wreath N/HP/Japan			
Sylvia, *91*	6603		N in wreath colorful	1963	Concerto	
Symphony	3915		M in wreath small bow			
Tahiti	8511		Folkstone	1975-1977	FOLK1	15-18
Tahiti	9151		Keltcraft misty isle	1986-1986	K-MI	37
Tahoe	2585		Contemporary FC Philip	1979-1997	Classic	25-57
Talara	4766			1976-1998	Empire	85
Talisman	B330		Versatone II	1978-1982	VER2	27-40
Tandem	8627			1979-1982	cas2	24-38
Tapestry	2405			1975-1979	Commander	22-32
Tara	2150		Cook'n Serve	1977-1977	CNS-R	19
Tarantella	2035			1976-1979	Commander	21
Tarkington, *83*	3695		Legendary Sri Lanka	1986-1993	Commander	50-54
Tartan	B953		Primastone	1975-1977	PRIMA4	20-23
Taryn, *50*	5912	0185448	N in wreath printed	1953-1977	Butterfly	
Tassel	4711			1992-1993	Masters Coll.	113-119
Tawny	8657		stoneware	1982-1986	CNCP1	33-36
Tecla	710		M in wreath small bow			
Temptation	2752			1977-1987	Remembrance I	35-53
Tenderly	2689			1978-1981		
Terrace Café	9203		Keltcraft	1995-1995	K-RIM	55
Terrain	8309		Primastone	1975-1977	PRIMA1	13-19
Thea	6875		N in wreath printed	1975-1977	LaSalle	20
Thelma Bassett			M in wreath N/HP/Japan			
Therese	5158		M in wreath small bow			
Thistle Garden	9105		Keltcraft	1980-1983	K-COU	35-36
Thornton	3160			1982-1988	Nor Ireland I	53-60
Thurston, *40*	6871		N in wreath printed	1975-1977	LaSalle	22-24
Tiara	3812					
Tiber				1998	epoch	
Tidal Song	B136		Sea & Sky	1985-1987	SS	33
Tiffany		0095640	M in wreath small bow	1935		
Tijuana	8350		Primastone	1979-1981	PRIMA1	24-27
Tilford, *91*	6712		N in wreath colorful	1967-1975	Concerto	
Timberlake	8689			1990-1995	CNCP1	43-53
Tina	8507		Folkstone	1975-1982	FOLK1	12-33
Tipperary	2771			1981-1983	Nor Ireland I	50
Tisdale	2893		Contemporary FC Philip	1978-1985	Classic	25-46
Together	9132		Keltcraft misty isle	1983-1986	K-MI	36-37
Tokay, *52*	5168		M in wreath big bow	1933-1979		
Tokio		0013714	M in wreath N/HP/Japan	1908		
Toloa	3841		M in wreath small bow			
Topaze	653		M in wreath small bow			
Touraine	3025		K in scroll shield Japan			
Tourmaline	7049		Expression	1975-1977	Victorian IV	18-19
Tracery, *119*	7258		N in wreath ivory china	1980-1984	Remembrance II	37-56
Tradition, *69*	2356		N in wreath blk/gld	1975-1980	Commander	21-37
Trailing Ivy	2760			1981-1983	Nor Ireland I	50
Tranquil Glen	9188		Keltcraft	1992-1998	K-RIM	58-75
Traviata, *123*	7327		N in wreath ivory	1991-1998	Imperial Baroque	72-88

Name, *Page #*	No.	Design	Backstamp	Time	Form	Value
Wildwood	B969			1979-1980	PRIMA1	
Williamston	9768			1989-1990	Sheer Ivory Bone	85-88
Willowbrook	9722			1980-1987	Sheer Ivory Bone	65-82
Wilshire	5224		M in wreath small bow			
Wimbledon	2022			1974-1975	Concerto	
Wimpole	3624		M in wreath small bow			
Wind Blossom	4719			1993-1994	Bone	88-92
Windham	3194		Contemporary FC Philip	1982-1988	Classic	45-46
Windrift	6117					
Windrift	6157			1953		
Windsor		0071432	M in wreath N/HP/Japan	1930	Original	
Windsor, *80*	5924	0185452	N in wreath printed	1953	rim	
Windsor Garden	7302			1987-1991	Imperial Baroque	64-72
Windsor White	9810			1994-1995	Cameo	70-75
Winona	511		M in wreath N/HP/Japan			
Winslow, *85*	5406		N in wreath printed	1953		
Winsome	B957		Primastone	1975-1981	PRIMA3	20
Winter Palace	7711		Fine China in wreath	1985-1985	New Traditions	60
Winter Park	9157		Keltcraft	1987-1988	K-COU,K-MI	37

Name, *Page #*	No.	Design	Backstamp	Time	Form	Value
Winter Rose	8590		Folkstone	1978-1981	FOLK2	27-30
Winter Whites	9436			1995-1995	PRIMAC	75
Winthrop	6430					
Winton, *66*	5521	0176126	N in wreath printed	1951-1953		
Woodfield	9135		Keltcraft	1984-1984	K-COU	53
Woodlawn	4735			1998-1999	Masters Collection	130
Woodley	6783		N in wreath colorful			
Woodmere				1919-1922	Original	
Woodstock	8354		Primastone	1983-1993	PRIMA1	41-58
Wrocklange	4706		M in wreath small bow			
Wynwood	6879		Contemporary FC Philip	1974-1975	Classic	
Yale (The), *35*			M in wreath N/Nippon	1912-1914	Original	
Ybry, *112*		0076832	M in wreath N/HP/Japan	1931	Original	
Yesterday	9112		Keltcraft	1982-1988	K-RIM	35-37
York	3830		M in wreath N/HP/Japan			
Yoshino	9983			1992-1993	Masters Collection	113-119
Young Love, *81*	118		Cook'n Serve	1975	CNS	19
Yukon (The), *24*			M in wreath N/Nippon		Original	
ZanZibar	3291			1982-1985	Commander	48-51

Numerical Cross-Reference

This numerical reference is designed to take the reader back to the more complete alphabetical listings on the previous pages. Please note that the patterns with no name are listed as such, and complete information about them may be found under *NO NAME* in the alphabetical listing, where they can be identified by their number or design. The first part of the list is organized by design number. The second part of the list is organized by Noritake Number. If a pattern has both numbers, it is listed twice.

Name	No.	Design	Name	No.	Design	Name	No.	Design	Name	No.	Design
Victoria		0010528	Chanazure		0061239	Floreal		0076839	Milford		0089486
Blue Willow		0011006	NO NAME		0061240	Romola		0076840	Althea		0089492
NO NAME		0010733	Chantaro		0061241	Aeolian		0076841	Rubigold		0089501
Sedan (The)		0011292	Tuscan		0061277	Chineblue		0076842	Luxoria		0091602
Hakone		0011298	Bedford		0068443	Sorrento		0076965	Luxoria		0091602
Valencia		0011632	Grosvenor		0068445	Mariana		0076972	Jacquin		0094549
Linwood (The)		0011657	Haverford		0068445	NO NAME		0077630	Galatea		0095632
(blue & white)		0011874	Atlanta		0068448	Fleurgold		0077631	Valiere		0095632
Vitry (The)		0013672	Chanesta		0068454	Biarritz		0078047	Garland		0095633
Portland		0013673	Chanlake		0068457	Amorosa		0078048	Glenmore		0095634
Regina		0013674	Vassar		0068465	Carltonia		0078048	Carmela	4732	0095635
NO NAME		0013680	Basel (The)		0068466	Minaret		0078049	Luray		0095638
Tokio		0013714	Lincoln		0068469	Fleury		0078052	Tiffany		0095640
Malay (The)		0013857	Savona		0068470	Perseus		0078053	Gloria		0095641
Ormonde Bassett		0014369	Chandella		0068478	Perdita		0078054	Marlene		0095642
Carmen		0014370	Knollwood		0068483	Favorita		0078057	Arlene		0095645
Inwood	1871	0014763	Angora (The)		0068585	Romeo		0080459	Glendola		0095648
NO NAME		0014800	Bellefonte		0068587	Athlone		0080460	Alvin		0095649
Edinburgh	7146	0015485	Baroda		0068596	Fairfax		0080461	Arnaud		0095654
Blue Willow		0016033	Deerlodge		0069531	Visalia		0080462	Gainford		0097893
White & Gold		0016034	Sheridan		0069533	Castella		0080463	Galavan		0097894
Azalea		0019322	Beaumont		0069534	Montebelle		0080466	Fernand	581	0097901
Black & Gold		0020056	LaSalle		0069535	Marilyn		0080467	Allure	586	0097902
NO NAME		0026979	Malvern		0069538	Sedalia		0080553	Allure	3706	0097902
NO NAME		0027462	Bellefonte		0069539	Elmonte		0080754	Mimi		0098141
Jenica	3471	0034921	Amiston		0069540	Fairmont		0080755	Acacia	509	0098212
Alicia	5762	0035762	Mayville		0069541	Severy		0081603	Loyalo		0098214
Raised Gold		0042200	Minerva		0069542	Nordich		0081857	Charoma		0098215
White & Gold	175	0043061	Paisley		0069543	Aubery		0082450	Linden	525	0098217
NO NAME		0044318	Daventry		0069544	Andalia		0083366	Nanarosa	682	0098218
Smartnis		0053569	Navarre		0069545	Estelle		0083367	Claudette	594	0098221
Chandova		0058438	Modesta		0069546	Florola		0083374	Gastonia		0098827
Comiston(The)		0058500	Doris		0071219	Eltovar		0083377	Cardinal	193	0098829
Ceylon (The)		0058581	Granada		0071422	Flodena		0085202	Exeter	604	0098834
Seville		0058584	Delhi		0071424	Oxford		0085963	Elvira	608	0098835
Alsace(The)		0058588	Cornwall		0071425	Roseglow		0086196	Lismore	609	0098836
Beverly		0058589	Delmonte		0071426	Ivanhoe		0086197	Muriel	611	0098838
Sahara (The)		0058590	Rosewood		0071427	Resilio		0086198	Garfield		0098845
Florencia		0058591	Chelsea		0071432	Marcell		0086199	NO NAME		0098846
Hanover		0058594	Windsor		0071432	Farland		0086200	Alcona	613	0100326
Montclare		0058595	Lafleur		0071432	Girado		0086205	Bluedawn	622	0100331
Monterey (The)		0058595	Charmeuse		0071435	Bantry Bay		0086209	NO NAME		0101207
Majestic		0058596	Marigold		0071436	Bantry		0086209	NO NAME		0101270
Argonne (The)		0058597	Gotham		0071437	Monarch		0086216	Devon		0108041
Lafayette		0058598	Rosemary		0071629	Goldinthia		0087195	Merlin		0108380
Coniston (The)		0058599	Burma		0071854	Marcisite		0087196	Revenna		0109493
Rochambeau		061228	Shila		0076593	Cheramy		0087197	Rainbow		0117791
NO NAME		0061229	Fleurette		0076831	Corinthia		0087198	Cimarron		1003006
Chainrose		0061230	Ybry		0076832	Kenwood		0089482	Claire	657	0103007
Louvaine		0061231	Juanita		0076834	Arvana		0089483	Phoebe	659	0103008
Laureate	2132	0061235	Romance		0076835	Elaine		0089484	Nerrisa (Nerissa)	673	0103009
Carmela			Penelope		0076837	Elaine		0089484	Trianon	676	0103034
Arleigh		0061237	Modjeska		0076837	Lanare		0089485	Juno	716	0103057

Name	No.	Design	Name	No.	Design	Name	No.	Design	Name	No.	Design
Salvador	303	0104529	Laveta	513		Augusta	2025		Spring Song	2354	
Alexis	3721	0108369	Pink Poppy	514		Keniworth	2026		May Garden	2355	
Coypel	3732	0108374	Merida	515		Waltz	2027		Tradition	2356	
Ciro	3744	0108378	Norma	518		Walden	2028		Maytone	2359	
Lorento	3852	0112926	Alameda	520		Kensington	2029		Venice	2360	
Valdina	3854	0112927	Linden	525	0098217	Barrington	2030		Rondeau	2361	
Grandeur	3870	0112930	Fernand	581	0097901	Savannah	2031		Early Spring	2362	
Mirabelle	3843	0114075	Hampton	582		Breeze	2032		Shangri-La	2363	
Camillia	3950	0117508	Claudia	583		Beguine	2033		Firedance	2401	
Harmony	3906	0117811	Joan	584		Dearest	2034		Nouveau	2402	
Sonora	3940	0117814	Jasmine	585		Tarantella	2035		Persia	2403	
Carmillia	4735	0117816	Allure	586	0097902	Bolero	2036		Chintz	2404	
Camelot	3031	0117817	Gramatan	587		Blythe	2037		Tapestry	2405	
Petite	5507	0176125	Oradell	588		Flanders	2038		Floris	2480	
Winton	5521	0176126	Rodista	590		Mediterranean	2039		Amor	2481	
Capri	5551	0176131	NO NAME	590		Eroica	2041		Blue Hill	2482	
Chatham	5502	0176133	Belvoir	592		Figaro	2042		Lilac Time	2483	
Charmaine	5506	0176135	Roberta	593		Aida	2043		Spring Meadow	2484	
Glenwood	5770	0181393	Claudette	594	0098221	Scheherazade	2044		Longwood	2485	
Stanwyck	5818	0182091	Aurora	600		Polonaise	2045		Oberlin	2486	
Glennis	5804	0182092	Trojan	603		September Song	2048		Raleigh	2487	
Edgewood	5807	0182094	Exeter	604	0098834	Pastoral	2049		Grace	2536	
Lucille	5813	0183980	Fondale	605		Highclere	2062		Spring Garden	2551	
Laurel	5903	0185444	Elvira	608	0098835	Burlington	2081		Harmony	2552	
Taryn	5912	0185448	Lismore	609	0098836	Clarinda	2111		Nantes	2553	
Windsor	5924	0185452	Farney	610		Laureate	2132	0061235	Delevan	2580	
Crestmont	6013	0187145	Muriel	611	0098838	Tara	2150		Biltmore	2581	
Claridge	6020	0187148	Alcona	613	0100326	Cielito Lindo	2151		Tahoe	2585	
Chaumont	6008	0187151	Bayard	614		Summerville	2152		Everett	2586	
Biarritz	6006	0187156	Cereus	615		Home-Town	2153		Noble	2600	
Barbara	6009	0189202	Lavegas	620		Amy	2154		Stardust	2603	
Fairmont	6102	0194925	Bluedawn	622	0100331	Sheila	2155		Arcadia	2604	
Colburn	6107	0194926	Lolita	631		Sue	2157		First Blush	2605	
Maya	6213	0196309	Allard	651		Paula	2158		Essence	2606	
Wellesley	6214	0196310	Hermione	652		Eugenia	2160		Inspiration	2607	
Hermitage	6226	0196311	Topaze	653		Mo-Bay	2162		Flourish	2608	
Buckingham	6438	0200495	Cynthia	655		Antigua	2163		Allison	2610	
Whitebrook	6441	0200484	Claire	657	0103007	Shasta	2167		Diana	2611	
Ramona	6504	1118708	Phoebe	659	0103008	Orange County	2168		Fairfield	2612	
Wild Ivy	102		Royce	660		Elloree	2169		Rosette	2651	
Belle Rose	102		Oberon	661		Kennesaw	2170		Karen	2671	
Roselin	103		Nerrisa (Nerissa)	673	0103009	Donegal	2179		Epic	2680	
Angela	107		Naomi	674		Iona	2180		Chorus	2681	
Namiki	108		Rochelle	675		Marywood	2181		Empire	2682	
Maplewood	109		Trianon	676	0103034	Andorra	2182		Tenderly	2689	
Young Love	118		Leslie	678		Leilahi	2206		Forever	2690	
White & Gold	175	0043061	Olympia	680		Monterey	2211		Culeton	2692	
Cardinal	193	0098829	Nanarosa	682	0098218	Dee	2212		Carolyn	2693	
Joy	227		Nanette	683		Ravel	2213		Laura	2694	
NO NAME	228		Fabian	684		Vicki	2214		Bella	2697	
Parnell	302		Swansea	685		Jennifer	2215		Brenda	2730	
Salvador	303	0104529	Tecla	710		Segovia	2216		Whiteview	2751	
Marvelle	304		Medean	712		Cordon	2217		Temptation	2752	
Georgette	305		Vanessa	714		Serenity	2218		Sweet Violet	2753	
Phyllis	318		Juno	716	0103057	Regency	2219		Enchantment	2754	
Mariposa	319		Moselle	723		Essex	2224		Embrace	2755	
Melrose	370		Goldora	882		Cumberland	2225		Jubilation	2756	
Ridgeway	400		NO NAME	1356		Fleurette	2226		Long Ago	2757	
Goldream	469		NO NAME	1357		Milford	2227		Trailing Ivy	2760	
Goldcrest	470		NO NAME	1359		Holly	2228		Scala	2761	
Fiesta	483		Contessa	1485		Peking	2229		Amapola	2764	
Amherst	501		NO NAME	1802		Kontiki	2231		Boliska	2766	
Eureka	502		Inwood	1871	0014763	Hula	2232		Morning Jewel	2767	
Arebella	503		Country Diary	1906		Mai-Tai	2234		Angel D'amour	2769	
Linda	0507		Anniversary	1979		Diamond Head	2236		Harvesting	2770	
Acacia	509	0098212	Pinnacle	2019		Mayflower	2351		Tipperary	2771	
Winona	511		Wimbledon	2022		Frolic	2352		Edenderry	2772	
Gramercy	512		Sedgwick	2023		Heirloom	2353		Kenmare	2773	

Name	No.	Design	Name	No.	Design	Name	No.	Design	Name	No.	Design
Astoria	2789		D'Azure	3091		Hyannis	3642		Gerome	3843	
Lynnbrook	2790		Carmine	3092		Flora	3643		Mirabelle	3843	0114075
Amsterdam	2792		Roselane	3093		Autumn Rhapsody	3660		Lace White	3847	
Heidelberg	2793		Summerfield	3095		Spring Rhapsody	3661		Dresalda	3849	
Granada	2794		Cache Pot	3132		Katmandu	3670		Lorento	3852	0112926
Sevilla	2795		Thornton	3160		Canastel	3671		Valdina	3854	0112927
Vienna	2796		Candice	3161		Remembrance White	3678		Marcia	3855	
Coventry	2797		Aubusson	3162		Parisian Lace	3680		Rigaud	3860	
Lorraine	2798		Fairfax	3190		Sutton Court	3681		Grandeur	3870	0112930
Valhalla	2799		Bordeaux	3191		Bonaventure	3682		Sierra	3871	
Horizon	2801		Chambray	3192		Grammercy Park	3684		Annabel	3872	
Cotillion	2802		Brookfield	3193		Washington Square	3685		Prescott	3880	
Concert	2803		Windham	3194		Chelsea Morn	3686		River Place	3881	
Nanking	2860		Quentin	3202		New Destiny	3687		Hartley	3882	
Carrie	2864		Smithfield	3203		Knightsbridge	3688		Lancashire	3883	
Brigette	2865		Elmsford	3204		Algonquin	3690		Lunceford	3884	
Glenbawn	2866		Swan Lake	3205		Ellington	3691		Azalea	3885	
Contentment	2880		Adoration	3260		Cote Basque	3692		Penrosa	3886	
Black Lace	2881		Waynesboro	3261		Brussels	3693		Hapsburg Rose	3890	
Memory	2882		Christine	3290		Tarkington	3695		Bavarian Blossom	3891	
Misty	2883		ZanZibar	3291		Kensington Palace	3696		French Charm	3901	
Pembroke	2892		Lisle	3292		Brookside	3697		Alcott	3902	
Tisdale	2893		Carthage	3330		Lake Worth	3699		Lynbrook	3903	
Green Hill	2897		Classic White	3330		Malibu	3700		Kelvin	3905	
Ming	2931		Alhambra	3331		Evening Sonnet	3701		Harmony	3906	0117811
Springfield	2932		Savoy	3340 3/340		Musetta	3702		Stanwyck	3913	
Virtue	2934		Sonata	3360		Allegra	3703		Lilac	3914	
Springlow	2935		Alexandria	3361		Ada	3705		Symphony	3915	
Memorable	2936		Blue Orient	3363		Allure	3706	0097902	Magnolia	3918	
Pledge	2938		Tullamore	3364		Decamps	3708		Royal Hunt	3930	
Inspire	2939		Rowan	3368		Stratford	3709		Sonora	3940	0117814
Anticipation	2963		Bambury	3369		Bassano	3720		Hibiscus	3942	
Patience	2964		Avalon	3390		Alexis	3721	0108369	Camillia	3950	0117508
Coquet	2981		Eden	3391		Gelee	3723		Belle Empress	3980	
Heritage	2982		Grenoble	3392		Dureer	3725		Goldenrose	3981	
Spectrum	2983		Mandalay	3393		Ribera	3727		Goldfleur	3983	
Holbrook	2994		Nancy	3402		Raphael	3730		Snow Petal	3986	
Barstow	2995		Cleo	3415		Coypel	3732	0108374	Lace Shadow	3988	
Chalmette	2996		Springtime	3417		Caliban	3733		Chadbourne	3990	
Poetry	2997		Sweet Marie	3430		Gerome	3743		Roseolyn	3991	
Fascination	2998		Deco Magic	3450		Ciro	3744	0108378	Van Orsdale	3995	
Ransdell	3004		Floral Dream	3451		Laramie	3754		Silk Ribbons	3996	
Veranda	3015		Belle Femmes	3452		Watteau	3755		Anaheim	3997	
Applique	3016		New Drama	3453		Jenna	3760		Arctic White	4000	
Murmur	3017		Deco Spirit	3454		Saddlebrook	3761		Arctic Gold	4001	
Effingham	3018		New Morn	3455		Café Versailles	3762		Acton	4001	
Benita	3019		Marblehill	3460		Ontario	3763		Savoia	4003	
Adrienne	3020		Fairburn	3461		Covent Garden	3786		Lauritz	4005	
Redlace	3024		Stockbridge	3462		Blossom Mist	3787		Hailey	4007	
Touraine	3025		Jenica	3471	0034921	Evening Mood	3788		Lurline	4007	
Camelot	3031	0117817	Secret Love	3481		Garbo	3790		Grape Arbor	4008	
Dresala	3033		Sweet Leilani	3482		Séance	3791		Walnut Hill	4009	
Dresgay	3038		Dream Street	3483		Silk Garland	3792		Cavatina	4011	
Rosalie	3052		Shrewsbury	3490		Southmoor	3801		Squirewood	4013	
Violette	3054		Easthampton	3491		Mariel	3802		Heatherwood	4015	
Carolyn	3055		Rangoon	3596		Lacewood	3803		Brenda	4017	
Sharon	3057		Malverne	3501		Columbine	3803		Queenanne	4018	
Sandra	3062		Sharon's Dream	3580		Vanity	3804		Oxford Lane	4020	
Granada	3063		True Love	3581		Sabetha	3805		Ricochet	4021	
Limerick	3064		Cadiz	3591		Glengarry	3806		Intuition	4022	
Roundelay	3065		Grand Monarch	3595		Oakmont	3808		Integrity	4023	
Romaine	3066		Commander White	3600		Aberdale	3808		Elevation	4024	
Audrey	3078		Newbury	3601		Tiara	3812		Border Bouquet	4025	
Melissa	3080		Blue Destiny	3602		Lavin	3814		High Sails	4026	
Tremont	3081		Night Life	3603		York	3830		Ashford	4026	
Colton	3081		After Dark	3604		Serena	3840		Briday Ribbon	4027	
Aldea	3083		Shelby	3623		Toloa	3841		Meadowcrest	4034	
Shahzada	3090		Wimpole	3624		Hermosa	3842		Enhancement	4035	

Name	No.	Design	Name	No.	Design	Name	No.	Design	Name	No.	Design
Adelpha	4036		Maison Fleur	4301		Killian	4763		Winslow	5406	
Sienna Sunset	4036		Foxboro	4302		Talara	4766		Fernwood	5406	
Paradise Tribute	4042		Antiquity	4304		Chavot Gold	4769		Stanton	5407	
Crystal Bouquet	4043		La Madeleine	4307		Hurley	4770		Wheaton	5414	
Ackley	4049		Palace Guard	4308		Edgemoor	4771		Crest	5421	
Golden Orchard	4049		Salutation	4309		Penelope	4781		Kent	5422	
Indigo Waltz	4050		Queens Mark	4310		NO NAME	4789		Debonain	5426	
Hannibal	4055		Floral Embrace	4311		Vornay	4794	0089527	Reverie	5431	
Club Stripe	4056		Caliph Place	4415		Naomi	4901		Sheridan	5441	
Brandywine	4057		Royal Emblem	4587		Nanarosa	4902		Regina	5442	
Forest Bounty	4058		Rose Legend	4702		Sonoda	4907		Fernwood	5444	
Lockleigh	4061		La Prada	4703		Hawthorne	4914		Rosa	5460	
Stoneleigh	4062		Brookhollow	4704		Empire	4916		NO NAME	5471	
Goldrina	4070		Chamberlain	4705		Valiere	4981		Bancroft	5481	
Castillo	4075		Philharmonic	4706		Goldkin	4985		NO NAME	5487	
Edgerow	4078		Wrocklange	4706		NO NAME	4986		Bordeaux	5496	
Sports Page	4080		Lyndenwood	4707		Rosemary	5007		Chatham	5502	0176133
Rose Sonnet	4081		Belcourt	4710		NO NAME	5020		Charmaine	5506	0176135
Oakleigh	4082		Tassel	4711		Canton	5027		Petite	5507	0176125
Whitecliff	4083		Fitzgerald	4712		Colby	5032		Candice	5509	
Homegrown	4088		Farentino	4713		Carleton	5034		Daryl	5510	
Arctic Blue	4089		Knottinghill	4714		Glendale	5038		Winton	5521	0176126
Arctic Green	4090		Bluedawn	4715		Roselace	5041		Diana	5522	
Newburg	4092		Lamelle	4715		Laurette	5047		Andrea	5524	
Greenbury	4094		Romanticize	4716		Rosemont	5048		Gaylord	5526	
October Light	4095		Dresdoll	4716		Margarita	5049		Canton	5527	
Summer Waves	4096		Mi Amor	4717		Peony	5053		Royal Pink	5527	
Brookvale	4098		Paris Opera	4718		Celeste	5070		Florence	5528	
Morning Poem	4100		Wind Blossom	4719		Gwendolyn	5083		NO NAME	5528	
Greenbrier	4101		Elms Court	4720		Goldlane	5084		Avon	5531	
Park Suite	4102		Dreamspun	4721		Floris	5088		Vanessa	5541	
Gateway	4103		Diamond Trace	4722		Madera	5106		Mavis	5543	
Ainsworth	4104		Mendelson	4723		Nuana	5129		NO NAME	5548	
Arlington Heights	4105		Voltaire	4724		LaSalle	5142		NO NAME	5550	
Metarie	4108		Lynbrook	4724		Adrienne	5143		Capri	5551	0176131
Bridal Waltz	4109		Purity Gold	4725		Remembrance	5146		Lilybell	5556	
Golden Twilight	4110		Purity White	4726		Roselane	5147		Bluebell	5558	
Landon	4111		Cerulean	4726		Avalon	5150		NO NAME	5559	
McKenzie	4112		Essex Court	4727		Dulcy	5153		NO NAME	5564	
Meadowside	4114		Rose Memento	4728		Therese	5158		Silverdale	5594	
Aristocrat Gold	4115		Lady Quentin	4730		Tokay	5168		Goldstone	5595	
Golden Myth	4116		Lady Quentin	4730		Joyce	5174		Helene	5602	
Kirkland	4117		Cardinal	4731		Ridgewood	5201		Arden	5603	
Imperial Jade	4118		Carmela	4732	0095635	Louise	5204		Margot	5605	
April Poem	4119		Hemingway	4733		Glenrose	5206		Granville	5607	
Emerald Crest	4130		Dresita	4733		Rosilla	5212		NO NAME	5612	
Gilded Blossoms	4134		Southern Estate	4734		Cordova	5215		Automne	5626	
Love Poem	4135		Woodlawn	4735		Edgemont	5216		Dover	5633	
Kipling	4141		Carmillia	4735	0117816	Stanford	5220		Holbrook	5635	
Brickhaven	4142		Azure Garden	4736		Arlington	5221		Laureate	5651	
Darnell	4154		Ashbury	4737		Wilshire	5224		Garnet	5656	
Bromley	4156		Sinclair	4738		Canterbury	5226		Goldkin	5675	
Engravings	4203		Shelton	4739		Greta	5272		Pinetta	5689	
Blue Treasures	4204		Crownpointe	4740		Goldart	5290		Grayson	5697	
Arctic Circle	4209		City Skies	4741		NO NAME	5295		Damask	5698	
Arctic Spring	4210		Summer Gold	4742		Shasta	5305		Alicia	5762	0035762
Kenwick	4217		Rose Gate	4743		Lynwood	5307		Lorene	5764	
Dearborn	4218		Autumn Estate	4744		Anita	5309		Oxford	5767	
Bellville	4219		Golden Mastery	4745		Argyle	5311		Glenwood	5770	0181393
Pacific Hill	4220		Christina	4746		Allison	5313		Ardis	5772	
Arctic Berries	4221		Stenmark	4747		Shelburne	5316		Danielle	5776	
Green Icicle	4225		Ashville	4750		Somerset	5317		Bessie	5788	
Fiesta Flowers	4226		White Palace	4753		Greencourt	5322		Revenna	5789	
Clemson	4227		Bellcrest	4754		Grayburn	5323		Rossina	5789	
Alamosa	4228		Rosslyn	4756		NO NAME	5329		Rosales	5790	
Holloway	4234		Delacroix	4759		Greenbay	5353		Bambina	5791	
Regis Blue	4235		Allaire	4760		Carole	5402		Beaumont	5796	
Astorbrook	4300		Palestra	4762		Esteem	5404		Arlene	5802	

Name	No.	Design	Name	No.	Design	Name	No.	Design	Name	No.	Design
Glennis	5804	0182092	Josephine	6240		Jacqueline	6670		Frangrance	7025	
Rochelle	5805		Roseberry	6241		Firenze	6674		Geri	7026	
Edgewood	5807	0182094	Margaret	6243		Leomore	6676		Darlene	7035	
Laverne	5810		Grayoak	6257		Kerri	6681		Moon Valley	7044	
Valerie	5812		Graytone	6257		Humoresque	6685		Chestnut Hill	7045	
Lucille	5813	0183980	Allenby	6302		Blue Orchard	6695		Alhambra	7046	
Natalie	5815		Barton	6305		Gail	6710		Jadestone	7047	
Stanwyck	5818	0182091	Pasadena	6311		Tilford	6712		Larkspur	7048	
Malibu	5823		Harwood	6312		Nicolette	6713		Tourmaline	7049	
Savoy	5825		Armand	6315		Inverness	6716		Jill	7052	
Rosamor	5851		Envoy	6325		Macon	6717		Connie	7085	
Clovis	5855		Silvester	6340		Nile	6719		Celia	7086	
Gracelyn	5856		Oriental	6341		Hyde Park	6720		Trudy	7087	
Blueridge	5858		Belda	6342		Kathleen	6722		Caledonia	7091	
Sanford	5860		Edenrose	6343		Belfort	6723		Carlyle	7121	
Graycliff	5861		Camden	6350		Jean	6724		Hawthorne	7122	
Laurel	5903	0185444	Sonoma	6353		Monaco	6725		Charleston	7148	
Garland	5905		Snowden	6354		Sutherland	6726		Edinburgh	7146	0015485
Croydon	5908		Baroness	6357		Aberdeen	6727		Moonbeam	7149	
Taryn	5912	0185448	Mesa	6370		Maureen	6728		Blossom Time	7150	
Waverly	5915		Embassy	6380		Marguerite	6730	0209009	Asian Song	7151	
Cheryl	5917		Simone	6407		Kathleen	6772		Summer Eve	7163	
Chartres	5920		Mariposa	6411		Woodley	6783		Serene Garden	7164	
Windsor	5924	0185452	Harley	6420		Espana	6805		Tribute	7165	
Dawn	5930		Winthrop	6430		Prosperity	6841		Atlanta	7166	
Derry	5931		Altadena	6437		Casablanca	6842		Cathay	7179	
Colony	5932		Buckingham	6438	0200495	Sezanne	6851		Reverie	7191	
Silverkey	5941		Georgian	6440		Soroya	6853		Affection	7192	
Melrose	6002		Whitebrook	6441	0200484	Swansia	6854		Miyoshi	7194	
Rosebud	6002		Goldvine	6444		Annabelle	6856		Brittany	7195	
Chevonia	6003		June	6448		Lamarre	6859		Ho-Oh	7196	
Biarritz	6006	0187156	Vineyard	6449		Thurston	6871		Debut	7210	
Chaumont	6008	0187151	Reina	6450		Warrington	6872		Cortege	7211	
Barbara	6009	0189202	Snowville	6453		Perdita	6873		Melody	7212	
Norwood	6011		Joanne	6466		Fay	6874		Finale	7213	
Crestmont	6013	0187145	String of Pearls	6480		Thea	6875		Viceroy	7222	
Claridge	6020	0187148	Glenwood	6500		Mirano	6878		Countess	7223	
Cathay	6029		Ramona	6504	1118708	Wynwood	6879		Flirtation	7227	
Graywood	6041		Glencoe	6505		Lucerne	6880		Amenity	7228	
Norwich	6042		Sweet Talk	6513		Nicosia	6882		Delight	7229	
Rosemarie	6044		Blair Rose	6519		Sharon	6883		Splendor	7235	
Fairmont	6102	0194925	Courtney	6520		Vienne	6885		Homage	7236	
Cavalier	6104		Seville	6521		Country Side	6899		Adagio	7237	
Colburn	6107	0194926	New Charm	6522		Patrice	6901		Gallery	7246	
Mayfair	6109		Compton	6524		Kendal	6903		Weyburne	7248	
Brooklane	6112		Gloria	6526		Harwyn	6904		Refinement	7249	
Whitehall	6115		Galaxy	6527		Eminence	6905		Meadow	7250	
Windrift	6117		Victoria	6528		Trilby	6908		Blue Peony	7251	
Sylvan	6118		Isabella	6531		Ranier	6909		Flower Maid	7257	
Gotham	6119		Royale Claret	6537		Geneva	6910		Tracery	7258	
Balboa	6123		Royale Mint	6538		Princeton	6911		Etienne	7260	
Richmond	6124		Royal Café	6539		Larue	6913		Cervantes	7261	
Almont	6125		Greenmere	6548		Elysee	6914		Fairview	7263	
Fremont	6127		Versailles	6565		Culebra	6921		Ivanhoe	7264	
Richland	6130		Pauline	6596		Bahama	6922		Baldwin	7265	
Windrift	6157		Irmina	6601		Bimini	6923		Nightsong	7268	
Ashby	6201		Sylvia	6603		Esperanza	6924		Behold	7269	
Benton	6204		Janette	6604		Dominica	6925		Devotion	7271	
Melita	6205		Ivyne	6605		Barbados	6926		Scarborough	7272	
Concord	6207		Primadonna	6608		Cho-cho-san	6936		Susan Anne	7273	
Rosemead	6210		Ninon	6609		Naples	6975		Ivory & Ebony	7274	
Maya	6213	0196309	Duetto	6610		Benedicata	6976		Ivory & Azure	7279	
Wellesley	6214	0196310	Blue Dawn	6611		Fellicia	6977		Ivory & Mist	7280	
Rosay	6216		Goldlane	6612		Pilgrim	6981		Mayfield	7280	
Athena	6221		Goldhill	6613		Norma	7016		Ivory & Sienna	7281	
Brandon	6222		Barcarolle	6655		Primavera	7017		Spring Venture	7282	
Hermitage	6226	0196311	Diaden	6663		Isolde	7019		Goldette	7286	
NO NAME	6234		Nina	6667		Ponchartrain	7024		Moonlight Rose	7288	
Roseville	6238								Platinum Lights	7292	

Name	No.	Design
Rothschild	7293	
Imperial Blossom	7294	
Midnight Majesty	7295	
Burgundy Royale	7296	
Suddenly	7297	
Orient Point	7298	
Salzburg	7299	
Southern Lace	7301	
Windsor Garden	7302	
Ming Treasure	7304	
Chandon	7306	
Solemn Amber	7320	
Solemn Sapphire	7321	
Solemn Emerald	7322	
Crown Flower	7324	
Traviata	7327	
Adornment	7330	
Berringer	7335	
Afton	7337	
Auburndale	7340	
Halls of Ivy	7341	
Fairchild	7345	
Vintage Rose	7349	
Edwardian Rose	7353	
Gilded Age	7354	
Ashland	7357	
Christmas Garland	7358	
Allendale	7359	
English Flowers	7360	
Imperial Gold	7361	
Greelay	7362	
Imperial Platinum	7366	
Chandon Platinum	7367	
Harveston	7524	
Montblanc	7527	
Fantasia	7532	
Selene	7536	
Rosalind	7537	
Marquis	7540	
Lorelei	7541	
Rhoda	7542	
Candlelight	7544	
Nora	7546	
Heather	7548	
Suffolk	7549	
Marseille	7550	
Patricia	7551	
Linton	7552	
Champlain	7553	
Parkridge	7561	
Tulane	7562	
Virgina	7564	
Virginia	7564	
Sorrento	7565	
Ambrosia	7567	
Weston	7568	
Monteleone	7569	
Prelude	7570	
Cornelia	7572	
Enchanteur	7701	
Sweet Surprise	7702	
Blue and Gold	7703	
Breathless	7704	
New Delight	7709	
Turtle Bay	7710	
Winter Palace	7711	
Queen's Guard	7712	
Gold & Platinum	7713	
Golden Serenade	7714	
Platinum Serenade	7715	
King's Guard	7716	
Golden Cove	7719	
Sterling Cove	7720	
Society Satin	7722	
Bentley	7723	
Royal Britannia	7724	
Edgewater	7728	
Halifax	7729	
Satin Gown	7730	
Night Jewel	7731	
Golden Lily	7733	
Momentum	7734	
Portfolio	7736	
Evening Gown	7738	
Golden Tide	7739	
Sterling Tide	7740	
Awareness	7741	
Grand Vision	7742	
Variation in Gold	7744	
Cecile	7801	
Merina Gold	7802	
Merina Platinum	7803	
Khira	7804	
Joely	7805	
Dignity	7901	
Noblesse	7902	
Aristocrat	7903	
Coram	7910	
Copper Bud	7911	
American Flowers	7912	
Dutch Tile	7913	
Clearlake	7914	
Conservatory	7915	
Memorabilia	7916	
Floral Song	7918	
Fruit Parfait	7919	
Country Fences	7920	
Fruit Passion	7921	
Crossways	7922	
Twilight Melody	7923	
Sonoma Gardens	7936	
Aspen Flowers	7938	
Silphium	7940	
Coreopsis	7940	
Primula	7940	
Pansy	7940	
Sweet Pea	7940	
Daffodil	7940	
Clematis	7940	
Amaryllis	7940	
Iris	7940	
Carnation	7940	
Castleberry	7960	
Snow Field	7961	
Love Song	8002 W81	
Fidelity	8003 W81	
Wedding Veil	8004 W81	
Engagement	8009 W81	
Peonia	8010 W81	
Innocence	8011	
Nadine	8035	
Twas the Night Before Christmas	8100	
Always	8101 W82	
Bridal Rose	8102 W82	
Champagne	8161	
Normandy	8162	
Golden Dawn	8163	
Impression	8164	
China Song	8165	
Westport	8166	
Mantigo	8167	
Honor	8220 W80	
Promise Me	8221 W80	
Cherish	8222 W80	
Paradise	8223 W80	
Cantata	8224	
Medallion	8225	
Troubadour	8226	
Malaga	8301	
Sundance	8302	
Bay Roc	8303	
Spinnaker	8304	
Campobello	8305	
Quadrangle	8306	
Pacifica	8307	
Malabar	8308	
Terrain	8309	
Sea Mist	8310	
Image	8315	
Counterpoint	8316	
Fantasy	8317	
Gaiety	8318	
Primary	8319	
Decision	8320	
Wild Plum	8321	
Radiant	8322	
Love Bird	8327	
Green Tree	8328	
Napa Valley	8336	
Colonial Times	8340	
Desert Flowers	8341	
Bounty	8342	
Mountain Flowers	8343	
Pleasure	8344	
Rapport	8345	
Floralee	8346	
Kerrie	8347	
Homeward	8348	
Eastwind	8349	
Tijuana	8350	
Atlantic	8351	
Madrigal	8352	
Autumn Day	8353	
Woodstock	8354	
Knickerbocker	8355	
Penzance	8358	
Welcome Spring	8359	
Blue Sky Glow	8401	
Lilac Glow	8402	
Sunrise Glow	8403	
Nile Glow	8404	
Rainbow End	8405	
Lily Pond	8406	
Tulip Magic	8407	
Mushroom Magic	8408	
Little Daisy	8409	
Choral Island	8410	
Channing	8411	
Oak Hill	8412	
Roswell	8413	
Circle Bay	8415	
Saddle Hill	8416	
Sand Ring	8418	
Lindsey	8426	
Contemplation	8428	
Options (Black)	8440	
Options (Yellow)	8441	
Options (Green)	8442	
Sand N Sky	8443	
Fragments	8445	
Aspiration	8447	
Grosveno	8448	
Pueblo Moon	8457	
Kachina	8458	
Rapids	8467	
Tweeds	8468	
Warm Sands	8472	
Madera Ivory	8474	
Madera Spruce	8475	
Madera Blue	8476	
Madera Sea Foam	8477	
Madera Peach	8478	
Safari	8501	
Silk Road	8502	
South Pacific	8503	
Inca	8505	
Equator	8506	
Tina	8507	
Cosmos	8508	
Oceanic	8509	
New Sante Fe	8510	
Tahiti	8511	
Twilight	8512	
Snowflake	8523	
Lilac	8527	
Oriental Garden	8528	
Orinda	8540	
Happy Time	8541	
Hello Spring	8551	
June Buds	8552	
May Song	8553	
County Fair	8554	
October Fest	8555	
Summerlike	8556	
Providence	8572	
Plenty	8573	
Bliss	8574	
Essay	8575	
Rapture	8579	
Rejoice	8580	
Shenandoah	8581	
Pizzicato	8582	
Riviera	8583	
Gingerbread	8584	
Marshmallow	8585	
Blueberry	8587	
Pueblo	8588	
Lily	8589	
Winter Rose	8590	
Volcano	8602	
Painted Desert	8603	
Moor	8604	
Aquarius	8605	
Polar	8606	
Sorcerer	8620	
Fanfare	8621	
Oceanica	8623	
Seafoam	8624	
Casino	8625	
Wayfarer	8626	
Tandem	8627	
Nimbus	8628	

Name	No.	Design	Name	No.	Design	Name	No.	Design	Name	No.	Design
Summer breeze	8629		Homecoming	9002		Petal Perfect	9140		Santa Barbara	9405	
Autumnwind	8630		Sunnyside	9003		Aventura	9144		El Parador	9408	
Junenight	8631		Blue Haven	9004		Christy's World	9145		May Breeze	9410	
Springlike	8632		Southern Glow	9005		Costa Mesa	9146		Dawn Blush	9411	
Brighteyes	8633		Pearl White	9006		Pacific Grove	9147		River James	9413	
Fallsong	8634		Blue Chintz	9014		California Dreaming	9148		Brighton Springs	9414	
Watercress	8635		Mardi Gras	9019		Mendocino	9149		Harris Grove	9415	
Pomegranate	8636		Verde	9020		Deerbrook	9150		Royal Orchard	9416	
Banana	8637		Blue Moon	9022		Tahiti	9151		Ocean Melody	9417	
Snowcap	8639		Aloha	9023		Barcelona	9152		Marble Canyon	9418	
Durango	8647		Felicity	9028		Lindsay	9153		Morro Bay	9419	
Sierra	8648		Tressa	9029		Evangeline	9154		Pacific Winds	9420	
Captivate	8649		Sunglow	9042		Montego Bay	9155		Le Parc	9421	
Festival	8650		Ole	9043		Chardonnay	9156		Fair Wind	9422	
Mallard	8652		Shenandoah	9054		Winter Park	9157		After The Rain	9423	
Mountain View	8653		Ming Garden	9066		Morning Melody	9158		Lemonade sky	9424	
Russet	8656		Happy Days	9069		Deerfield	9159		Home for Christmas	9425	
Tawny	8657		Berries'n Such	9070		River Oaks	9161		Marine Buffet	9434	
Cycle Brown	8658		Petals Plus	9071		Spring Orchid	9165		Damask Bouquet	9435	
Country White	8659		Flower Time	9072		Hennessy	9167		Winter Whites	9436	
Cycle Frost	8660		Au Naturel	9073		Pursuit	9170		(blue & white)	9488	
Sunset Mesa	8663		Bewitch	9078		Eastfair	9171		Rosalia	9558	
Sierra Twilight	8667		Bright Side	9079		Peachtree Manor	9175		Contrast	9569	
Strawberry Delight	8671		Clear Day	9080		Harvest Ribbon	9176		Lyric	9570	
Victory Blue	8673		Good Times	9081		Cortland	9178		Rhapsody	9582	
Boulder Ridge	8674		Berredin	9083		Ivy Lane	9180		Canterbury	9627	
Raindance	8675		Georgetown	9084		Stepping High	9181		Aldridge	9702	
Prairie Song	8676		Overture	9086		Summer Rain	9185		Kimberly	9703	
Arizona	8677		Summer Dreams	9090		Maple Shade	9187		Sakura	9704	
Blue Adobe	8678		Café du Soir	9091		Tranquil Glen	9188		Canterbury	9705	
Centennial White	8679		Spring Blush	9092		Belgravia	9189		Venus	9706	
Desert Fire	8682		Café du Jour	9094		Abbotswood	9190		Fairbanks	9707	
Tulip Ridge	8683		Gotham Gray	9096		Southwood	9191		Elegante	9708	
Olive Wreath	8684		Society Orchid	9097		April Sky	9192		Imperial Garden	9720	
Aspen Nights	8685		Plum Orchid	9098		Valmorea	9193		Randolph	9721	
Mendon	8687		Peonytime	9100		Watervale	9194		Willowbrook	9722	
Sand Painting	8688		Daisygarland	9101		Apple Crisp	9196		Salisbury	9723	
Timberlake	8689		Oriental Dream	9102		Spring Debut	9197		Ruby Garland	9723	
Mystic Ridge	8690		Wild Rose	9103		Wicklow Green	9198		Chalfonte	9724	
Metronome	8691		Blue Chintz	9104		Nature's Bounty	9199		Southgate	9725	W32
Destination	8691		Thistle Garden	9105		Shannon Spring	9200		Troy	9726	
Ignition	8694		Roscrea	9106		Lemonique	9202		Paris	9727	
New West	8696		Wicklow	9107		Terrace Café	9203		Buenavista	9728	
Surf Blue	8754		Shamrock	9108		Meadow Spray	9204		Shenandoah	9729	
Picnic	8755		Kilkee	9109		Summer Magic	9205		Brently	9730	
Mahogany	8756		Julie	9110		Midnight Fest	9206		Bellefonte	9731	
Calypso	8757		Santa Rosa	9111		Harvest Treasure	9210		Spell Binder	9733	
Polka	8758		Yesterday	9112		Berryvine	9211		Parkhill	9734	
Rumba	8759		Ice Rose	9113		Summer Estate	9212		Evermore	9735	
Blue Sky	8760		Trinidad	9115		Floral Sonnet	9216		Magnificence	9736	
Ragtime	8761		Azure	9116		Blue Estate	9222		Barrymore	9737	
Midsummer	8762		Nutmeg	9117		Orchard Spring	9224		Hermitage	9740	
Morning Song	8763		Slate	9118		Countrywood	9226		Garden Empress	9741	
Buttercup	8769		Dutch Treat	9120		Watergreen	9227		Sandhurst	9742	
Trees	8770		Harlequin	9121		Greens Farm	9228		Mandarin Garden	9743	
Medley	8771		Dreamer	9122		Rainbow Fruits	9229		Victorian Lace	9744	
Flower Power	8775		Blue Shadow	9126		Asian Bouquet	9301	W4	Queen's Splendor	9746	
Joy	8777		Partners	9127		Floating Garden	9302		Vancouver Gold	9747	
Cheer	8780		Sherwood	9129		Kashmir	9303		Stanford Court	9748	
Harvest Time	8782		Fairday	9130		Tulip Time	9304		Churchill	9750	
Springtide	8783		Ringlet	9131		Dutch Weave	9305		Chancellor	9751	
Potpourri	8786		Together	9132		Summer Blossom	9306	W	Van Buren	9752	
Dominique	8788		Kerry Spring	9133		Santiago	9307	W41	Bridgehampton	9753	
Annelisa	8789		New Hope	9134		Chanteuse	9308		Highland Park	9754	
Whimsy	8789		Woodfield	9135		New Castle	9309		Embassy Suite	9756	
Marie Claire	8790		Roxy	9136		New Yorker	9400		Grand Terrace	9757	
Claudette	8791		Black Tango	9137		New Orleans	9401		Gold & Sable	9758	
Up-Sa Daisy	9001	0211655	Eternal Blush	9138		Florida	9402		Kiev	9759	

Name	No.	Design	Name	No.	Design	Name	No.	Design	Name	No.	Design
Lylewood	9760		Before the Wind	B134		Homestead	B337 W21		Running Free	B968	
Sestina	9761		High Fliers	B135		Surprise	B338		Wildwood	B969	
Lyndhurst	9762		Tidal Song	B136		Rochelle	B339 W10		Merry Mushroom	B970	
Williamston	9768		Sea Gems	B137		Akaye	B350 W30		Moonflight	B971	
Golden Tribute	9769		Foam White	B138		Summer Dreams	B351 W10		Arctic	B972	
Sterling Tribute	9770		Glimmer	B301 W10		Sumiye	B351 W10		Ice Flower	B976	
Pacific Majesty	9771		Patches	B302 W10		Sometsuke	B352		Ankara	B977	
Carnegie	9772		Verse	B303 W10		Kiseto	B353		Seaview	B978	
Palais Royal	9773		Matchmaker	B304 W11		Fjord	B951		Fantasia	B979	
Lady Eve	9777		Outlook	B305 W10		Fruitful	B952		Floral Frost	B980	
Imperial Gate	9778		Lineage	B306 W12		Tartan	B953		Free Flight	B981	
Sunswept	9781		Happy Talk	B307 W10		Clinging Vine	B954		Rosina	BS54	
Cousteau	9782		Crazy Quilt	B308 W10		Elation	B955		Kent	CAB30	
Venetian Rose	9783		Parkside	B309		Up Up and Away	B956		Sedan	D1441	
Icon	9784		Evendale	B316		Winsome	B957		Garland	D167	
Cabot	9785		Bleufleur	B319 W30		Tundra	B959		Norway	E2003	
Astair	9795		Hofgarten	B320		Frey	B960		Country Ridge	E2007	
Hyannis Port	9797		Parchment	B329 W30		Odin	B961		Oakbrook	E520	
Commemoration	9798		Talisman	B330		Softly	B962		Apple Magic	E523	
Opulence	9799		Fallriver	B331 W15		Whisper	B963		Spice Blossoms	E527	
Windsor White	9810		Frost Flower	B332 W16		Sonoma	B964		Berry Grove	E528	
Yoshino	9983		Abundance	B333 W17		Salem	B965		Summer Hill	E530	
Simplicty in Blue	B132		Bristol	B334 W18		Alpine Flowers	B966		New Stockholm	E701N	
Elegance in Blue	B133		Seabreeze	B336 W20		Vale Flowers	B967		New Sweet Dream	E940N	
									New Apple Blossom	E941N	

rice Guide

The condition of the piece, the rarity of the piece, and the age of the piece usually determine price. So these guides are just that— guides. Prices vary in different parts of the United States. When shopping for a complete set, it is usually harder to find the dinner plates and the cups and saucers, as these pieces are more often broken. The column for the year 1947 includes the Occupied Japan era and accounts for the higher price of some of these pieces. Occupied-Japan marked pieces of any kind get into another area of collecting.

Starting with the year 1953 or the N in wreath era, pieces are usually too modern looking to entice many collectors, though the retro or 50s look is enjoying a comeback. Many of these pieces go for original price or less. (Hint, buy them now and hold them. In twenty years they will be collectibles.) Another oddity about collecting old china, the less made of a pattern the less collectible it usually is. This accounts for the highly collected Azalea pattern, many people remember it and now want to collect it. If a pattern was only in production for a year or two, probably very few are aware of it and its collectibility suffers. This, of course, is extremely different from the one-of-a-kind collection of original art where the fewer created the more valuable.

Place settings	1915	1925	1935	1947	1953	1965	1980
Bowl cereal/soup	18	16	15	20	13	12	10
Bowl fruit	14	12	10	18	7	6	4
Cup & saucer, (oversized)	25	23	21	-	-	-	-
Cup & saucer, flat	22	20	-	-	20	18	18
Cup & saucer, footed	-	-	20	22	16	16	16
Cup & saucer, coffee mug	-	-	-	-	16	15	14
Cup & saucer, demitasse flat	20	20	-	-	-	-	-
Cup & saucer, demitasse footed	-	-	20	22	16	16	16
Cup & saucer, bouillon	22	22	20	28	-	-	-
Egg cup, single	20	20	20	20	-	-	-
Egg cup, double	40	40	40	-	-	-	-
Plate, bread & butter	10	10	8	10	6	6	6
Plate, salad	15	15	10	14	8	8	8
Plate, luncheon	25	25	22	-	-	-	-
Plate ,dinner	30	28	24	26	20	20	20
Tea & toast, & cup	25	25	23	28	20	20	20

Serving pieces	1915	1925	1935	1947	1953	1965	1980
Bon bon	40	30	30	-	-	-	-
Butter tub	80	60	50	-	-	-	-
Butter, covered round	100	80	75	100	-	-	-
Butter, covered rectangle	-	-	-	-	50	50	40
Cake plate w/ handles	75	70	65	75	-	-	-
Chip and dip	180	170	170	-	-	-	-

Serving pieces	1915	1925	1935	1947	1953	1965	1980
Chop plate	-	30	35	-	20	20	20
Coffee pot	-	-	-	-	160	150	150
Chocolate pot	150	140	130	160	100	100	100
Creamer	45	40	35	40	25	20	20
Gravy boat attached plate	90	80	70	50	40	40	40
Mustard w/ lid & spoon	65	50	40	-	-	-	-
Platter, oval, large 16"	150	90	80	70	70	65	50
Platter, oval, med. 14"	90	80	70	60	55	40	40
Platter, oval, small 11"	70	60	60	50	40	30	30
Relish	30	30	20	20	20	30	30
Salt and pepper	30	35	35	40	40	30	30
Shakers, salt & pepper, individual	25	25	25	-	-	-	-
Salt dip	20	20	20	-	-	-	-
Spoon holder	70	70	70	-	-	-	-
Sugar bowl with lid	60	50	45	35	30	30	20
Syrup with lid and underplate	50	40	30	-	-	-	-
Tea pot, round	150	130	120	140	90	90	80
Tea pot, top handle	-	-	-	-	60	50	-
Tea tile	50	40	30	-	-	-	-
Vegetable ,open oval	60	55	55	45	45	40	40
Vegetable, covered oval	150	90	80	60	40	40	40
Vegetable, open round	80	70	60	50	45	35	35
Vegetable, covered round	150	140	130	120	110	100	100

Bibliography

Alden, Amee Neff. *Early Noritake China,* Lombard, Illinois: Wallace-Homestead Book Company. 1987.

Chefetz, Sheila. *Antiques for the Table*, New York, New York: Penguin Studio Books, 1993.

Plante, Ellen M. *The Victorian Home*, Philadelphia, Pennsylvania: Courage Books, 1995.

Rinker, Harry L. *Dinnerware of the 20th Century: The Top 500 Patterns*, New York, New York: House of Collectibles, 1997.

Schiffer, Nancy N. *Japanese Porcelain 1800-1950,* West Chester, Pennsylvania: Schiffer Publishing Ltd., 1986.

Spain, David. *Noritake Collectibles, A to Z: A Pictorial Record & Guide to Values*, Atglen, Pennsylvania: Schiffer Publishing, Ltd., 1997.

Van Patten, Joan. *The Collector's Encyclopedia of Noritake*, Paducah, Kentucky: Collectors Books, 1984.

White, Carole Bess. *Collector's Guide to Made in Japan Ceramics Identification and Values Book III.* Paducah, Kentucky: Collector Books, 1998.